JB'S

The Story of Dudley's
LEGENDARY LIVE MUSIC VENUE
in words and pictures
by Geoff Tristram

First published in 2014 by The Drawing Room Press.

Printed and bound by CPI Antony Rowe Ltd.

First Edition 2014

ISBN 978-0-9926208-3-7

Book design, layout and typography by Steve Jolliffe.

Cover design adapted by Steve Jolliffe from Pete Beardsmore's iconic original membership cards.

Additional photography and illustrations by Steve Jolliffe.

Edited and proofread by Laura Tristram (BA History of Art; MA Publishing).

Contact the author at gt@geofftristram.co.uk

Book Sales:
www.jbsbook.com

DRAWING ROOM

Published by
The Drawing Room Press

This book is dedicated to my good friends, the JB's committee, namely, Sam, J.B., Roy, Sid, John, Larry, Colin and Dermott, not forgetting Gezz, Mick and Big Dave, who are sadly no longer with us.

I also want to say thank you to the many hundreds of musicians and bands that played at the club, and last, but definitely not least, the lovely, colourful, diverse, mad people who frequented the old place and made it what it was – arguably the best small music venue of all time.

IV

Contents

Other works by the author:

A Nasty Bump on the Head

The Hunt for Granddad's Head

Monet Trouble

Vincent Gough's Van

The Curse of Tutton Common

Painting by Numbers

Stealing the Ashes

David's Michelangelo

The Curious Tale of the Missing Hoof

Mr Maori Goes Home

Losing the Plot

The Last Cricket Tour

Geoff Tristram's comedy novels can be purchased from his website – www.geofftristram.co.uk – or ordered from all good bookshops, and a few bad ones as well. He can be contacted by email on gt@geofftristram.co.uk – but not if you just want to complain about something.

The Author

When I was asked to write the JB's book, I felt obliged to explain that, much as I would love to, I was really only a comedy writer – novels mainly, of which I have now published twelve, plus the odd humorous article for local newspapers. My area of expertise, if you can call it that, is the complex, farcical plot, the cast of crazy but somehow believable characters, the hilarious set piece, and the occasional poignant moment.

The seven-man committee that sat drinking at the Foresters Arms pub in Wollaston weighed this carefully, and then assured me that I'd be perfect for it. An hour later, after hearing just a small sample of the anecdotes they had to offer, I had to agree with them. The one about Freddie Mercury and Queen alone (more about that later) was enough to persuade me to take on the job, and there were hundreds more where that came from, they assured me. This book, I felt, deserved to be far more than a mere photograph album interspersed with page after page of historical statistics about who played there and when (though all that is quite rightly included too).

The JB's book is an adventure story, a comedy, a tragedy, a rock-and-roll history lesson, and several fascinating biographies all rolled into one. I had been a regular patron of the club myself when it was based in King Street, and had met my wife-to-be Susan there (after many years I have eventually managed to forgive JB's for this). The band I used to play guitar for back in the 1970s, a progressive rock outfit by the name of Still, even played there two or three times. Being asked, many years later, to compile this book, at first filled me with fear and trepidation, I have to admit. It was an enormous project, which seemed to get bigger by the day, and it was inevitable that I would be lining myself up for criticism if I took it on. Important facts would almost certainly be omitted here and there, either on purpose or by accident. Fellow members might complain that I'd spelt the name of the bass player in Hackensack incorrectly, or that I'd stated that The

Manic Street Preachers played there on Saturday, when in fact it was Friday. That said, I am confident that any small errors will be more than compensated for by the wonderful story I am presenting to you now. I hope you enjoy reading it as much as I enjoyed writing it!

Geoff Tristram
Curriculum Vitae

Geoff Tristram has been a professional artist, illustrator and cartoonist for forty years, working for a diverse range of clients including Penguin Books, Embassy World Snooker, the BBC, Tarmac, Carillion, Past Times, Ravensburger Puzzles, Reeves, Winsor & Newton, Trivial Pursuit and the television show 'They Think It's All Over', to name but a few. He has created artwork featuring the likes of Jonathan Ross, Jeremy Clarkson, Ian Botham, David Vine, Steve Bull, Alan Shearer and Ayrton Senna, not to mention virtually every famous snooker player that ever lifted a cue. You may even have noticed him at the Crucible World Championships on TV, interviewing the players whilst he drew their caricatures!

He has also illustrated many book covers, advertisements, album sleeves for bands such as UB40, The Maisonettes and City Boy (all of which played at JB's), and postage stamps, notably 'Charles and Diana – The Royal Wedding', 'Bermuda Miss World', 'Lake Placid Winter Olympics' and 'Spain 1982 World Cup Football'. More recently, his incredibly detailed 'Cat Conundrum', 'Best of British' and 'What If?' jigsaws have enthralled and exasperated thousands of dedicated puzzle fans all over the world. Geoff's younger brother, David, is a well-known and extremely successful comedy playwright and film-maker (check out the hilarious Doreen's Story and the Inspector Drake films on YouTube), so it was no real surprise when Geoff eventually turned his hand to comedy writing. He has now written and published twelve comedy novels and of course, this wonderful book about the legendary live-music venue, JB's.

Johnny Bryant, who, according to Sam, was like George Best but better looking.

Introduction

Tipton in 1969

"Last year we drove right across the USA. We had one cassette tape to listen to on the entire trip... I don't remember what it was"

Steven Wright

"People try to put us d-down (Talkin' 'bout my generation)
Just because we get around (Talkin' 'bout my generation)
Things they do look awful c-c-cold (Talkin' 'bout my generation)
I hope I die before i get old (Talkin' 'bout my generation)
Why don't you all f-fade away (Talkin' 'bout my generation)
Don't try to dig what we all s-s-s-say (Talkin' 'bout my generation)
I'm not trying to cause a big s-s-sensation (Talkin' 'bout my generation)
I'm just talkin' 'bout my g-g-g-generation (Talkin' 'bout my generation)

Pete Townsend

Most self-respecting disc jockeys will have hundreds, if not thousands, of records in their collection. Johnny Bryant and Sam Jukes had precisely six, and, to make matters worse, they were singles.

It was fair to say that their 'discotheques', staged for the inmates at Coneygre Youth Centre in Tipton, could get fairly repetitive. When someone is treated to the same song approximately every twelve minutes, it can tend to wear thin. The listener begins to experience more than the occasional feeling of déjà vu.

This failing was pointed out to Mr Bryant in memorable, if faltering fashion, by another Johnny – Johnny Higgs, who, like Gareth Gates, could sing like an angel but had real trouble speaking.

'W-w-w-what y-y-you n-n-need, m-m-mate, is more f-f-f-f'king records,' he tried his best to say.

The Who could well have been thinking of Johnny Higgs when they recorded 'My Generation'. His tortured voice seemed to speak for the youth of Great Britain – well, those at Coneygre Youth Centre anyway, and thankfully, his sagely advice was not wasted on J.B. (as we will call him for the time being to distinguish him from the other Johnny). This stammering critique of his shortcomings seemed to galvanize him into action, once he'd discreetly dabbed his face dry with the cuff of his denim shirt. Meanwhile, somewhere deep inside, a Richard Branson-like entrepreneurial spirit was struggling to burst forth, and Higgs' rebuke had inadvertently lit the metaphorical blue touch paper.

Little did J.B. or Sam know that this small, seemingly insignificant encounter at a Black Country youth centre would eventually lead to the creation of one of the country's legendary live-music venues, a club to rival such venues as The Marquee and the 100 Club in London, and The Cavern in Liverpool. It was a place where many of our best and most famous bands would cut their teeth before going on to international fame – and a place they were grateful to return to on the way back down the ladder, years later.

This book charts the history of the legendary JB's club from its humble beginnings right through to its golden era as one of the country's most influential small clubs, and beyond that to its sad decline and eventual closure. Those who were lucky enough to spend their evenings there in its heyday will know that this was no mere music venue. It was a spiritual hub that attracted like-minded people: musicians, writers, comedians, poets, free spirits, intellectuals, oddballs, hippies, and a good many honest working-class folk who just loved good music – in short, all human life was there, and quite a few species yet to be categorized too. It was a place where relationships were formed, a good many of which have survived to this day. It was a place where bands were formed too, and where rival outfits met on their nights off from gigging to swap ideas and occasionally steal each other's vocalists, drummers, guitarists or girlfriends – sometimes all four at once. Rock stars rubbed shoulders with bricklayers, accountants, teachers and those who resisted work in all its forms, because in that hot, sweaty, noisy, heaving little room, they were all the same.

Hopefully, this book will delight and entertain you with amazing, and, frankly, bizarre anecdotes, incredible facts and rare photographs provided by the bands, the management and the club members alike. If you were one of those lucky people who were there most weekends, it will no doubt help to bring the memories flooding back and probably cause you to feel deeply nostalgic, uncharacteristically sentimental and a little sad – the way you'd feel at the passing of a loyal old friend. You will discover things you didn't know or had completely forgotten, and you will certainly laugh until it hurts at some of the strange but true stories you are about to read. If you don't, well, there's probably something wrong with your mouth. And to those unfortunate souls who never got the chance to know the place, this book will hopefully help to make up for the glorious, golden times you missed.

Now fasten your seat belts, ladies and gentlemen. It's going to be an exciting ride!

The Loft, where Dermott, Gezz and Co. used to live. See page 50.

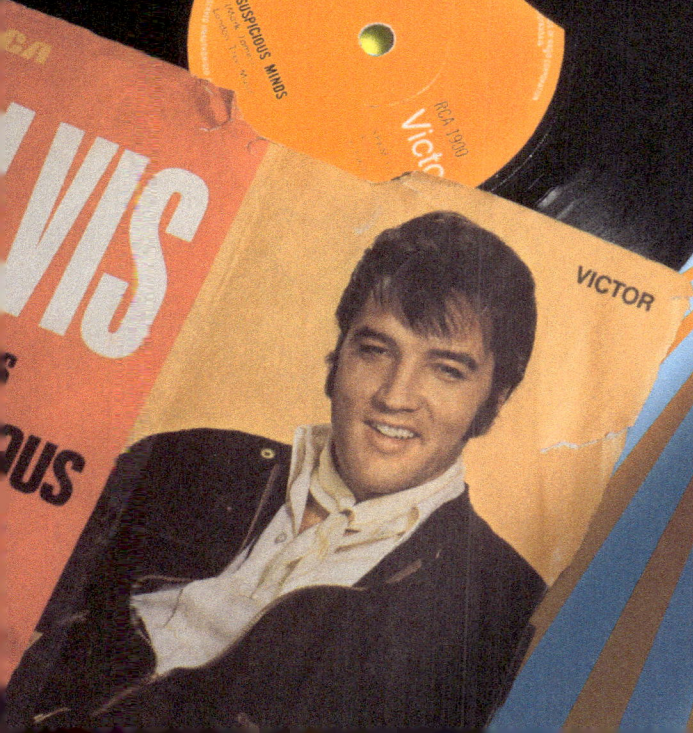

The derelict Dudley Town F.C. site. The original JB's club is just out of shot.

An extremely rare photograph of the Dudley site, showing the nearby cricket pavilion burning down.

The First Year

The Football Club

*"I've got to admit it's getting better (better)
A little better all the time (It couldn't get no
worse)"*

Lennon and McCartney

1969

The Black Country town of Tipton, it was fair to say, was not on the shortlist for 'Centre of the Universe' in 1969. It was not even on the very long list, but elsewhere in the world, things were happening. Led Zeppelin had released their eponymous first album, and in France, the first Concorde test flight was successfully conducted. Mario Puzo published the first of his Godfather novels, and over in Gibraltar, John Lennon and Yoko Ono got married. In America, the first case of AIDS had not long been diagnosed, and Midnight Cowboy was released. Neil Armstrong set foot on the moon, watched by some 500 million people, and The Beatles were photographed crossing Abbey Road. Charles Manson's deranged followers murdered Sharon Tate, The Rolling Stones played a free concert in Hyde Park, London, and the Woodstock Festival took place in upstate New York. As if all that wasn't enough for one year, the Vietnam War began, and seemed to last forever. Meanwhile, back in Tipton, youth leaders Johnny Bryant and Sam Jukes still only had six singles to play at their disco.

Not far away, in Upper Gornal, another club, The Quarry, was doing its level best to entertain the bored youth of the area. To this end it was mooted that its inhabitants might benefit spiritually from a change of scenery now and again, and by this they didn't mean a short walk down the road to Lower Gornal. Regrettably, the budget did not extend to a fortnight on the Isle of Wight, so The Quarry youths instead linked up with Tipton's Coneygre Club and embarked on a kind of casual exchange system, whereby one week, everyone would pile into the Lower Gornal building to sample its delights, and the next, the charabanc would fetch up at the Tipton venue to do likewise. This was how Johnny Higgs, the stammering vocalist that you will recall from the introduction page (unless you foolishly skipped it like some impatient readers do), came to berate Johnny Bryant about the sparsity of his record collection. This influx of new blood and new ideas seemed to do both clubs some good. Over at The Quarry, Higgs and his rock band, The Arnold J. Contingent had been regularly entertaining the troops, alongside others such as The Band of Joy, Chicken Shack and The Locomotive, plus a decent soul and Motown disco (presumably boasting more than six singles). At the risk of holding up the flow of this tale for a second, I'll throw in a quick piece of trivia. Stan Webb's band, Chicken Shack, part of which eventually morphed into the mighty Fleetwood Mac, was named after a tiny tin-shed rock venue situated behind the Foresters Arms pub in Wollaston – the very pub where, coincidentally, the JB's committee first met to discuss the creation of this book!

The marrying of the two youth clubs not only produced some long-lasting friendships, but also an inspired cross-pollination of ideas. The Coneygre Club was now staging rock nights of its own, featuring bands such as the St. Louis Blues Band (where are they now?), and film evenings, courtesy of a young man by the name of Sid Weston.

Sam Jukes had first met Johnny Bryant at Coneygre, where Bryant ran the youth football team. Sam, a talented professional footballer, and later, accident-prone speedway rider, often played football with him, and a friendship ensued. The Quarry Club connection introduced Johnny Higgs to the mix, and he was to reappear in various musical collaborations from that point onwards. Roy Williams first encountered J.B. and friends at the nearby Safari Club, which was a regular meeting place that hosted a few early discotheques for them. Before long, Roy was roped into the committee, and would eventually become a sound engineer and booker of bands.

Having travelled all of around four miles to Lower Gornal, it began to dawn on the Coneygre lads that the world was now their oyster, and they soon became more and more adventurous and positively thirsting for chances to explore this wonderful and diverse planet of ours. Sid and his brother, John, knew a man by the name of Ray Davenport, whose father owned several coaches, and during one of their presumably alcohol-fuelled brainstorming sessions, the youth club movers and shakers decided to create an excursion which they christened 'The Magical Mystery Tour', after The Beatles song of the same name. The idea was that only Ray the driver and Sid would know the end

destination (classified information that they guarded with their life), and those interested in broadening their minds would pay a nominal sum in return for being promised a night to remember, even if, by the end of it, they were longing to forget it. The organizers' carefree, hippy-like take on the world, coupled with a decidedly abstract sense of humour, resulted in several wondrous excursions. One early sortie to the Catacombs, a Wolverhampton music venue, was placed in serious jeopardy when Mr Davenport completely forgot that his services were needed that evening and stayed at home to wash his hair, meaning that his coaches were noticeable only by their absence. Unperturbed by this, the youth leaders simply marched their flock in conga formation down the road to the nearest trolleybus stop, commandeered every seat on the next vehicle that arrived and asked the driver nicely to get them to the church on time. Once inside the Catacombs, the crowd was treated to a showing of The Beatles' film, The Magical Mystery Tour, which had been hired from the Arts Lab in London. Colin Pugh was the designated projectionist, thanks to his impeccable film-industry credentials (he owned a cine camera), but unfortunately the take-up spool was quite a bit smaller than the film spool, which meant that The Beatles' classic ended up in a tangled mess inside a hastily provided empty Walkers' crisps box.

Not all of the Mystery Tours went as smoothly as the Catacombs event, if smoothly is the right word. One coach tour destination was Kinver Edge, a local beauty spot. For those who don't know the place, what makes this area so interesting is not just the spectacular views in all directions from the top of the Edge, but also the strange sandstone rock formations dotted around the vicinity, some of which were inhabited by locals until as late as the 1950s. These Black Country cave dwellers carved out rooms within the rocks and transformed them into cosy cottages. A few, namely the Holy Austen Rock Houses, have been restored to their original condition and are open to the public, whilst others remain as shells. It was planned that the crowd would make its way on foot to these disused caves, in order to hold a party there. A team of Sherpas trudged up the hillside carrying provisions, mainly alcohol and dodgy home-made fireworks, and once there, campfires were lit and the show began. Colin, later to become JB's club's trusty barman, remembers that one party-goer had strewn the severed limbs of mannequins around the cave in a bizarre attempt to decorate it, and there was a huge pot of baked beans bubbling away in the corner. He also recalls that someone, somehow, managed to capture a small bat. All went well until a young man by the name of Gerald 'Gezz' Tobin (later to become one of the main JB's disc jockeys) discovered that his girlfriend, Eva, was missing, and decided to leave base camp to look for her, armed only with a lit candle. Whether or not he uttered the famous last words, 'I'm going out now, and I may be some time,' is not on record, but what is well documented is the fact that he staggered off shouting 'Eva!' at the top of his voice, and immediately fell over the edge of a cliff, breaking his hip. That evening, the Mystery Tour party was treated to visits from the police, the ambulance and the fire brigade, none of whom were best pleased. The following day, the ill-fated event made the front cover of the Express and Star newspaper, with the headline, 'Hippy Falls from Kinver Edge and Breaks Hip'. Gezz's mother, on reading this, was so incensed that she immediately set fire to her son's clothing, including his prized sealskin coat, in a futile attempt to curtail his wild ways before he ended up killing himself. As to Eva, it is hoped that she was eventually located, none the worse for her adventure. If she ever reads this book, maybe she could write in and tell us where she had been, to put our minds at rest.

Another eventful expedition saw the Mystery Tour revellers boarding a canal narrowboat at Brewood (pronounced 'Brood', for those who don't already know), just outside Wolverhampton. The boat was supposed to be ferrying the clientele to a country pub and back, but the best-laid schemes o' mice an' men gang aft agley, as Rabbie Burns so eloquently put it, and it all went 'agley' on this occasion when one of those present discovered his girlfriend in the arms of the coach driver. The lovelorn partygoer took this very badly indeed, his feelings almost certainly heightened by copious alcohol consumption, and he decided to commit suicide. Having presumably studied Hamlet at A level and been impressed by it, he chose the same method of self-destruction that Ophelia had opted for, and threw himself into the canal. What he hadn't reckoned on, however, was that in Shakespeare's version, the watery grave was a deep, babbling brook strewn with wild flowers, whereas in the Brewood Mystery Tour version, it was a shallow, smelly canal full of old shopping trolleys. Consequently, the water was only just over knee-height, which seldom proves fatal for someone who's standing up in it. The broken-hearted young gentleman, who must have looked and felt quite silly at that juncture, was dragged out to safety by his fellow partygoers. Feeling the need to be alone, a bit like Marlene Dietrich, he decided to squelch back along the muddy track to the coach, rather than rejoin the boat, and to add to his woes, the surly coach driver and love-rival would not allow him onto the vehicle because he was plastered in pungent black mud. There may well have also been deeper-rooted reasons, given the events that took place earlier that same evening. However, a compromise was finally agreed, and the lad was forced to sit shivering in the stairwell all the way home to Dudley. Just to cap a memorable evening, once back in town, Big Dave Hodgetts, one of the many revellers, somehow managed to rip the taxi rank's telephone from the wall as he attempted to arrange his transport home. Unfortunately, he was observed by a local beat bobby, and was subsequently invited to spend the night contemplating the error of his ways, whilst sobering up in Dudley Police Station.

The perils of water-based entertainment should have put the organizers off, but they persevered. On one memorable night, they hired a boat with a licensed bar to chug down the river Severn in Stourport, and while the crowd busied itself drinking the bar dry and accidentally falling into the river, Mick Ralphs' girlfriend, Wendy (not Mick Ralphs of Bad Company fame, sadly, but another, lesser-known Mick Ralphs), and her two sisters, Heather and Jill, provided a charming piece of theatre based on 'The Three Billy Goats Gruff'. Sid collected a few shillings from all on board to cover expenses, and when he realized that, after paying Ray's diesel and the boat fee, there was still a lot of cash left, he busied himself trying to reimburse everyone. It was this kind of shrewd, Wall-Street-style business acumen that would stand them in good stead for their future projects.

Not all excursions were local. The usual suspects went to see The Stones in Hyde Park, Led Zeppelin, Santana and Pink Floyd at the Bath Festival of Blues, and Bob Dylan at the Isle of Wight. A friend by the name of Big Pete Bunn had connections with the Boys' Brigade, and was able to borrow a tent from them for the Isle of Wight trip. The only problem was that the trunk the tent was stored in was huge and incredibly heavy. They battled on bravely, nevertheless, dragging it inch by inch to its final destination, Sid leading the

The Citizens featuring Sid Weston (far left) in his pre-moustache days.

Sid Weston and Pauline Wells, Larry Oakley, John Weston, Sue Evans and Sam Jukes.

Even in the '60s, Sid and John Weston were interested in rock.

Sam Jukes playing school football, wearing the dark shirt.

A Magical Mystery Tour day trip to see Dr. Feelgood at the Hope & Anchor, London.

Sam Jukes astride his JAP speedway bike, being handed a red oil can by Sid Weston.

Sam broadsiding into the first turn, as the photographer runs for cover!

Sam and Sue on their wedding day.

11

way, wearing a rather fetching pith helmet. When they finally got the tent to the festival and tried to erect it, it suddenly became clear why it was so weighty and cumbersome. The Boys' Brigade had actually lent them a massive marquee that would have held an army. That night, huddled up in a lonely corner of this huge canvas monstrosity, they watched as hundreds of strangers piled in, had shallow, meaningless sex in the dark, and piled out again. Homely it was not.

Meanwhile, back at the youth club, Johnny Bryant, Sam Jukes, Sid Weston and Co. continued to amuse and baffle the locals in equal measure by organizing tiddlywinks championships on Burnt Tree Island – regrettably not some exotic palm-tree-lined earthly paradise, but instead a busy traffic island a few miles down the road. Sadly, until JB's club was born, this was what passed for entertainment in Tipton, circa 1969.

One of the many Magical Mystery Tour destinations was the Swan Pub in Yardley, Birmingham, which hosted a soul discotheque, presided over by a slick, verbally incontinent disc jockey who insisted on addressing his audience as his 'soul brothers and sisters'. His glib, professional-sounding patter between the records greatly impressed the Tipton lads, and spurred them on in their attempt to create something similar for themselves, back in the Black Country.

We now turn our attention to Colin Jukes. He was christened Colin but was renamed Sam by friends after the nightclub pianist character who sang 'As Time Goes By' in Casablanca. The reasons for this are lost in the mists of time, but the nickname stuck, and he has been Sam ever since to everyone except his wife, Sue, and his mother. Sam would eventually become the manager of JB's club, and run it as a labour of love for an incredible forty-one years.

Born in 1946, just a year after World War Two had ended (is that how his parents chose to celebrate?), he attended Park Lane Secondary Modern Boys' School. He eventually became Deputy Head Boy, and was captain of both the cricket and football teams, so a career in sport seemed to be the natural choice. During a game against Stoke Schoolboys, in which he excelled, he was spotted by a talent scout from Wolverhampton Wanderers, who told him that his was the finest individual performance he had seen in all the years he had been involved in youth football. The scout's

approach, it transpired, was highly irregular, not to mention illegal. At that time, for reasons no one could quite fathom, professional clubs were not allowed to approach schoolboy players, whereas nowadays, lads are signed up as they emerge from the womb if the mother had experienced a higher than average number of kicks during her pregnancy. Sam was subsequently invited to the Molineux Stadium to meet the manager, his hero, Stan Cullis, but, disappointingly, he was only offered amateur status forms. Instead, Sam signed for nearby Walsall as an apprentice professional, but still had to work each afternoon for Triplex Foundries Ltd. When it became obvious that he was never going to be offered a single game in midfield, he moved to Dudley Town, hoping to at last be offered his favoured position. Alas, it was not to be, and he had to be content as a winger, which didn't suit him. He picked up an injury shortly afterwards, and, disillusioned, he quit Dudley with the intention of becoming a speedway rider instead. In order to pursue this new venture, he purchased a second-hand speedway bike from top riders, Ron Mountford and Ricky France of Coventry Bees. Worryingly, however, when Sam met up with Mountford to collect his new bike, the rider's leg was in plaster, and his colleague, France, had his arm in a sling and was nursing a broken collarbone. This did not bode well, and in fairness, both gentlemen did try their level best to dissuade young Jukes from a life in the fast lane. In spite of this good advice, a determined Sam began practising at the King's Lynn and Sheffield Speedway Stadia, and did sufficiently well to be offered the number 7 spot in the Sheffield team. For those not au fait with the sport, a speedway team has seven riders. Those that wear the 1, 3 and 5 race jackets are considered the stars of the team, with the numbers 2, 4 and 6 next in the pecking order. Number 7 is the last but least member of the team 'proper', and beneath them is a pool of reserve-team hopefuls, each trying to impress the selectors. This, it must be stressed, is no slight on what Sam had accomplished. To get the number 7 slot in a top team is one hell of an achievement in itself, especially in a short space of time. Once you've got that far, the next step is to put in some good performances and outpace the lads wearing the number 2, 4 and 6 race jackets, which he was already doing on a regular basis.

In order to get a little bit of practise in before his inaugural league meeting at Sheffield, Sam arranged to ride in a reserves heat at his local Cradley Heath

Speedway a few days before. This, in hindsight, was a pretty serious mistake. In an accident that was not his fault he managed to break his femur and shatter his knee cap. Those watching this awful spectacle reckon that they had never seen a speedway crash quite like it. Sam was, so we are told, unceremoniously shunted into the starting gate by another rider who wasn't looking where he was going. Nowadays one could probably put this down to the rider texting as he raced, but back in the 1960s there was no such diversion. The lad was probably just hopelessly inexperienced and Sam paid the ultimate price. Ironically, the culprit walked away unscathed. The word 'unlucky' doesn't do justice to what befell poor Sam. Some higher authority just didn't want him to be involved in sports. After all his hard work, he never made it to Sheffield. Maybe it was meant to be – fate, if you will, and God had bigger and better plans for Mr Colin 'Sam' Jukes.

What followed was a painful stint at Dudley Guest Hospital, where his femur was reset and placed in traction, and the knee joint and severed ligaments stitched back together. This was followed by a depressing three months spent lying on his back at The Limes Hospital.

It was during his tedious convalescent period, when all he had to do all day was lie in traction and stare out across the garden at a vegetable patch full of courgettes, that his thoughts turned to forming a music club for like-minded people. His first step was to become more involved in the club's fledgling discotheque project, and to this end, he set about building the record decks, falling back on his training as a pattern maker and electrician. After an initial hiccup, when the decks insisted on rotating in the wrong direction, he and J.B. were up and running. Now all they needed were a few records to play on them and someone to front the operation.

The committee, as we will call them, for now at any rate, needed a disc jockey with a certain amount of charisma. It was agreed that, whilst their mothers obviously loved them, sadly, most of the lads had features that were best suited to radio, and even worse, possessed the vocal delivery of a particularly dour undertaker.

All, that is, except one. Johnny Bryant – it has to be said, albeit begrudgingly – was a very handsome young man who not only possessed the necessary physical attributes, but could also talk the talk. In fact, it was hard to shut him up. Johnny, as Sam Jukes remembers, looked just like a young George Best back in '69, only if anything, better looking. Women loved him, and he had a quick wit, even though he could have benefitted from a purifying filter between his brain and his mouth on occasion. After a quick show of hands, it was unanimously agreed that Johnny should be the man in charge of Sam's new record decks. The lads became determined to set-up their discotheque at a brand new, larger venue of their own, which would also provide local bands with somewhere to play. It was Sam who suggested to Sid that Dudley Town's Football Club pavilion might be worth considering, because of his connection with the place. The two of them took a look around and immediately realized that there was a problem. There was no electricity, thanks to the football club somehow forgetting to pay the bill. This initial hurdle was overcome, however, thanks to Sam and Sid agreeing to settle the unpaid invoice between them. The decks were duly installed, chairs and tables dusted off, spiders rehoused, light bulbs replaced, and the old place was opened for business, initially on Thursday evenings. The word was passed around, and the football club's inaugural event saw fifteen or so punters entertained by Johnny Bryant, who had managed to find a few more records in the interim. So far, so good, but now the committee needed a name for their venture. Most of the suggested names from that time are best confined to the pedal bin of history, to spare the blushes of those who misguidedly created them. In their defence, it is important to remember that this was 1969, and not all cigarettes consumed were of the legal variety. Larry Oakley favoured 'Hedonics Inc.', for reasons best known to himself. Sid, on the other hand, liked the word 'Smaug', which, rather predictably, emanated from the pen of J. R. R. Tolkein, whose books were required reading for just about everyone with long hair in those heady, Hobbitty days. Mick Ralphs liked the sound of 'The Club', which, in fairness, was quite acceptable. However, it became known as JB's, named in honour of their new figurehead, Dudley's cut-price answer to George Best.

Originally, the committee's intention was to create a mobile disco, but such was the popularity of their new venture, they never really needed to travel. Within a few weeks, the jungle telegraph had spread the news, and in no time at all the club, which legally held around 80 to 100 people, was attracting crowds of some 300 to 400. This, as one can readily imagine, was creating problems of its own, as success often does. Inside, the club was soon rammed to capacity each Thursday, and those who could not find a space within gathered on the terraces outside. This meant that in the summertime, extra speakers had to be located outside the building, to accommodate the al fresco punters. The crowded interior also caused problems for J.B. The football club's malodorous lavatory block was situated outside the pavilion, so if he needed to relieve himself, he had to fight his way through the crowd,

J.B. with his glass of beer. Or is it?

and this seething mass of inhumanity would seldom, if ever, move aside to facilitate his hasty evacuation, possibly due to the fact that there were no available spaces left to move aside to. This left J.B. with two options – one being the deployment of a lengthy music track ('Slip Jigs and Reels' by Fairport Convention, or 'Keep on Chooglin' by Creedence Clearwater Revival were favourites), and the other being the empty pint mug placed discreetly just under the record decks. Option 1 was favoured, despite the inevitable wrestling bout needed to vacate the room, because it allowed our intrepid disc jockey time (albeit limited time) to pee, smoke, and chat up stray girls. Option 2 may have seemed, on the surface, a less frenetic choice, but in a dark, noisy club, illuminated by a barrage of dazzling lights, it was all too easy to mistake something vile and unpalatable for a welcome glass of cold lager.

From the very beginning, the committee had wanted their club to be primarily a live-music venue, and not only that, but they didn't want to insist on a membership or an entrance fee. The club initially opened only on Thursdays, but quite soon Sid was running a quieter film night on Tuesdays, and showing gems such as Cream live at the Albert Hall, Pink Floyd live at Pompeii, Bob Dylan's 'Don't Look Back', 'Chelsea Girls' by Andy Warhol, and 'Murder, Inc.', a popular gangster film. He'd hired a projector from Warner's in Chapel Ash, Wolverhampton, for this purpose, and during one visit to the shop he'd encountered an employee throwing unwanted slide projection equipment into a skip. Possessing an inquisitive mind and an eye for a bargain, Sid commandeered the unloved paraphernalia and took it to a secret underground laboratory, we fondly imagine, where Mick Ralphs converted it into a light show for the JB's disco, ably hampered by his friend and fellow lighting boffin, Larry.

If you have ever seen footage of swinging London clubs from the psychedelic 60s, the first thing you will notice is that young ladies with Vidal Sassoon bobbed hair and miniskirts are usually performing some cringeworthy dance routine alongside cool-looking fellows wearing Grattan's catalogue leather coats, polo necks and slacks. No doubt there are also Biba or Mary Quant posters on the wall and a row of bright-red E-Type Jags and Lotus Super 7s parked in the mews outside. The next thing that takes your eye is the strange, swirling, modulating blobs of psychedelic colours, courtesy of the liquid light show, as the party-goers groove away to an early Pink Floyd track such as 'See Emily Play'. This lava-lamp effect was the kind of lighting that Mick was striving to achieve at JB's. The problem was, in 1969, it was not possible to buy anything locally to create this effect, as far as he was aware, and even if you could, no one at JB's had any money anyway. Admirable though it undoubtedly was, the club's policy of free admission, which in turn meant no revenue, did rather restrict any grandiose schemes. However, necessity is the mother of invention, as Frank Zappa always used to say, and besides, it's always far more satisfying to create something for yourself, rather than to splash the cash and simply buy your way out of every tricky situation you find yourself in, and this is precisely what Larry and Mick did. After much experimentation that probably went on into the wee small hours and caused many theatrical explosions, they eventually emerged bleary-eyed but triumphant. They'd tried filling the glass slides with ink, cooking fat and engine oil, and all manner of

An ancient photograph of the Dudley Football Club venue. From left to right: Barrie Birch, Roy Williams, an unidentified gentleman, Sid 'The Moustache' Weston, Johnny Bryant and another unidentified gentleman, possibly Brian May of Queen (well, we can pretend!). The shady men lurking behind the Newcastle Brown crates are Larry Oakley and Mick Ralphs, the lightshow boffins.

other household liquids, none of which did the job, but they had finally experienced their eureka moment when they married together Mick's mother's food dye and a Toilet-Duck-style lavatory cleaner (which gave them their elusive sought-after blue colour). These ingredients, plus a few drops of paint stripper, caused the liquids within the slides to melt, mingle and bubble beautifully when heated by the projector lights. In fact, so successful were the results of their experimentation, that quite soon, they were not only doing the light show for JB's on Thursdays but also for numerous other local events.

With the free-admission policy, the psychedelic lighting, the live bands, and George Best's better-looking brother at the turntables, JB's club quickly went from strength to strength, so much so that at no time did the club feel the need to advertise. Incredibly, everything was still done by word of mouth. When not at the football club, the committee and other like-minded music lovers would meet at Dudley Zoo's Safari Club nearby, from where they would formulate their plans for world domination. It was here that they got to know Roy Williams though he had met them

before during the youth club exchanges, and before long he too was involved in helping to run JB's. Roy recalls them organizing a few pre-JB's discos at the Safari, and a planned gig by Leicester band, Gypsy, which was cancelled at the last minute when the roof caught fire. Roy later worked for the Astra Agency with director, Jake Elcock, and would become responsible for booking the larger, better-known bands for JB's.

When they were not sat around drinking copious amounts of alcohol, smoking dubious cigarettes and reading the International Times, or Richard Neville's Oz magazine, they would be planning more mad Mystery Tours, or venturing over to darkest Erdington to the well-known rock club, Mothers, to check out the competition. Meanwhile, the list of live bands that graced the JB's stage was increasing, with the likes of Anubis, the excellent Tommy Burton Quartet and the Artesian Hall Stompers jazz band, just to prove how all-embracing their musical tastes were. In addition to this, the JB's club committee members were spreading their wings further, and staging larger events at neighbouring venues such as Netherton Arts Centre and St Michael's Church in Tividale, which played host to the likes of Judas Priest, Travellin' Redwing, and Bronco, featuring the world-class soul singer, Jess Roden.

As with any new venture, JB's experienced a few growing pains. A deal had been done with the brewery by Sam, who now found himself in charge of managing the place. Film projectionist, Colin Pugh, a tall, genial, ginger-haired fellow with an impressive beard, and Sid's non-identical twin brother, John Weston, had joined the team as bar staff alongside Sue Jukes, Sam's wife, and it was a job which could get a little frantic, come Thursday evening. With some 400 punters arriving every week in an attempt to drink every available drop of alcohol within a square mile, the proceeds were healthy, but there was a snag. All the profits from the bar went to the football club, and not to JB's, even though it was the music club that provided the vast majority of drinkers. There was also the vexed question of the entry fee, or rather, the lack of it. It was all very well to retain a hippy ideal of free entry to all, but this meant that Johnny Bryant could not afford to buy new records. Thanks to begging and borrowing he was considerably better equipped than he had been at Coneygre, but with so many people turning up each week, he could only play Led Zeppelin '1', Free's 'Fire and Water', and Credence Clearwater Revival so many times. The situation worsened when the PA amplifier blew up, which meant that Sam had to part with his hard-earned cash to pay nearby Modern Music's repair bill. Then there were the bands to consider. If the audience wanted live music, and they did, they could hardly expect five or six people and two roadies to drive for hundreds of miles down the M5 in a sweaty, unroadworthy old van, set up forty tons of gear, play music for three hours, put the gear back in the van well after midnight, and drive for miles in the opposite direction to get home, all for the promise of free beer and a packet of stale smoky bacon crisps. The committee might have been altruistic, but it wasn't fair to force the bands to be altruistic too. It was decided after much wailing and gnashing of teeth that a modest entry fee should be introduced, albeit with a lot of mixed feelings from those who feared that their pure principles were about to be betrayed. An entry fee of 1/- was therefore levied at the door by Roy Williams, and, as he remembers it, one might as well have asked people to part with one of their kidneys. Sue Jukes was a little more commercially aware than her fellow committee members, and eventually stood at the club entrance, where she began levying the princely sum of 1/6d, stopping cars and customers until they paid up.

Things came to a head one evening when this exorbitant entry fee was shamelessly increased for the Tommy Burton Quartet, led by one of the Midlands' top jazz pianists and comics.

'2/6d for Tommy Burton?' the baying crowd snarled at poor Roy, who had drawn the short straw and ended up on the door that evening. 'Who the bloody hell is he when he's at home? We've never even heard of him!'

In spite of this, history tells us that the punters reluctantly coughed up nevertheless, and were then treated to a wonderful evening of slick jazz and witty repartee, which made them feel a lot better about it. And so it came to pass that the committee members were subjected to a steep learning curve, the gist of which was, 'It's all very well having high-minded principles, but they don't pay your mortgage.'

The regular crowd was problematic in other ways too. Many of them, finding that the club was heaving, would instead elect to lurk around the outside of the pavilion, drinking and smoking exotic cigarettes. Some, presumably fuelled by alcohol and illegal substances, would kid themselves that they were at Woodstock, and duly begin mating with anyone who would let them, though most drew the line at painting multicoloured floral designs on their faces and naked breasts, probably due to the fact that they had to catch the 244 bus home afterwards and the conductor tended to frown upon such things. It was only a matter of time before this outlandish sexual behaviour and drug abuse came to the attention of the local constabulary, who soon paid JB's a visit. Roy, who was on the door that evening too, recalls the police officer explaining to him that the club was about to be raided for drugs. Unfortunately, for the boys in blue at any rate, the place was so crowded that entry was impossible, and after several aborted attempts, the officers simply gave up trying and went away. There followed what might be best referred to as an uneasy pact – a Mexican stand-off between the club and the law after that incident. Quite often, the police would insist on parking a blue van outside the venue in an attempt to scare off the unwanted element, but all this did was provoke them. Sam Jukes remembers a gentleman by the name of Cliff Whiteley standing beside the police van one evening singing the song, 'Piggies' by The Beatles, at the top of his voice in a somewhat drunken and atonal fashion. Others, who didn't possess Cliff's vocal ability but were still desirous of making a statement, simply urinated up the side of it. After suffering this kind of abuse every Thursday, eventually the raids subsided, and instead, if we are to believe Sam (and why wouldn't we?), the officers would pay their 1/6d like everyone else and just drink there.

From the very beginning, JB's had been created by a group of close friends with the same sense of humour and love of music, simply acting on impulse, without giving anything too much thought. In fact, had they bothered to think about what they were doing, they would probably have ended up not doing it. Now, all of a sudden, they were having to grow up and become slightly more professional. Against all the odds, they found that they had concocted a winning formula, but as ever, nothing was easy. Controlling such relatively large crowds was a real problem, and in any sizeable gathering of people, there would inevitably be a small percentage of troublemakers. After one particularly fraught evening, the lavatories were seriously vandalized, and no one had the money to put things right. The Dudley Town football pavilion had seemed perfect when they set out, but now, after two years of madness, they needed something bigger and better. The vandalism had been a turning point, and the football club helping themselves to JB's profits had begun to stick in the collective throat of the committee somewhat. It was now time to look for new premises and move on.

☞ A delightful early press ad for Possessed – three of whom were later tragically killed in a motorway accident (see page 95) – and Anubis, courtesy of Phil Cunniffe. Note that the newspaper misspelt it as JD's and Phil has taken the trouble to correct this with his 13-colour biro.

☞ Anubis, namely Moss Drew, bass guitar, Phil Cunniffe, drums, and Dave Onions, guitar and vocals.

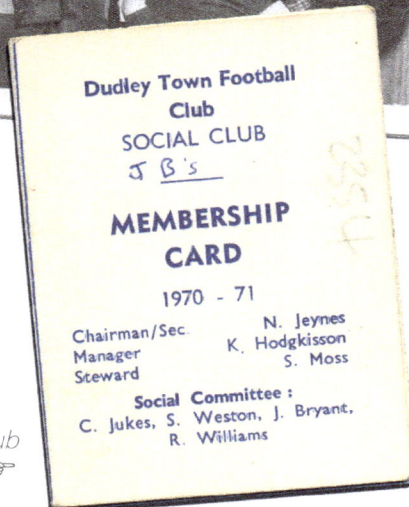

Phil Cunniffe's Football Club membership card. ☞

☞ *The Pathfinder showroom on King Street. JB's was immediately behind it.*

The King Street club, front view. How on earth did up to 400 of us cram into that tiny place every weekend? ☞

King Street

Back of Pathfinder

"We gotta get out of this place
If it's the last thing we ever do
We gotta get out of this place
'Cause girl there's a better life
For me and you "

The Animals

A young employee of the Pathfinder Gentlemen's Outfitters store, situated in King Street, Dudley, was a regular visitor to the football-club discos. Unfortunately, we have no name for this unsung hero, and this is rather sad, because it was he who mentioned to the committee that his boss, Percy Hill, owned a small, disused, Victorian infants' school building immediately behind his store that was in need of some loving care. Percy, who was in his fifties at that time, was not only a store owner but a town magistrate. He had been approached by members of the Jamaican community about the building, which they were keen to use as a social club, but their intention was for Percy to renovate the old St Thomas's School, and for them to rent it from him

once the redecoration was completed. The project stalled, and it was at this juncture that Sam and Sid came a-calling with their own plans for the place. They were shown around, and liked what they saw. After a brief discussion with their colleagues, they proposed to Percy that they would undertake the renovations on the days that the football club was not open for business, and pay him a suitable sum in rent – a figure of around £20, as Sam recalls. Percy agreed, presumably reasoning that Sam's agreement to refurbish the old place for him would suit him better than the Jamaican alternative. Nowadays, £20 might not sound a lot of money, but as Johnny Bryant explains, 'In 1970 I was earning £3.17.6d a week as a pattern maker. I had to give £2 to my mother for board and lodgings, and I spent a quid on bus fares from Dudley Port, Tipton, to Dudley town centre. The rest, I'm ashamed to admit, was blown on high living, all 17/6d of it.'

News of this deal with JB's club inevitably filtered back to the Jamaicans, who complained that they had been the first to moot the idea, and so a compromise was agreed, whereby JB's would run the place during the week, and they would have use of it on Saturdays.

None of this was ideal, but nevertheless, a deal was struck, and work began. A stage and a bar were fitted, and the building was given a coat of paint. Barmaid Glenis Jones (now Smythe) remembers that the place was full of creepy old mannequins and wooden counters and cabinets, presumably rejects from the Pathfinder store. Anyone who had a little spare time was commandeered, and Colin the barman recalls that one of the least inviting jobs was the painting of the ceiling. On this occasion, it was Larry who drew the short straw. He spent several uncomfortable hours perched precariously atop a wobbly stepladder, paint dripping into his eyes, like a low-rent version of Michelangelo in the Sistine Chapel, only to be informed after finishing two-thirds of the ceiling that those observing his endeavours down below were of the opinion that it would have looked better in dark blue. Sighing one of his heavy sighs, Larry began again, only to discover that a decision had been made to invest in a suspended ceiling instead.

As is par for the course when workmen are left to their own devices in eerie old deserted school buildings, tales were told of ghosts, usually men in military uniforms, curtains that moved when there was no wind, and a piano that played tunes even when no pianist was present.

Aggrieved that JB's seemed to be paying for the renovations in order that the Jamaicans could take advantage of the facilities come Saturday, Sam and Sid had a word with Percy, who reluctantly coughed up for materials, sourced from Smith's timber yard, just down the road.

Within a few weeks, things had gone awry, at least from the Jamaican perspective. Licensing laws were ignored, and a lot of late night/early morning drinking went on, which did not please the landlord. Percy, as we know, was a magistrate, and magistrates tend to take a dim view of such matters, as did Monty Walker, of the local drug squad. In fact, after observing the comings and goings at the old school, his view was, if anything, even dimmer than Percy's had been. However, it's an ill wind that blows nobody any good, as the old saying goes, and before long, the Jamaican connection was a mere brief footnote in the history of the place, which quietly suited Sam and the lads. JB's was up and running, even though no one seems to remember calling it JB's at the time. It was simply referred to as The Club for a while, before the old name crept back and stayed for good. It was not all plain sailing thereafter, though. Not having the foggiest idea about such matters, the committee had overlooked one vital requirement. They didn't have a proper liquor licence either. They had been relying on Ray Hingley from nearby Quarry Bank, landlord of the Robin Hood pub (much later, coincidentally, to become The Robin Rock Club under the new owner, Mike Hamblett), to provide an 'occasional' licence, but the law dictated that the licensee should be present on the premises, and of course, Ray was busy a few miles down the road at his own pub, which in those days hosted such events as the famous Black Country Night Out and the Citizens' Theatre.

Consequently, the club was again raided by the police, but thankfully, Sam was allowed to apply for his own licence, and, mercifully, was granted one. Now, the fledgling club could really move forward. Mick Ralphs had installed his psychedelic light show, there was a raised section created for the DJ's decks and the bands' mixing desk, a very sticky carpet (a traditional feature of all rock clubs), beer barrels that acted as tables, and, of course, a dartboard. When more money became available, they also planned to invest in an in-house PA system. Sam, by now, was in effect the club's manager, but would often be found on the door, greeting the customers and taking their money. In August 1972 Sam employed a solicitor, R. J. Evans, Bullock and Co., to form a company with the name JB's Promotions Ltd., with Sam nominated as a director. Susan Evans, who eventually married Sam in 1982, became a founder director, and her computing and accounting skills helped greatly in the smooth running of the club's financial affairs. It was Susan who held the first bank account at Lloyds Bank, in the name of Susan Evans trading as JB's Promotions. She later became appointed as Company Secretary, and was responsible for the audited accounts. Suddenly, it all sounded very grown up!

A plethora of young ladies, Glenis Jones and Carol Hayden to name but two, helped out with bar work, and supplied a much-needed sprinkling of glamour. Sue also worked at the club, turning her hand to whatever task needed doing, as soon as she finished her day's shift at West Bromwich Council's IBM computer department. It was all hands to the pump, as ever.

The brewery, Scottish & Newcastle plc, had recently expanded into the area, looking for new customers, so Sam invited them to the club, and as a consequence of this, Newcastle Brown Ale, with its distinctive label and clear-glass bottle, immediately became synonymous with JB's. 'Big' Dave Hodgetts, aka Newcastle Dave, the fellow who you will recall had earlier demolished the taxi-rank telephone thanks to a mixture of potent alcohol and heavy-handedness, was a particular fan of the brewery's products, and reckoned that Newcastle Exhibition Ale was eleven-ninths stronger than Newcastle Brown, based on the less-than-scientific theory that he could drink eleven bottles of Newcastle Brown but only nine bottles of Exhibition before he collapsed in a giant heap onto the sticky carpet. It was the same Dave Hodgetts who, if you will allow this slight digression, heard a bizarre radio advert for Sid Riley's car showrooms in nearby Dudley Port and decided to act upon it. Apparently, a free second-hand car would be given to the first person to arrive at the flashy, American-style car lot wearing a top hat and carrying a tin of Andrews Liver Salts (it is easier not to question why). This he duly did, and was rewarded with a nice vehicle for his efforts, the only snag being that our prize-winner did not possess a valid driving licence at that time. Dave eventually became local superstar Robert Plant's right-hand man and fixer. It would be nice to imagine canny Robert thinking, 'Anyone who can wangle a free car just for doing that deserves to be part of my organization.'

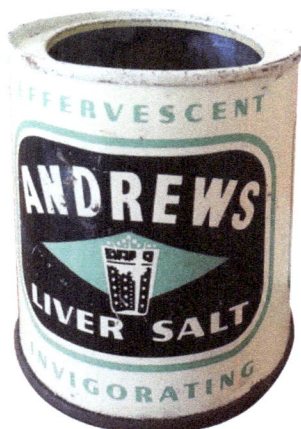

Meanwhile, back at the club, Sid's non-identical twin brother, John Weston, in one of his shrewder moments, decided from almost day one (shall we agree on not long after day two?) to have the bands sign a visitors' book, similar to the type favoured by seaside bed and breakfast establishments. Thanks to what must now be seen as an important historical document in rock-music terms, we can now be more or less categorical about who played there and when, during that early period. The new King Street JB's club opened quietly and without fuss on Thursday the 1st of July 1971 with a disco, and Colin Pugh recalls that everything behind his bar had to be locked away before the short-lived Jamaican social club moved in on the following Saturday. He also remembers disconnecting a huge barrel of Guinness behind the bar, which resulted in a five-foot high, thrusting arc of gushing black stuff, which, to the casual observer, gave the impression that some lucky ginger-bearded prospector had struck oil in the middle of Dudley. JB's might not have struck oil as such, but they had certainly struck gold. A Thursday disco could see at least ten crates of Newcastle Brown alone disappear down the throats of the thirsty crowd, and at Christmas, this increased to twenty crates. The good news was that, for the first time, the music club, and not the football club, was reaping the financial benefits.

The first Friday evening that the club opened, however, was poorly attended. As with any new venture, it took time for the jungle telegraph to do its work. Someone – alas, another name lost forever in the mists of time – played a set at the piano to the bar staff and a few Victorian ghosts, but at least got paid for his trouble. The committee, who, it has to be said, can barely agree about anything most of the time, are of the opinion that a local outfit by the name of Pahana, fronted by Elmer O'Shea, was the very first 'proper band' to appear at the club, closely followed by Travellin' Redwing and legendary percussionist Jon Hiseman's band, Colosseum. Those who now fear that the rest of this tome will be a mass of befuddled speculation and guesswork can relax, however, because it was at this juncture that John's visitors' book was introduced, just in time to record that on the 20th of August, 1971, the excellent Bronco graced the JB's

Glenn Hughes sprays the JB's audience with testosterone. ☞

☞ Terry Reid, looking very psychedelic thanks to the famous JB's liquid light show.

☞ A rare old photo of Travellin' Redwing in the days when beards were compulsory. Did you spot a young Johnny Bryant (centre) or did the facial fuzz confuse you?

☞ Argent raise the roof. Shouldn't that bloke on the right be holding his head up?

☞ Tír na nÓg at King Street.

☝ *A stick-thin Phil Lynott of Thin Lizzy.*

☝ *Thin Lizzy autographs in John Weston's visitors' book.*

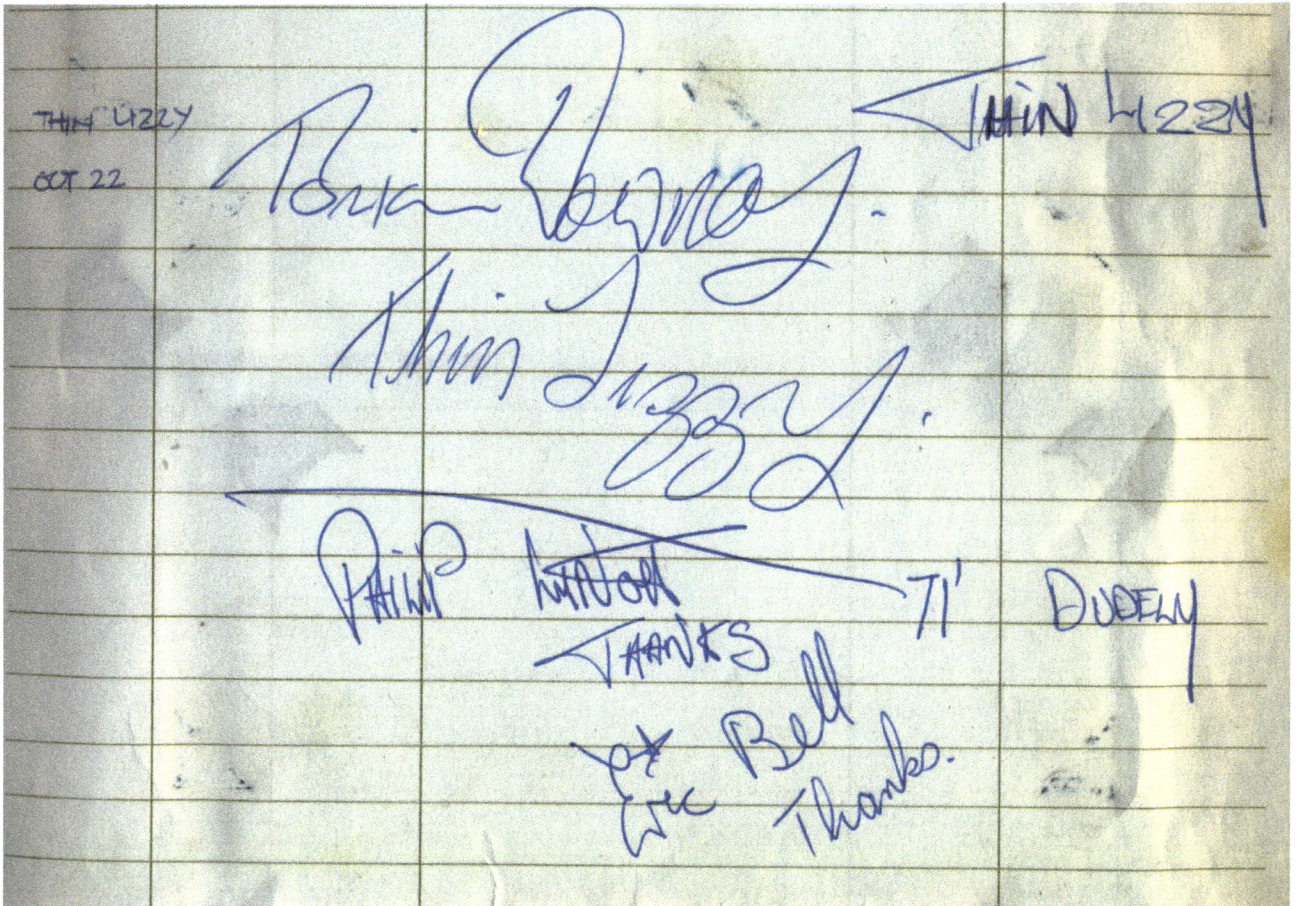

☞ Bronco pose in a farmyard setting, as befits a country rock band. Jess Roden must be hiding behind the tractor on this shot.

☞ This is either Long John Baldry or a very large garden gnome.

stage, featuring Jess Roden on vocals, John Pasternak on bass, Pete Robinson on drums, an d Robbie Blunt and Kevin Gammond on guitars. The band's second country-rock album, 'Ace of Sunlight', was about to be released, following their equally beautiful debut album 'Country Home'.

Jess began his career in The Alan Bown Set, a well-known sixties band that helped develop the careers of Robert Palmer, Mel Collins (King Crimson), John Helliwell and Dougie Thomson (Supertramp), before forming Bronco, which was essentially a country-rock outfit. He later formed The Jess Roden Band, which leant more towards soulful funk, and became one of England's best, if somewhat underrated, white soul singers. It was as a testament to Roden's talent that he was asked to replace the late Jim Morrison in the reformed 21st Century Doors, which toured briefly.

Determined to keep this standard up, the following week welcomed Trapeze, a powerhouse heavy funk-rock trio featuring Mel Galley on guitar, Dave Holland on drums, and, of course, Glenn Hughes on bass guitar and vocals – a man who would later become one of heavy rock's superstar singers, courtesy of Deep Purple.

Having set the bar high, Sam and Co. needed to keep the momentum going, and they certainly did. The Alan Bown Set, Jess Roden's original band, played there the following week, followed by Terry Reid, who was quite a coup for the fledgling rock club at the time. The committee had been to see him perform at the Roundhouse in London and Mother's in Erdington, loved him and booked him to play at JB's. Reid's band that night featured Alan White on drums, Dave Linley on guitars (Jackson Brown) and Lee Miles on Bass (Ike and Tina Turner Band). His public profile had been considerably enhanced back in 1966, thanks to landing a job as vocalist with The Jaywalkers, who were invited to support The Rolling Stones at their Royal Albert Hall concert. Shortly after this, impresario Mickie Most began to manage Reid, and in 1968 his new band was busy touring the USA alongside Cream. A song-writing liaison with Graham Nash of The Hollies, and later Crosby, Stills, Nash & Young, also helped to ensure that Reid's career continued to blossom. It was only a matter of time before The Yardbirds' guitarist Jimmy Page took notice, and consequently asked Reid to

be the frontman in a new band that was to become Led Zeppelin. As is often the case, the timings were not convenient, and Reid had already committed to the Cream tour. His hands were tied, but instead he recommended a young singer from West Bromwich by the name of Robert Plant, having been impressed by Plant's Band of Joy, which had supported Reid in the past. Not only did Reid give away one of the best jobs in rock music to Plant, but he also lost out to Ian Gillan as frontman to Deep Purple not long afterwards!

Sound engineer, Roy Williams, will always remember Terry Reid's gigs at JB's, not only for his musical excellence, but also because of a conversation he had with Reid's drummer at the time, Alan White. White, a highly rated percussionist, has been around the block, and had done stints with the likes of The Alan Price Set, Ginger Baker's Air Force, Steve Winwood, Joe Cocker, and later on, progressive rock giants, Yes, but back in 1971, he was to be seen and heard playing drums with Terry Reid. Roy Williams had arrived early to open the club, ready for the band's arrival, and was surprised to see Alan White arrive alone, carrying his sticks and a snare drum. When asked why he wasn't in the van with the rest of the band, White explained that he had been recording in London, but had been allowed to leave early in order to fulfil his commitments at JB's club that evening. Unfortunately, he had leapt off the train at Dudley Port, believing it to be situated in the centre of Dudley. Sadly, it is not. The confusingly named station is in fact three miles shy of Dudley, in Tipton, not far from the Coneygre Youth Club where this tale began. As a result of this error, White was forced to flag down a bus, but still arrived at the club in good time. Roy asked the perspiring percussionist what he had been up to in London, and White informed him that he had been at Ascot Sound Studios, which was John Lennon's newly built home studio at Tittenhurst Park, recording a new tune by the name of 'Imagine'.

As ever, JB's club seemed to find itself linked in some way to what was hot in the world of rock music. Sometimes, the link was direct, and other times slightly more tenuous, but the place had a knack of never being far from the musical action. Sam Jukes has a plethora of amusing tales about the many bands that have played at his club, and in the following case, the ones that didn't.

at in his cramped little office one afternoon, Sam answered a phone call from a rather well-spoken agent from London, who had recently taken a new band and was keen for them to venture out into the provinces. He had heard that JB's was one of the places to be seen, and was enquiring about how he could secure a gig at the venue. Sam explained that new bands had to perform on Friday nights initially, in order to prove their worth, before being allowed the more prestigious Saturday night gig. The typical fee paid to a band at that particular time in the club's history was £150, plus a crate of Newcastle Brown Ale and fish and chips all round (presumably the roadies only got roe and chips, as befits their status). If this inaugural evening was successful in terms of crowd reaction, the band would then be offered a Saturday in the near future, with an increased fee of £200, plus of course the usual brown ale and fish supper thrown in. This seemed to give the well-spoken Londoner much to think about, and there was a slightly awkward silence, after which he rang back, asking questions about the distance from dressing room to stage, and similar irrelevant twaddle. He then cleared his throat, and politely asked for 'at least £175' for the initial Friday evening, whereupon Sam, who had not been to the same finishing school as the gentleman on the other end of the phone, promptly told him to 'fuck off!', the debate now being, to Sam's mind at least, concluded.

Whether or not he might have been tempted to change his mind, had he realized that the caller was ringing on behalf of Freddie Mercury and Queen, is another story. On another occasion, later in the club's history, Sam was sent a tape to listen to from a band angling for a booking. Having heard a few tales about some of the band's performances and not caring over-much for the tape either, he declined the band's request, which meant that JB's was never to play host to Debbie Harry and Blondie either. It is worth noting that ALL tapes sent to JB's did get listened to, unlike a lot of other clubs. Whether they booked them or not was another matter.

eptember 17th, 1971, saw Tír na nÓg play at JB's. They were an Irish folk band from Dublin who specialized in lyrical Celtic songs that featured close-harmony singing, a genre that was at the other end of the musical spectrum to bands such as, for example, Trapeze, but this was, for many people, the secret of JB's longevity. The committee members were always keen to promote all forms of music, and the clientele seemed equally willing to turn up and appreciate whatever was put before them. In many ways, the club came first. It was the place that everyone went to, because of, or sometimes in spite of, which act was performing there that evening. It was their social club where they met like-minded people, and if the band that night was a particular favourite, even better. This attitude inevitably engendered a broader understanding and appreciation of the many forms of music on offer at that time, which was all to the good.

Tír na nÓg was followed by Glenn Cornick's group, Wild Turkey. Cornick had recently left the highly successful Jethro Tull to venture out on his own, but the band was never to set the world alight, and after a tour with Black Sabbath, Wild Turkey disbanded. No matter. JB's was booking bands that were – at the very least – connected to the big acts that were currently filling large concert venues, and this in itself was no mean feat for what was, in truth, a small, tatty old primary-school building hidden from the world behind a big, ugly old clothing store on a nondescript road leading out of Dudley town centre.

Chicken Shack's. Stan Webb.

The mighty Trapeze, fronted by Glenn Hughes.

Climax Chicago Blues Band pose with the band member who didn't much care for their 12 bars.

There is an amusing parlour game entitled 'Six Degrees of Separation', which argues that it is possible to link anyone in this world to anyone else, in no more than six moves. At JB's, audience members could usually link themselves to any famous band in just two or three moves. By way of example, October began strongly with Stan Webb's Chicken Shack, who had also appeared at the Quarry club in Gornal. Any person present on that evening would probably know that Webb's original female vocalist had been Christine Perfect, until she left the band in 1969, married John McVie and joined Fleetwood Mac. Thus, a JB's member who had stood chatting to Stan Webb in the lavatory could boast that he could connect to Fleetwood Mac in just two moves. In those heady days of the early seventies, it seemed as if every musician was somehow related to every other musician. It was all quite magical, if a little incestuous, and the town of Dudley – and its surroundings – was all too often the unlikely catalyst. Take another, even more remarkable example. Alan White played at the club with Terry Reid, who could have ended up as vocalist for Led Zeppelin, or Deep Purple. White also played for John Lennon, which instantly links a tiny rock club in a seemingly dull Midlands' town to The Beatles, Led Zeppelin and Deep Purple – again, in just two moves. The connections go on and on, ad infinitum, but surely the prize for the most fascinating and unexpected connection to rock royalty has to be awarded to none other than Johnny Bryant, the man who gave his name to the club. That, however, is a story for a little later down the line, so you'll have to be patient! I'm such a tease!

Before we get to that particularly fascinating chapter, there's the small matter of Thin Lizzy, who played at JB's on the 22nd of October, 1971 (fee – £50, a crate of brown ale and a few bags of chips). Sam recalls that they were extremely good, but then added, somewhat mysteriously, that they were not invited back. Having already witnessed Sam's no-nonsense approach vis-à-vis the Freddie Mercury and Queen affair, and realizing that he ran a tight ship, further probing eventually revealed that one of the band had 'borrowed' a bottle of whisky after the gig, which did not go down well with the manager. Presumably, they purloined it to put it in their jar-o.

Bands such as Philip Goodhand Tait, Gypsy, Barclay James Harvest, America, Roy Young, Climax Chicago Blues Band, Argent, Brett Marvin and the Thunderbolts, and Long John Baldry, took the fledgling club into the New Year, and several of them became extremely well known and commercially successful. Sid remembers that America – largely known for their singles 'Desert Song' (later renamed 'A Horse with

*America, the band that loved to rehearse **after** a show!*

No Name') and 'Ventura Highway' – played their set, and once the audience had eventually gone home in their Mark 1 Cortinas and MINI Clubmans to their cosy three-bar electric fires, their polystyrene ceiling tiles and maybe a mug of Horlicks before turning in for the night, the band availed themselves of the facilities to rehearse for another two solid hours, much to the bemusement of the exhausted staff. Sid also recalls America's manager, Jeff Dexter, a man that 'no one quite took to', standing in the cramped little reception area, counting in the punters with a small clicker device to make sure that JB's did not rob him, having done a deal with Sam for a fee based partly on the amount of tickets sold on the night. America had arrived fresh from performing at The Oval with The Who, and were very much in the ascendancy, so it was natural that a manager might be looking after their interests, but somehow, to a small group of friends that had created JB's in the pure spirit of altruism, a group that, to this day, has never betrayed that ideal, this slightly arrogant man accounting for each and every punter like a modern-day Ebenezer Scrooge was galling, to say the least. Perhaps someone should have explained to Mr Dexter that every member of staff, from Sam down, was working long, antisocial, unpaid hours to provide the people of the Black Country with some good live music. It wasn't in their nature to be as sharp as he obviously was.

Some fifty years on, as the committee discussed the creation of this book in the Foresters Arms, it was interesting, not to mention quite moving, to note that, when the subject of advertising was mooted as a means of paying for the book's printing costs, each of them pretty quickly dismissed the idea, instead favouring a whip-round amongst themselves. That way, they explained, it kept the book pure, and also, more importantly, beholden to no one. It is to their credit, in these cut-throat, commercial times, that they have each remained true to the original spirit that helped create JB's in 1969.

That said, if a slightly annoying manager wielding a clicker was the worst that ever happened, Sam and the boys and girls who worked at the club would have been more than happy. Alas, it was not. Just as there had been trouble at the old football-club venue, it was inevitable that there would be the odd incident at King Street. One evening, before the club was open to punters, Sam was busying himself in the main room,

when he heard a commotion in the reception area. He poked his head around the door to find a character by the name of Dougie the Drunk, who was helping out at the time, staring down the twin barrels of a shotgun, wielded by a person unknown at the front door. Dougie, a gentleman who was overly fond of the demon drink (the more astute reader will probably have already ascertained this fact from his nickname), was remonstrating with the armed man, and Sam arrived just in time to hear him slur the words, 'You pull that fucking trigger, mate, and I'll punch your earole!'

Thinking on his feet, as footballers are prone to do, Sam yanked Dougie back into the club and quickly slammed the front door, locking it as he did so. The two of them then made a dash for the main room and hid there, quaking, until it was deemed safe to peer outside. The gunman had thankfully left the premises by this time, and to this day, Sam does not have a clue who the man was or what he wanted. What he is certain of, is that the incident provided the best cure for constipation he had yet discovered.

Before we dispense with the services of Dougie the Drunk, impeccable sources inform us that this gentleman occasionally lived in the cellar at JB's, like some low-rent, sozzled version of the Phantom of the Opera. One has visions of this poor man – this cellar-dweller – chained to a sweating wall, wearing a gimp mask and awaiting Sam's pleasure, but the truth was somewhat more prosaic. Sam allowed him to bunk there occasionally because the man had nowhere else to go, bless him.

It was incidents such as the case of the stranger with the shotgun that confirmed the need for a bouncer, and fortunately the committee knew the perfect candidate, a man they had seen working at the Safari Club on many occasions, striking fear into the heart of every ne'er-do-well in the area. The word 'legend' is badly overused, but in this particular case, it is justified. JB's King Street and Jimmy the Con were synonymous, pretty much from the start. The two were inseparably intertwined, and if JB's club is destined to become part of rock and roll history, then the untamed, explosive tornado that was the late Jimmy Fisher must be part of it also.

It must be stressed that Jimmy did some bad things – some extremely bad things – and this section of the story is not an attempt to repaint him whiter than white. There will be certain individuals who have found themselves on the wrong side of this man, and 'legend' would not be their adjective of choice for him. What follows is hopefully a fair assessment of Jimmy's life, as it revolved around JB's club, with all the anecdotes, the contradictions, the humorous incidents, and the general madness that that entailed. We do not judge here, for it is not our place to do that in a book that is first and foremost about music. We will simply record a few of the more noteworthy tales that we know to be true, and then move on.

Gypsy guitarist Robin Pizer at JB's, November the 12th, 1971. ☞

☞ *JB's regulars, Leicester band, Gypsy, not to be confused with the American band of the same name.*

Jimmy the Con

*"Everywhere I hear the sound of marching,
charging feet, boy
'Cause summer's here, and the time is right
For fighting in the street, boy
But what can a poor boy do
Except to sing for a rock and roll band
'Cause in sleepy Dudley town
There's just no place for a street-fighting man!"*

(With apologies to The Rolling Stones)

One evening circa 1970 at the nearby Safari Club, Johnny Bryant and his friend, Johnny Higgs, were visiting the men's lavatory when they came across Jimmy Fisher (known to all as Jimmy the Con), who was explaining to three trouble-making Teddy boys (yes, they still existed as late as 1970) that their custom was not required. The precise reasons for this decision are lost in the mists of time, but what happened next would stay in Johnny Bryant's head for ever. The largest of the Teddy boys made the massive mistake of questioning the bouncer's judgment, and, squaring up to Jimmy, added the obligatory, 'And who's going to make me?'

After that, all hell broke loose. The first two men were punched once and instantly collapsed, unconscious. The third put up a certain amount of resistance, so Jimmy, who had now seemingly transformed into the Incredible Hulk and was red-faced and raging, tore into the third man.

Johnny remembers experiencing a troubling mixture of emotions at that juncture, as befits a man of peace. He was overawed and impressed by the sheer animal power of the man, but also terrified, in equal measure. If JB's could maybe harness that power and use it solely for the benefit of the club, he reasoned, then it might be a good move. The last thing anyone wanted at King Street was an environment that was modelled on a Viking-style fighting, raping and pillaging den. It was a place where gentle hippies and music lovers mingled, but, as had been demonstrated at the football club on several occasions, sometimes idiots with a completely different agenda found their way into such places and caused mayhem. It was akin to allowing a rabid fox to gain entry to a large hen house. It only took one troublemaker to cause absolute chaos for the entire place. The consensus at JB's was, if

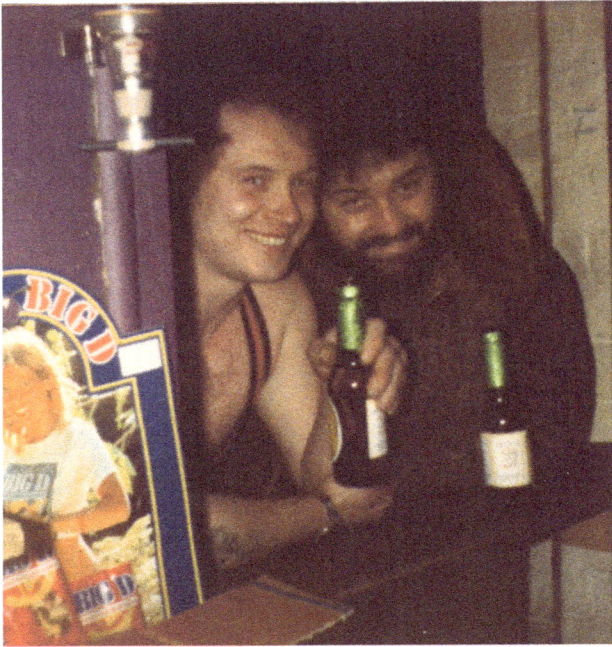

☞ Jimmy the Con and friend indulge in a quick Pils.

☞ Dexys Midnight Runners, who, in spite of their boy-next-door looks, were quite a handful.

☞ A fine shot of Jimmy the Con in his prime. Not sure about the pink T shirt though.

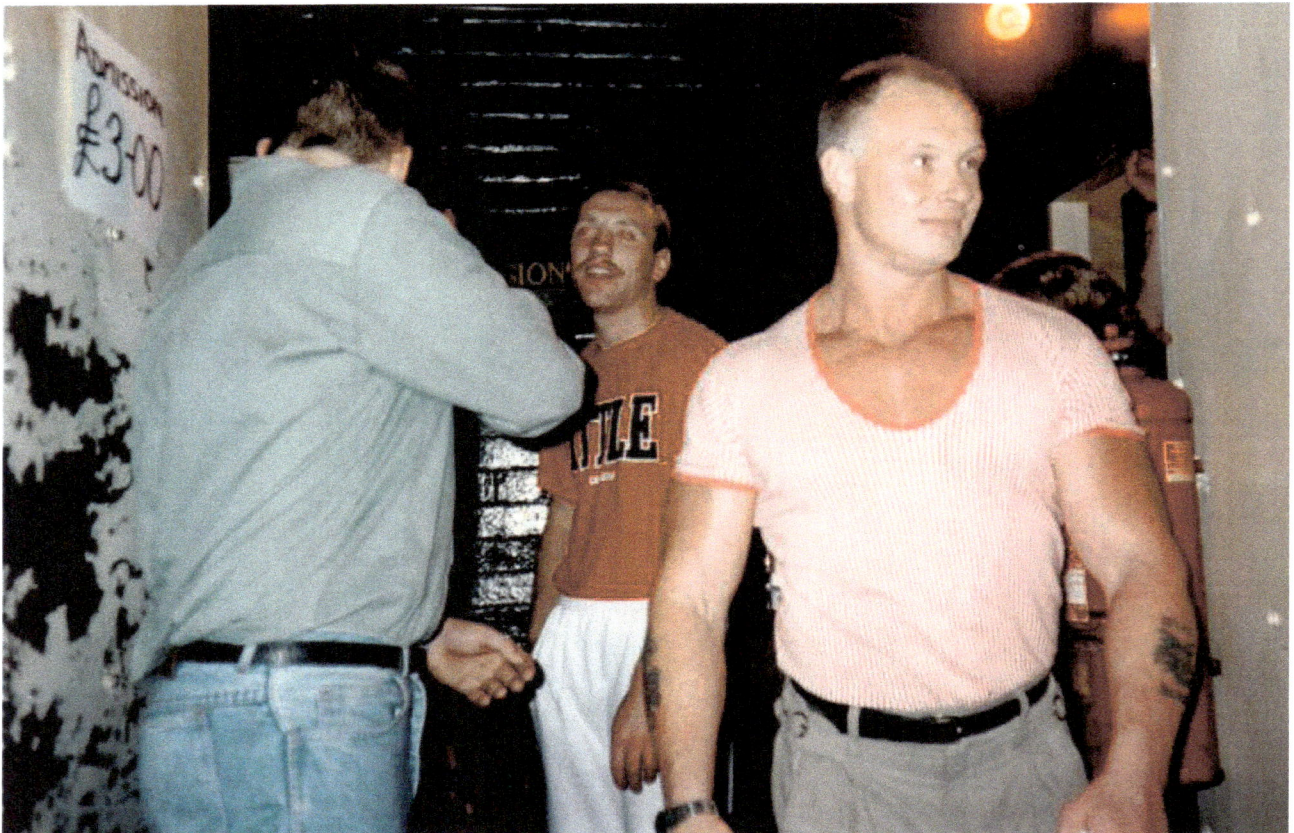

Jimmy, loose cannon that he was, became the club's bouncer and human nuclear deterrent, the wayward punters would be so scared to start anything that an atmosphere of peace and love would naturally prevail. The vermin would be turfed out, leaving the peaceful hens free to go about their lawful egg-laying business. In other words, if you ever find yourself constantly troubled by a rabid fox, buy yourself a large grizzly bear.

The expression 'bouncers', or the more modern, politically correct alternative, 'door staff', instantly conjures up images of huge gents with bent noses, dressed in regulation black overcoats, often with a security pass swinging on a chain around their neck and a microphone fixed to their ear. Jimmy the Con was not that kind of bouncer. These were the dark days before regulations, certificates and council approval. Jimmy looked more like a small, muscle-bound pirate circa 1720, with a shaven head, a single earring and a sweaty vest. All he needed to complete the ensemble was a red and white spotted bandana and a cutlass; maybe a flintlock tucked into his Levi's and a talking parrot. He was nick-named 'The Con' because, in the words of Sid Weston, he'd seen more courts than John McEnroe.

Ex-boxer Jimmy settled in as the bouncer at King Street, settling disputes and disturbances in his own inimitable style. Sam explains that 'The Con' was the only person at JB's to get paid, which seemed fair enough, given what he potentially had to do each evening. Perhaps it also had something to do with the fact that no one was brave enough to suggest that he worked for nothing, like the other staff did.

Countless tales of Jimmy's exploits exist, and doubtless, many have been suitably embellished with each re-telling, but even given the occasional exaggeration, here was a man who struck fear into the hearts of the customers, and in so doing, managed to keep the club fairly peaceful, a vindication of the committee's choice of bouncer. It is also fair to say that most, if not all of those who were on the receiving end of Jimmy's violence, had it coming. He was not prone to picking on innocents, just because he could. The only bone of contention was that he often meted out far more than was necessary to subdue a troublemaker, rather than just throwing them out into the street and dusting off his hands, like they used to do in 1950's westerns. Take, for example, the evening when a tough, unruly, drunken soldier began to pester the house DJ and tamper with his record decks. Jimmy was asked to intervene, and did so in his own, inimitable way. Let's just say that the man would think twice before doing it again.

In addition to his JB's duties, Jim was also employed by artistes such as Ian Gillan (of Deep Purple) and Dexys Midnight Runners, as a minder. Kevin Rowland, Dexys frontman, had a reputation for rubbing people up the wrong way, and needed looking after. Those who remember their keyboard player, Andy Leek, sporting a black eye on Top of the Pops during the 12 weeks they spent at number one with 'Geno', might have wondered how he came by it. Word has it that it was inflicted during a brawl in the tour van, before the TV show was filmed, but those who are keen to know which member of the band actually hit him on that particular occasion should perhaps ask Andy. It is not for us to speculate! Let us just say that theirs was a volatile relationship.

One evening at a Dexys gig, Rowland had somehow managed to displease five burly rugby players, but thankfully, Jimmy was on hand to talk to them. He began diplomatically enough, by asking the men to disperse, but when this tactic failed, he once again explained who was going to be hit and in what order, and once again, the recipients of his talk chose to ignore his warning. There has already been far too much talk of violence, so suffice it to say, without having to go into detail, things were settled the Fisher way.

An interesting postscript to this story is supplied by legendary JB's disc jockey, Dermott Stephens (of whom, more later). He remembers that Rowland had a punk band by the name of The Killjoys, before he finally found fame with

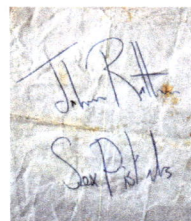

Dexys, and when they played at JB's, a violent row erupted between the band and Jimmy (were they insanely foolhardy, we ask?). This resulted in Jimmy ejecting the lot of them out of the club, 25 minutes into their set. Surely there must have been a lot of kissing and making up to follow, given that Jimmy ended up working for Rowland.

In the mid-70s, when the Sex Pistols had been banned

from performing and their records removed from playlists, due to their carefully stage-managed, anti-social, headline-grabbing antics, they cleverly changed the name of their band, temporarily, to The Spots ('SPOTS' standing for 'Sex Pistols On Tour Secretly'), and using this pseudonym, they were able to play incognito at venues around the UK. One such venue was the Club Lafayette in nearby Wolverhampton. Once the band had sound-checked at the nightclub, they were at a loose end and getting restless, so Roy Williams, who was working at the Astra Agency at the time (which was based at the Lafayette and where Sam often turned to when booking bands for JB's), suggested they might benefit from evading the spotlight for a few hours by slipping over to JB's in nearby Dudley for a drink. Roy and Maurice Jones, a director of Astra, duly ferried the band over to the club, which was all but empty as it had only just opened. Colin the barman recalls that the band members were quite subdued and polite, considering their demonic reputation. Johnny Rotten, he distinctly remembers, came to the bar and meekly requested a half of lager and a packet of plain crisps, even adding 'please'. The worst that Sid Vicious managed to do was to scrawl his name on the lavatory door. Understandably nervous about the coming evening, Jimmy the Con and his friend, Carly, were asked by the promoter to beef up the security at the Lafayette, which they duly did. In fact, without them, there would almost certainly have been a riot. The Sex Pistols was a band that would need a lot of looking after, that was for sure.

Sam's wife, Sue, recalls an evening when a visiting band had a valuable guitar stolen. The thief hid it in a skip outside the club and returned to collect it when the coast was clear, but tragically for him, he had been wrong about the clarity of the coast. Jimmy the Con was waiting, and feeling mean. Suffice it to say that, unlike ankle tags and ASBOs, Jimmy was a very effective deterrent for the criminal fraternity. Sadly, this didn't prevent him from indulging in a little criminal activity himself. Jimmy, looking unusually apprehensive, approached Sid, desirous of a word. Apparently, the police suspected him and two other gentlemen of stealing a large safe, full of valuables.

'They have to prove it first,' advised Sid. 'Do they have any evidence?'

'Well, they caught me running down the road

with it under my arm,' admitted Jimmy.

Expecting the worst, nevertheless Sid asked Percy the magistrate for advice, and wrote a heart-rending defence, explaining that, even though Jimmy was a rough diamond and had undeniably been in trouble before, he now had a steady job at JB's, and was determined to turn over a new leaf, and begin a life of honest toil (if duffing up hoodlums at JB's could be described as honest toil). Remarkably, Jimmy received no more than a suspended sentence, whereas his two colleagues ended up in jail. Quite how Jimmy, Sid and Sam pulled off this Houdini-like escape is still one of the great unsolved mysteries of the time.

Meanwhile, back at the club, Jimmy continued to deal with unruly customers, which was beginning to unnerve the committee. They did not want punters to be so scared of the man that they spent their hard-earned cash elsewhere. The problem was, Jimmy seemed to think that he had to be seen to be earning his wages, and the most effective way to do this was to be seen ejecting the riff-raff on a regular basis. Fundamentally, he was acting in a similar way to the farmer's cat, forever bringing dead rats into the farmer's wife's kitchen to prove his worth. Someone had to quietly and tactfully mention to Jimmy that this was not necessary. If there was no commotion at the club, and his services were not required, that was to be seen as a good night. No one minded a jot if he got paid for not doing anything. That was how the committee liked it, no matter how boring it may have been for Jimmy. The only problem was, who should tell him? Eventually, this unenviable task fell to Sid, though it is not clear whether he and Sam drew straws for the privilege or whether Sid was overcome with a rare injection of courage, Dutch or otherwise. Thankfully, Sid lived to tell the tale.

Another worry was Jim's developing interest in the Hell's Angels. One evening, he arrived at the club wearing the outfit of the Oakham Chapter, which caused a few palpitations amongst the committee, who feared their peaceful little club being taken over by marauding gangs of bikers. The following week, the Wolverhampton Chapter of the Hell's Angels, the most feared biker organization outside of the Los Angeles Chapter at that time, decided to pay the Oakham Chapter a visit, and one sensed that it wasn't to engage in a few games of whist over cucumber sandwiches. The two gangs faced each other briefly, before the Oakham bikers decided that discretion really was the better part of valour, and they disappeared sharpish whence they came. All, that was, except Jimmy the Con, who stood in the street by himself, inviting anyone who was interested to take him on. This may have been the action of a mad man, but it worked. The Wolverhampton gang seemed to be impressed by his bravery, and even asked if he'd care to join them. Thankfully, he declined their kind offer, and his Hell's Angel days were quickly put behind him, much to the committee's relief.

Not all Jimmy the Con anecdotes are related to violence. Larry Homer, a talented guitarist, originally from nearby Old Hill, recalls the evening that his progressive rock band, Still, played at JB's. Still was very much in debt to Genesis, musically speaking, with their complex arrangements and lengthy songs containing intricate instrumental sections, though they drew the line at dressing in strange costumes. The band used an opening tape of orchestral music, as was de rigueur in those days for this type of band, and towards the end of the piece, by Vangelis Papathanassou, for those who like the detail, the band members would sidle onto the stage, take up their positions, looking suitably solemn, magnificent and intellectual. As the piece ended they would seamlessly segue into their rousing opening number, probably amid a sea of dry ice if the budget ran to it. The only problem was, no one seemed to know where the opening tape had gone. Larry swore that Nick had it, and Nick suspected that John or Rob had it, but Rob was certain that Trev or Graham the roadie had it and had left it in the van. People were running around like headless chickens, searching every nook and cranny, and this was seriously delaying the start time for the gig and making the management twitchy. Eventually, Jimmy the Con stormed onto the stage, grabbed the nearest microphone and bellowed, 'Put the fucking tape on!', which wasn't quite the ethereal effect that Still was striving for. Then, as if by magic, the opening bars of Vangelis' 'Heaven and Hell' wafted out from the PA speakers. It is funny how one sharp sentence from Jimmy could concentrate the mind and make things happen.

A friend of Larry's remembers arriving at the club to watch Still, offering his 50p entrance fee to Jimmy, who was sat behind the table in reception that evening, taking the money and checking credentials.

'Where's your membership card?' he snarled. The skittish young man handed over the card with a trembling, sweaty hand. Jimmy studied it at length and threw it back across the table.

'Think that's fucking funny?' he asked, studying the terrified young man as a mongoose would a snake. The sallow youth looked down at his card, and realized that it was in fact his student bus pass. Quickly pocketing it and fumbling inside his blue Air Force greatcoat for his membership card, he eventually offered it to the bouncer to inspect.

'Keep it still, I can't read it, you fucking idiot,' said Jimmy. The Con could have that effect on a person's nerves.

Shaun Payne and Carol Harrison (left) frolic in the woods.

Shaun Payne, a regular JB's goer, and the man who created the psychedelic Knave of Hearts playing-card backdrop that once graced the stage, had a similar experience. JB's had a strict 'no drugs policy' within the club, because, amongst other things, it could be closed down if the police raided the place – which they often did – and found that everyone within it was stoned senseless. It was part of Jimmy's remit to control this, as best he could. Shaun, who arrived at the club slightly the worse for wear after an illegal cigarette or two, was dancing around in carefree fashion when he experienced an extremely painful stabbing pain in his shoulder, which caused him to spin around. He found himself inches away from Jimmy's glaring eyes, for it was he that had poked him in order to attract his attention.

Path Lab Diplomats
next match
4

☞ The JB's football squad. Note Jimmy the Con's sleeveless shirt.

v

J. B. WARRIORS   0

at GUEST HOSP. RECREATION GROUND
on SUNDAY 3rd APRIL 83 K.O. 2.30pm
Team :-

1. MARK (NOBBY) STOCK
2. ANDY (CHOPPER) MILES
3. NICK (GUST OF WIND) PARRY
4. MARK (NOT SO DICKY LEGS) DAVENPORT
5. STEVE (CRANE FLY) GENNER
6. ROGER (DISGRACED) DOUGAN - CAPT.
7. PHIL (DA SCORE IN LAST GAME) STEWART T (MANAGER)
8. AL (NAR-SURPLUS HAIR DO) HOMER
9. COLIN (MUDS) JOHNSON   2
10. DEAN (CARRY ME OFF NEXT TIME) IRONMONGER
11. GARY (THE GHOSTIE) YARNDELL
Subs DOUG (FEET TURNS UP) HEGGIE (AWOL)

☞ A football team-sheet for the Path Lab Warriors versus JB's Diplomats, circa 1983, complete with match report, which mentions Jimmy the Con performing 'orthopaedic surgery' on a Path Lab player. For those not familiar with medical jargon, substitute the phrase, 'kicked the shit out of'.

The author as a handsome young rock god, with the band Still.
☞

Local prog rock band, Still, showing Larry Homer on guitar, Rob Lake on vocals and you can just about see David Tristram (creator of the hilarious Doreen's Story and Inspector Drake films) on bass.

'I bet you think you're really somebody because you smoke dope, don't you?' he asked, strongly suspecting that Shaun had been indulging in illegal substances.

Quaking with fear, Shaun recalls replying somewhat pitifully, 'No Jim, I don't think I'm anybody.' Thankfully, this little warning was all that was required to set Shaun back on the straight and narrow, and miraculously, the two even became quite matey with the passing of time. Shaun also remembers with great fondness arriving at JB's one Christmas to watch a festive band, just as the snow began to fall heavily, instantly coating the car park in a crisp, white blanket that seemed to twinkle with a thousand fairy lights. It was, he recalls, 'like something from a Hollywood film – It's a Wonderful Life starring James Stewart, maybe. It was all quite magical.'

Sadly, as he rounded the corner, the illusion was shattered when he saw Jimmy in his sweaty vest, standing outside the front door on the top step, urinating into the snow (thanks to the club being so packed that he couldn't get to the toilet), without a hint of embarrassment, as gaggles of young lads and their girls arrived for the party.

'Happy fucking Christmas!' grinned Jimmy,

greeting his flock. One can't help thinking that James Stewart wouldn't have handled it that way.

Andrew Miles, nowadays a pharmaceutical company executive, remembers Jimmy turning out for his company's football team on one occasion, many years ago, thanks to another player who also ran the JB's football team. Jimmy was handed a smart, brand new, red and white football top bearing the pharmaceutical company logo, and asked to play in defence. His reputation as a ferocious bouncer was well-known, and players asked, in hushed voices, if any of them would be brave enough to tackle him, and if a foul occurred as a result of this, would the referee be brave enough to book Jimmy for it? When it was time to begin the game, the teams trotted out onto the pitch, with Jimmy noticeable only by his absence. A few minutes later, he emerged from the clubhouse wearing his new red and white top, minus the sleeves, which had been roughly torn off and left on the changing-room floor. Jim had such large biceps that any form of sleeve restricted his movement, and his first action, upon purchasing a shirt of any kind, was to wrench the sleeves from it. One wonders what his wedding photos looked like.

John Weston, twin brother of Sid, has his own favourite Jimmy the Con anecdote. Having given

Jimmy a lift home after a night at the club, Jimmy asked if John and Larry would like some 'real' coffee before heading home. Thrilled that Jimmy was finally getting to grips with domesticity, they gladly accepted. Moments later, as they sat on his old settee, Jim emerged from his kitchen carrying two mugs of boiling water with several large coffee beans floating around in them, like turds floating around in a pet rabbit's water bowl.

So far, little has been said about Jim's love life. This, like everything else in Jimmy Fisher's world, was paradoxical. He'd married his second wife, Jeanet, (spelt this way by the Express and Star so blame them if it's incorrect), a Jehovah's Witness convert, in the mid-seventies, and Sam remembers their wedding day being a raucous affair. The couple were married at Dudley Registry Office, with the extremely drunken reception held at Yates's Wine Lodge afterwards, followed by a stint at the North Bank of the Molineux Stadium, as the Wolves played (who ever said romance was dead?). On the surface, this union seemed a very strange and unusual one, but somehow it worked. Even more intriguingly, Jeanet was, by all accounts, a member of Mensa, and extremely bright. She would often lie in bed at night studying extracts from the Bible, with Jim lying beside her, taking it all in. Not an image one could readily imagine, given what we know about Jim and his volatile career. Even more intriguing is the fact that in later life, Jim took up weightlifting, and with typical dogged determination, eventually became the Over-50s Powerlifting World Champion. This, needless to say, pleased him greatly. It was as if, after a troubled and often violent life, he had finally found something worthwhile to channel his aggression into. Around this time, Jimmy drifted away from the club, presumably to concentrate on his new sport.

Not long afterwards, in 1998, Jimmy was battling with skin cancer. He fought and beat this illness, as one would expect from Jimmy, but succumbed to lung cancer not long afterwards. Sadly, even someone as strong and seemingly indestructible as Jimmy Fisher can sometimes lose battles of that magnitude. Jim promised Jeanet that he would still be around for their 25th wedding anniversary, but it was not to be. Jimmy, of Wolverton Road, Kates Hill, Dudley, died on his 57th birthday, after insisting on making arrangements for his own funeral. He chose a scripture,

and a Jehovah's Witness song entitled, 'Keep Your Eyes on the Prize'. He left behind a sister, Dawn, two daughters from his previous marriage, and a 7-year-old grandson. Jeanet said that, even though he knew he was dying, he had never seemed happier. She added that, in spite of his terrifying exterior, he was loyal, had a heart of gold and would do anything for anyone. The funeral at Gornal Crematorium was an interesting affair. Sam recalls that the church was full of bodybuilders, Jehovah's Witnesses, JB's members, musicians, Hell's Angels, and around half of the Dudley police force. Presumably they were there in case Jim decided to cause any trouble.

The death of Jimmy the Con, as reported by the Express and Star.

☞

Jimmy Fisher

Champ of the weights dies, 57

A Dudley bodybuilder and weightlifting champion has died of cancer on his 57th birthday – after making arrangements for his own funeral.

Former boxer Jimmy Fisher died at his home in Wolverton Road, Kates Hill, on Friday.

The former bouncer at Dudley's JB's nightclub, nicknamed Jimmy the Con, beat skin cancer but a year later developed lung cancer.

His wife of 25 years Jeanet today said hundreds of people would be at his funeral on Thursday, including powerlifters, bouncers and Hell's Angels on a cavalcade of motorbikes.

The couple were both Hell's Angels years ago before Jeanet became a Jehovah's Witness in 1971 and Jimmy used to go with her to services.

She said Jimmy, who leaves a sister, Dawn, two daughters from a previous marriage and a seven-year-old grandson, knew he was dying but said he was happier than he had ever been.

Dream

He even arranged his own funeral deciding on who should carry out the service, choosing a scripture, a Jehovah's Witness song called Keep Your Eye on the Prize and asking for a speech to made about his life.

Mrs Fisher said her husband had achieved his dream to be bodybuilding champion of the world and then power-lifting world champion before discovering he had cancer in December 1998.

She said: "He had a heart of pure gold and would do anything for anybody.

"He was loyal and the love just poured out of him.

"He had the mind of a champion and his dedication and attitude helped him fight the skin cancer."

The funeral will be at Gornal Wood Crematorium.

Mr Fisher was convicted for the manslaughter of a homosexual customer while he was a bouncer in Wolverhampton in 1984. The conviction was quashed on appeal after he served eight and a half months of a three-year jail term.

Jimmy 'The Con' Fisher, Over-50s Powerlifting World Champion.

The 1970s

The Way We Were

"Memories
Light the corners of my mind
Misty water-coloured memories
Of the way we were
Scattered pictures
Of the smiles we left behind
Smiles we gave to one another
For the way we were
Can it be that it was all so simple then?
Or has time rewritten every line?
If we had a chance to do it all again
Tell me, would we?
Could we?
Memories, may be beautiful and yet
What's too painful to remember
We simply choose to forget
So it's the laughter
We will remember
Whenever we remember
The way we were"

Barbra Streisand

"Fat-bottomed girls you make the rockin' world go round"

Freddie Mercury

We begin this chapter with a belated apology, not as some might suspect for quoting the lyrics of a Barbra Streisand song in what is supposed to be a book about a rock club (they are rather nice words though, in fairness, and the gay community in particular will enjoy their inclusion), but for managing to get this far without any meaningful references to the fairer sex in general, and more specifically with regard to the running of JB's. Behind every great man, as the old saying goes, is a great woman, and none was greater than Sue Jukes, wife of Sam, who worked at his side from day one, along with several other ladies who we will mention in the fullness of time. While Sam was trying to earn a living at the Triplex Foundry, in between running around most of the local football pitches and breaking the odd leg or two in theatrical fashion at local speedway tracks, Sue worked in the IBM office at West Bromwich Council. Each day she would leave at 4pm to open up the club, and get the beer, crisps, KP nuts, Wigwams, Hula Hoops and pork

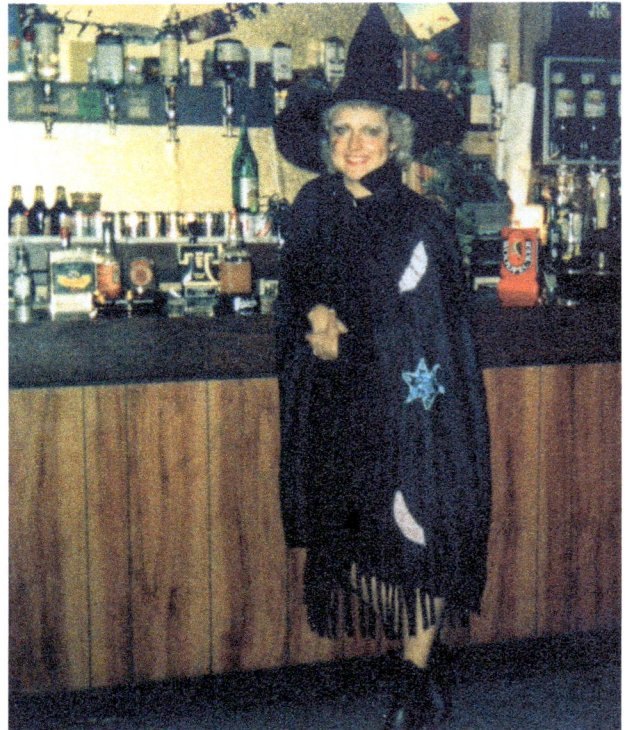

☞ No, it's not J.K. Rowling, it's Sue Jukes at one of the New Years' Eve fancy dress events.

☞ Can anyone give this poor bloke a lift back to Hull?

☞ Ace, starring Paul Carrack, (below, top left), played at JB's regularly throughout the '70s.

scratchings ready for the coming evening. Later on, she would be joined by various regular barmaids who would put in a gruelling shift each evening in a packed, smoky, noisy club.

In these days of health and safety consciousness, with the nationwide enforcement of the no smoking ban now long-established, it is easy to forget how eye-wateringly smoky our pubs and clubs were, and how badly our clothing and hair stank when we got home after visiting them. In sharp contrast to the 'Red Robbo' trade union shenanigans at companies such as British Leyland, at nearby Longbridge, there were no specific job titles or demarcation of labour at JB's. Whatever needed doing, if a committee member happened to be at a loose end, he or she would chip in and help, whether that meant cleaning a blocked lavatory, serving behind the bar or taking money on the door. Sue recalls that clubs such as the Lafayette in Wolverhampton were run as hard-nosed, money-making businesses, whereas the JB's ethos was all about having fun and helping each other. This attitude obviously stood them in good stead. In spite of never advertising, the place was packed to the rafters each weekend.

One of the JB's regulars was 'little' Carol Harrison, a pretty, petite girl who helped out doing bar work or whatever was required. Carol was such a regular fixture, she even had her own stool, which no one else was allowed to sit on. One evening, she arrived at the bar to find that some unsuspecting rock star was sat on it, or at least, he was, until the feisty dark-haired beauty explained to him that he would have to relocate. A member who often frequented the place during the 70s remembers seeing Carol trying her best to call a halt to one of Jimmy the Con's altercations with a rowdy punter. Seeing that the unfortunate man was on the wrong end of a severe battering, she attached herself to the back of Jimmy's vest and tore it from his back. None but the bravest would attempt that manoeuvre, and those who did so seldom survived. Happily, Carol is still here to tell the tale. In those days, even the toughest men (on the whole), didn't hit women. Sadly, that unwritten rule has now been superseded.

Sue Jukes not only made sure that the bar was well stocked, she also began to cook dinner for the visiting bands – usually curries, rice, salads, and plated meats. For most bands, this treat was the highlight of their visit. Spencer Davis and Steve Winwood (who was playing with The Spencer Davis Group at that time) were so impressed with the food that they jokingly suggested that Sam and Sue would be better off abandoning JB's and setting up a restaurant. Winwood was also a huge real-ale fan, so he was sent to visit the nearby Lamp Tavern, whence he returned with a huge jug of Batham's beer. Annie Lennox, Dave Stewart, Chrissie Hynde and The Wonder Stuff all waxed lyrical about Sue's prowess with the frying pan.

Sue remembers catering for one band that had sent the club a contract, stipulating in detail the kind of food they wanted before the gig. Sue was to provide a large, cooked chicken for one member of the band, who was renowned for his big appetite. This she duly did, but to her dismay, by the time the band arrived and were sitting down to enjoy their pre-gig meal, persons unknown at JB's had already devoured the specially ordered chicken. Thankfully, in those days, the 'riders' (specific requests for certain items and conditions) within the band's contract were easily met. Most bands were just thrilled to be asked to perform there, and as long as they were fed by Sue, and given a crate of Newcastle Brown Ale, they were as happy as pigs in mud. Sadly, as the years went by, this would change, and the stars would gradually become more prima-donna-like. John and Sid Weston would often go the extra mile and allow visiting bands to stay at their house. John remembers Tony Capstick, the well-known folk musician, comedian and actor, staying at Chez Weston on several occasions. Sid and John's mother would cook the bands bacon and eggs the following morning, before they set off home, or to their next show. John even took respected singer-songwriter, Michael Chapman, home to Hull on one occasion, and can still remember the address to this day! It was, he assures us, 60 Louis Street. One presumes that Michael made enough money from music to eventually relocate, so die-hard fans should think twice about tracking him down.

Larry too found himself running a part-time bed and breakfast business for passing musicians, and in the early days he played host to various impoverished bands, including Bees Make Honey. Though not a household name nowadays, certain members of the band found fame to varying degrees with other outfits, such as Barclay James Harvest, Ace (with Paul Carrack) and Supertramp.

☞ The much loved Gezz Tobin in action.

☞ A very young, sexy and rather potty-mouthed Chrissie Hynde.

A piece of rock memorabilia to treasure. Ginger Baker, Pahana and Anubis, plus a disco, for 60 pence!
☞

JBs PRESENT at the 'LAFAYETTE'
THORNLEY STREET, WOLVERHAMPTON
MON., MARCH 13th
FELLA RANSOME KUTT 70
FEATURING
GINGER BAKER
ALSO PAHANA, ANUBIS, JBs DISCO
TICKETS 60p ADVANCE   70p ON NIGHT
TICKETS FROM JBs KING STREET, DUDLEY & LAFAYETTE

☞ Queens Head F.C.
(circa 1977).
Top row:
P. Bellamy,
M. Cartwright, R. Plant,
P. Gwilliam, T. Leath,
K. Small.
Front row:
O. Donaghey,
K. Keady, J. Bryant,
J. Boothley, A. Kaye.

Roy Williams surveys the aftermath of a good night at the club.

Bill Gladwin's collection of King Street membership cards.

One band that had travelled all the way from Scotland and were too broke to check into a bed and breakfast, were allowed to sleep on the club floor after their gig, and told to lock up and drop the keys off on their way home. This was always a pretty difficult judgment call for Sam to make, not helped by the fact that the band, believed to be Contraband, stayed overnight and helped themselves to all the beer, by way of saying 'thank you'. Between the hours of midnight and 10am the following day, they had somehow managed to drink the club dry.

As the club was technically a social club at that time, it required a membership card, and this was designed by a young artist by the name of Pete Beardsmore and his wife, Babs. Pete 'borrowed' the look from an Art Deco design, and adapted it to suit,

adding a block sans serif JB's logo on a panel towards the bottom. This logo was later replaced, on everything but the membership cards, by a typeface which was created by Sid. Its no-nonsense, workman-like, home-made stencilied look is now almost a metaphor for the club and its ethos at that time, if that doesn't sound too pretentious. The logo was not professionally designed by a Birmingham advertising agency at great expense, but that echoed the way things were done at JB's. Everyone chipped in and did their best. Over the years, this humble, cheaply produced membership card was printed in a variety of colours, and became truly iconic – so much so that it seemed only right and proper that it should be revamped for the cover of this

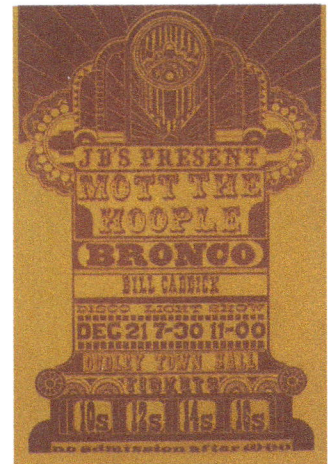

☞ *Two more distinctive posters by Pete Beardsmore, in his typical retro style.*

☞ *A lovely old poster for America and Brinsley Schwarz, a JB's gig at Dudley Town Hall.*

☞ *Brinsley, Nick and the boys enjoy a post-gig Newcastle Brown.*

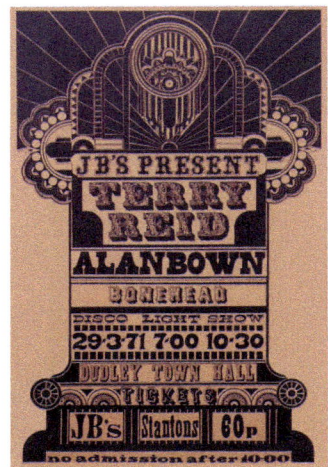

book. We hope you agree that, whatever your feelings about it, no one is going to mistake it for anything else!

Inside the card were the simple rules of the club:

Members must agree to abide by the club rules as displayed on the club premises.
All members of this club must be over 18 years of age.
The committee may cancel the membership of anyone causing a disturbance in or near the club.
The committee reserves the right to refuse admission.

On the right-hand inner page was the card's number (which inspired us to number the First 1000 books too!), plus a space for the date acquired, the name of the member, their address, and their signature.

On the back were the words:

This membership card is issued for the sole personal use of the registered holder.

JB's, King Street, Dudley

One club rule not mentioned on the card was that you weren't allowed to dance on Sundays. Presumably, anyone daring to break into a quick twist, foxtrot or quickstep would be taken to one side by Jimmy the Con and given a stern lecture about the dangers of such unruly behaviour.

In conjunction with having to show the card, members arriving at the club were required to be stamped on the hand with what is known in printing terms as a 'dingbat'. These were illustrative woodcut flourishes that were originally used to augment type, especially in Victorian and Edwardian times, on adverts, posters, and so on. They could take the form of flowers, swirls, borders, hearts, arrows, or whatever, but JB's usually used a small drawing of a pointing hand, for reasons unknown. A rubber stamp was dipped into a small tin of blue ink that sat on the reception desk, and visitors were branded like cattle, so that they could pop outside for a breath of fresh air (the air inside was not fresh) and then return with visible proof that they had paid. The only problem was, the ink was a devil to remove, and regular visitors, especially those not too keen on personal hygiene, would be plastered in little pointing hands by Sunday night. This was not a

good look, especially for the women, who began to resemble Lydia the Tattooed Lady, or for our younger readers, Amy Winehouse. Sadly, nowadays, everybody and his dog has tattoos, so no one would probably notice these small, pointing-hand stamps. One evening, a young lady, upon hearing that she was to be stamped, unbuttoned her top and bared her breasts in reception, and asked to be stamped there. Suddenly, every male member of staff seemed to be taking an interest in this mundane nightly chore, with some even volunteering to take over the role on a full-time basis.

Pete Beardsmore also produced many of the early posters that were used to promote bands – such as Mott The Hoople, America and Wishbone Ash – at the larger venues, including Netherton Town Hall, Dudley Town Hall, and Dudley Technical College, some of which are illustrated in this book.

On the 29th of April, 1971, the day that JB's promoted the Bronco, Mott The Hoople, and Bill Caddick gig at Dudley Town Hall, Johnny Bryant stepped down as resident DJ, due to work and domestic commitments. He had been dating a lady by the name of Shirley Wilson, whom he'd met at the Adelphi Ballroom in West Bromwich, the town where he worked each day as a pattern maker at Grews, of Carter's Green. Shirley had a sister, who, Johnny discovered, had recently married Robert Plant. Inevitably, Johnny was then invited to Plant's home, along with his new girlfriend, and the four became close friends. This in turn led to Robert Plant asking Johnny to become the farm's manager, leaving him precious little time to continue spinning the records at JB's. Not long afterwards, in 1972, Johnny and Shirley were also married. Johnny remembers commandeering his new sister-in-law's car to act as the official wedding vehicle. It was a huge, futuristic-looking Citroën DS, only slightly larger and thirstier than a Sherman tank, with weird hydraulic suspension that caused it to sink into the pavement each time it parked.

The wedding took place at the West Bromwich registry office, with the reception afterwards held at a pub in the town. Johnny recalls having to help break up two fights, one of which was an enthusiastic bout between Shirley's brother, Bruce, and his girlfriend at the time. Thankfully, everyone seemed to have made up and forgiven each other by the time the party ended. By sheer coincidence, Johnny had now

Little Acre, from left to right: Jock Evans, George Northall, Glenis Jones, Laura Spencer, Johnny Higgs, John West, Jim Hickman, Johnny Bryant, John Ogden, and Elmer O'Shea.

morphed from a DJ who played Led Zeppelin records at a local rock club, to being Robert Plant's brother-in-law. As farm manager, it was also Johnny's responsibility to look after Robert's wife, Maureen, and their children, while Robert was away on tour, or during the concerts if they were in the UK. In the mid-70s, Johnny, who, like Sam, was a keen footballer, became captain of the Blakeshall Bashers, a loose arrangement of enthusiasts that included Robert, who was a decent sportsman and dedicated Wolves fan, in spite of him hailing from West Bromwich. The team soon amalgamated with the players at the Queen's Head. A fact that is borne out by the many framed photographs of the team hanging in pride of place in the bar room. Sharp-eyed visitors will spot many pictures of Messrs Plant and Bryant, arms folded across their chests, beaming proudly. The story goes that Bryant, as captain, would often threaten to not select Plant for the team if his hair wasn't just so, and Plant would retaliate by threatening to sack Bryant as farm manager. When Johnny decided to step down as resident disc jockey, he was replaced by Gezz Tobin (the man who fell off a cliff at Kinver Edge and broke his hip), Roy Williams, Graham 'The Bus Driver' and Trevor Long. Gezz had quite an avant-garde taste in music, and introduced many of the JB's regulars to the delights of Captain Beefheart, Frank Zappa, and musicians of that ilk. We have already touched on the delicate matter of how difficult it was for Johnny to relieve himself at the old football club, due to the impenetrable crowd, and described his clever ploy of playing the lengthy 'Keep on Chooglin' so that he could take a comfort break. Compared to those days, the new disc jockey, Gezz, was positively spoilt at King Street. He could slip down from 'The Loft', as it was fondly known, and cut sideways across the hall to the men's lavatory in a couple of minutes, even if the room was rammed with people. 'Willie the Pimp', from Frank Zappa's Hot Rats album, and sung by Captain Beefheart (timed at 9.25 minutes), was plenty long enough to get the job done!

Johnny Bryant pulls another bird.

Meanwhile, Johnny busied himself with his musical projects. His original band had played at the old football club, and his new project, Salty Dog, an acoustic-based folksy outfit, first hit the King Street stage on Sunday the 31st of December, 1972, and again on Saturday the 31st of March, 1973. Next, he joined Thunder, a rock band featuring Geoff and Greg Falkner, and Frankie Lea, brother of Slade's Jim Lea. The band toured with Wizard, and on one memorable evening at Green's Playhouse, Glasgow, Johnny recalls having several bottles thrown at him and his fellow band members. As one particularly close one whistled past his ear, he suddenly began to have grave doubts about packing in his pattern-making job to pursue a life in music.

Next up was Little Acre, a band gathered together and organized by sound engineer Roy Williams, who had become concerned by the amount of good local musicians who were hanging around with nothing to do. To this end, he ran an audition that 16 or so musicians turned up to. After a bit of judicious pruning, he ended up with 10 finalists, which made Little Acre one of the largest rock bands in the Midlands, and as a consequence, also one of the worst paid. Despite that, they played at JB's many times and became firm favourites. There was even interest from record mogul, Mickie Most, but he was worried about the size of the outfit, and insisted that they cull a few more members, which didn't go down overly well. Shortly after this, Johnny took some time out to concentrate on his farm-manager duties, in between babysitting while Led Zeppelin performed at Knebworth, Earls Court, and other venues. One evening, he was approached by Peter Grant, Led Zeppelin's manager, who thanked him for taking care of things at home so that 'his boys could go off and play'. Those who are familiar with some of the legendary tales of the band's excesses will not doubt that Peter's boys liked to 'go off and play'.

Johnny was, and still is, an excellent singer, and currently sings with a band from Kinver, The Stubble Brothers, who, remarkably, are still together after some 25 years, or at least, they were at the time of writing this piece. Given their habit of arguing like an old married couple and then making up again the next day, one is never sure. Johnny divorced Shirley in 1985, and has been happily co-existing with the delightful Lucinda Brightwell ever since. They live in an idyllic location,

near to Kinver, in a small barn conversion. 'Lu' rides her beloved horse in the countryside all day long, and Johnny apparently cooks and vacuums up a lot. At least, this is Johnny's version of events.

Having become friendly with Johnny Bryant and others, Robert Plant became a semi-regular visitor to JB's, often playing darts on a Thursday evening with the locals. It was a place where he could go to relax, safe in the knowledge that no one would pester him there.

1972 saw many more wonderful bands come and go, after a fairly major setback, when the club was broken into, and speakers and records were stolen. This was particularly upsetting as it had taken a long time to install the Vox speakers, because the engineering bricks used in the club were incredibly tough, and hard to drill into. The thieves had also left their calling card – a nice pile of shit on the floor (why do they do that?). Afterwards, steel shutters were installed, and everyone involved became a lot more security conscious.

Vinegar Joe, featuring the late, great Robert Palmer, ('Every Kinda People', 'Addicted to Love', 'Johnny and Mary', and many more) and Elkie Brooks ('Pearl's a Singer', 'Fool If You Think It's Over', 'Lilac Wine', etc.), played on the 3rd of March, 1972, much to the delight of the committee, who seemed to be mesmerized by Elkie's raunchy stage presence. Argent and America were rebooked, but this time were offered the Lafayette and Dudley Town Hall,

A young Robert Palmer with Elkie Brooks in Vinegar Joe.

respectively, in accordance with their growing status. Glenis Jones remembers Elkie popping into the old back room behind the bar, where Glenis was busy washing glasses. Elkie asked where the dressing room was, and Glenis replied, 'Er, this is it!' Apparently, the look on Elkie's face spoke volumes, but she laughed it off and got on with it. Glenis did think of handing her a tea towel and asking her to help with a spot of wiping up, but thought better of it.

Then came Brinsley Schwarz, featuring the very influential Nick Lowe, who seemed to have an involvement in virtually every up-and-coming hot act at the time. He also did rather well in his own right, with hits such as 'Cruel to Be Kind' and 'I Love the Sound of Breaking Glass'. This new association with Brinsley (their guitarist) and the band also forged a very useful link with London. Brinsley Schwarz was part of the burgeoning London pub rock circuit at the time, which revolved around the famous Hope and Anchor venue. Roy Williams spoke to Dave Robinson at Stiff Records about a reciprocal deal, which enabled Little Acre and Steve Gibbons to get gigs at the Hope and Anchor and other London venues, and, just as in the early days, when resources were shared between the Coneygre and Quarry youth clubs to their mutual advantage, so now were the smaller London club bands able to get gigs in the Midlands, courtesy of JB's. This in turn increased the listenership, which led to more record sales for all concerned.

A hand-drawn flyer, a few items from Howard Williamson's badge collection, an old Capability Brown sticker, a hand-drawn poster by Pete Beardsmore to advertise the new King Street club, a colour photograph of John Verity (Argent, Phoenix, The John Verity band) with his entry in the visitors' book, a lovely black and white snap of Planty on the JB's stage, and beneath, John Illsley of Dire Straits (the band Sam wanted to manage). Last but not least, Hackensack, who virtually lived at the club in the '70s.

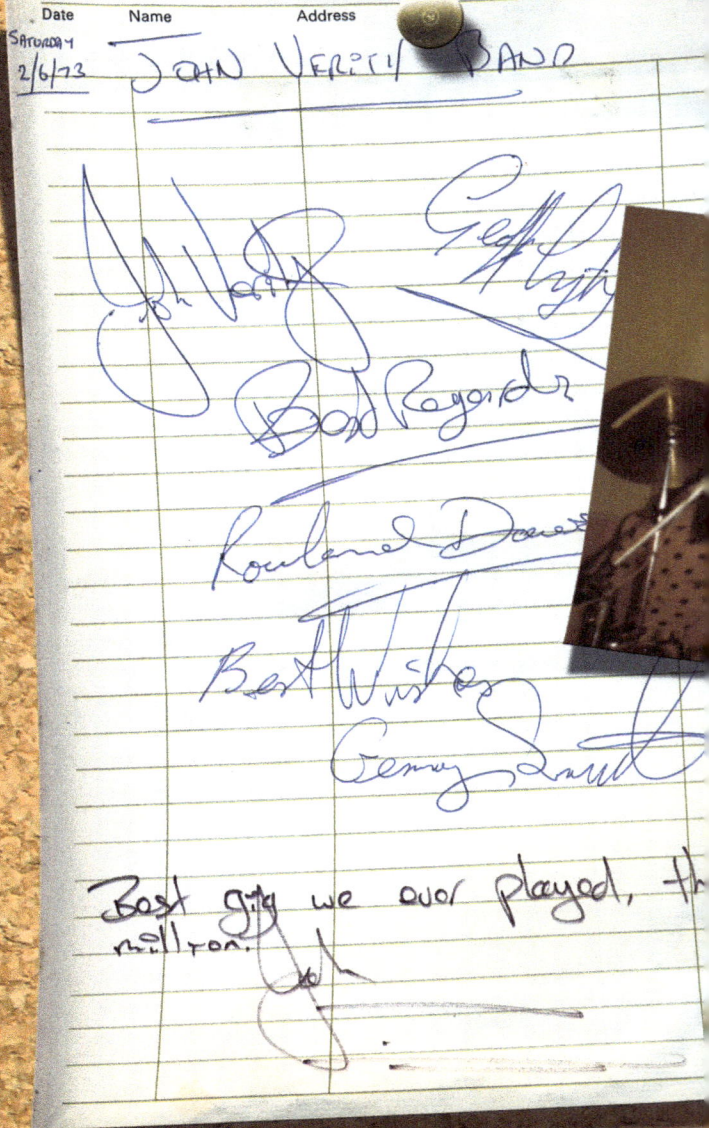

JB'S NEW CLUB OPENS SATURDAY JUNE 26

HACKENSACK

J.B.S. DUDLEY

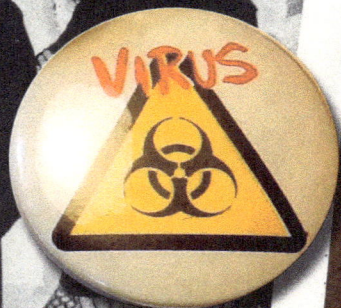

☝ Jasper Carrott, whose fee at the time was the princely
sum of £25! (See page 62.)

(See page 62.)

☟ Tony Capstick at one of the Tuesday evening folk sessions.

There's Nowt so Queer as Folk!

"Kumbaya my Lord, kumbaya
Oh Lord, kumbaya "

Accredited to Reverend Marvin V. Frey (1930s)

The committee, from the earliest days, had always striven to cater for many different musical tastes, and folk and acoustic music was no exception. Around the beginning of 1973, it was decided to dedicate Tuesday evenings to these gentler, more introspective forms of music, and create a more intimate atmosphere.

Just as the simple expressions 'rock', or 'rock and roll', cover a multitude of styles, so too do 'folk' and 'acoustic', and the club tried its hardest to represent artistes from all genres, from the 'finger in the ear' traditionalists and the sensitive singer-songwriters to the humorous/radical/political wordsmiths in the Bob Dylan mould.

On Tuesday the 14th of November, 1972, the first folk night saw Tony Capstick take the stage for an evening of folk and comedy. A regular on the folk circuit, Tony recorded many albums, presented a show on BBC Radio Sheffield, and was also a TV actor, his most well-known role being a policeman in the long-running sitcom, Last of the Summer Wine, though he occasionally appeared in soaps such as Emmerdale and Coronation Street. Tony was even given his own show in 1983 – Capstick's Capers, on Channel 4. Sadly, he was found dead at his South Yorkshire home in 2003.

Capstick's slot was followed, on Tuesday the 19th of December, 1972, by Jasper Carrott, now a household name and an extremely successful comedian, but in those days he was still an up-and-coming folk singer who told the odd joke or amusing anecdote between songs. These anecdotes proved so popular that quite soon the songs would become scarcer, whilst the anecdotes evolved as the main part of his act. Those who saw Carrott on TV, later on in his stratospheric career, would often wonder why he constantly had an acoustic guitar slung around his neck, but hardly ever seemed to play it. The truth is, old habits die hard, and he still needed something to hide behind, or at least, something to do with his hands!

The acoustic nights were run by Kidderminster teacher, Richard Rodgers, now better known as Ricky Cool, or 'Trix' to his friends. He began playing in folk

Gasolene, from left to right: Phil Cunniffe, Barry Anderson, Steve Jack and Paul Gooderham, were JB's King Street regulars. (Photograph courtesy of their roadie and art student, Paul Boswell.)

clubs in 1968, and at that time he was an apprentice doing day release at Dudley Technical College. He was living in Halesowen, where he was born, had become friends with some Dudley lads, and started going to JB's on Thursdays with them. He then got to know Johnny Bryant and the other members of the committee, who suggested he organize the new Tuesday night sessions. Trix knew Bill Caddick, Dave Cartwight and Mike Billington, who ran a Tuesday evening folk club at the King's Head in Quinton, his local venue. He also knew Mick Howson, Dan Fone and Alec Angel, all of whom later became members of his band, Ricky Cool and The Icebergs, and he got them involved in his new Dudley venture.

During 1973, Decameron, local band Gasolene, Pigsty Hill Light Orchestra, Contraband, Richard and Linda Thompson, Sonny Phobes, Willy Mason (from the USA), Dave Cartwright, Nigel Denver, and Jon Betmead all showed up on the Tuesday gig lists, but shortly afterwards, Tuesdays seem to have been commandeered by the London pub rock outfits such as Brinsley Schwarz, possibly so that they could fulfil their London bookings at weekends. From then

onwards, the Tuesday events seemed to thin out and eventually disappear altogether. On the main club nights, however, it was very much business as usual.

From 1972 to 1974 alone, JB's was treated to virtuoso guitarist, Gordon Giltrap, Jasper Carrott, Richard and Linda Thompson, v, Gary Moore, Steve Gibbons and Kevin Coyne, and the bands Gypsy, UFO (very loud indeed!), Capability Brown, Long John Baldry, Skid Row, Trapeze, The Climax Chicago Blues Band, Bronco, Chicken Shack, the Alex Harvey Band, Pigsty Hill Light Orchestra, Patto, Average White Band, Heavy Metal Kids (featuring Gary Holton from Auf Wiedersehen, Pet), Judas Priest, Medicine Head, Country Joe and the Fish, Ace (with Paul Carrack), Ducks Deluxe (an offshoot of Brinsley Schwarz and another of the up-and-coming London pub rock outfits), Kokomo, and Dr. Feelgood (featuring the wonderful Wilko Johnson and the late Lee Brilleaux), plus many, many more excellent bands that weren't quite as high profile or didn't have current hit singles – bands like Supercharge, for example, who were the band of choice when famous musicians decided to have a private party.

👆 Wilko Johnson with the late Lee Brilleaux, performing with Dr. Feelgood. Sa:n paid them a small fee, plus some milk and alcohol.

👆 The one and only Albie Donnelly of Supercharge.

👇 An old Supercharge flyer from the early JB's period.

SUPERCHARGE

Personal Management: ALAN COTTAM ENTERTAINMENTS LTD, 65 Renshaw Street, Liverpool 1   Tel: 051-709 0398

Supercharge were from Liverpool, and became firm JB's favourites, largely because they were not only an incredibly tight, well-rehearsed funk band with two drummers, but also because they were riotously funny. Fronted by Albie Donnelly (a huge, bald-headed, big-bearded, shades-wearing, loud, aggressive, sweary sax player with an absolutely wicked sense of humour, often at his band's expense), Supercharge blasted non-stop through song after song, mostly serious disco-funk numbers, but with the occasional crowd-pleaser containing ludicrous words peppered with sexual innuendos. When the band wasn't actually playing, the

The shy and retiring Albie Donnelly.

between-the-songs patter was often painfully funny. It is extremely difficult to illustrate their appeal on the cold page, but, in a brave/foolish attempt to do so, take, for example, 'She Moved the Dishes First', a little ditty about Albie's girlfriend, a woman of such good breeding that, even when desperate to relieve herself, she always moved the dishes in the sink first. This moving chorus would be sung by the colossus that was Albie, accompanied by a small, Chinese guitarist who often wore a National Front crash helmet (yes, you did read that correctly), and a shy bass player called Tony who was just trying desperately to keep himself to himself, ignoring constant requests from the front man to 'get yer knob out and show the audience'. Think of one of Frank Zappa's ultra-slick bands but with

broad Liverpudlian accents, one minute being childish or absurd, the next stunning the crowd with some blinding, complex jazz-funk. There are many clips of Supercharge on YouTube, so treat yourself to a couple of them. Even the legendary 'She Moved the Dishes First' is there, recorded live at a gig, but sadly, it has no visual to accompany it. To a great many JB's members, that song will be synonymous with the club, and extremely sentimental, in a strange sort of way. There was always a buzz of expectation and excitement in the room if Supercharge was playing that evening, and everyone would leave with huge smiles on their faces. During one of the band's many appearances, Albie had introduced the members, and inadvertently forgotten to name-check one of the two drummers he used at the time (the line-up has changed many times since then). The audience then began to shout at Albie, imploring him to correct this oversight. Albie, realizing his mistake, casually glanced round at the drummer and announced nonchalantly, 'Oh yeah, some c**t on drums!'

Oscar Wilde it certainly was not, but it brought the house down nevertheless.

Then, as if all this wasn't good enough, imagine the scene on the 5th of April 1974. The club is rammed full of people because Steve Gibbons and Supercharge are playing, but so too are John Bonham and Robert Plant, at a party to celebrate JB's club's 5th birthday. Legend has it that the Supercharge drummers relinquished their places to allow Bob Lamb (Steve Gibbons' drummer and the producer of UB40's albums) and John Bonham to use their equipment. Supercharge frontman, Albie, then led the customers out of the club and around the block in a spirited version of the conga, leaving the two percussionists with an empty hall to play to. The rather heavy-handed Led Zeppelin drummer had duly battered the kit so hard, he'd more or less demolished it. Quite how its owner felt about this is not known.

Before and after his occasional secret gigs at JB's, or whenever he was just there socially, Plant would always mix freely with the punters, and did not display the usual superstar airs and graces, remembers John Weston. He'd quite often bring 'Bonzo' Bonham along with him, and occasionally Maureen, his wife, to enjoy a quiet pint of mild at the bar. Admittedly, he'd arrive in a swanky Aston Martin, but that, on those evenings at least, appeared to be his one concession to fame. On the night of the 5th birthday party, shortly before he was about to perform, a young man collared the singer at the cigarette machine.

'I know who you are, mate!' said the young man. 'You go down the Wolves a lot, don't you?'

Robert admitted that this was the case. He saw it as a form of penance, presumably.

'Thought so,' smiled the lad, pleased with himself. 'Can you get me Stevie Bull's autograph then?'

The 5th birthday bash was a resounding success, and to finish off a classic year, the customers were treated to Man, from Wales, Country Joe and the Fish, and The Bonzo Dog Doo Dah Band – featuring Neil Innes and the late Viv Stanshall, Sonny Terry and Brownie McGhee (the latter two being legendary bluesmen from the USA). Not bad for a tiny, old school hall!

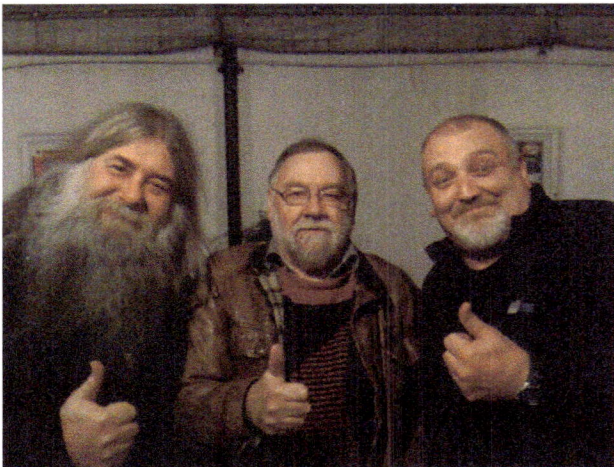

The 3 Sound Fellows – Big' Mick Hughes, Roy 'No Nickname' Williams, and Dave 'Shirt' Nichols

No, it's not ZZ Top, or even the Redbeards from Texas, it's Mick, Roy and Dave. All three of these intrepid fellows were JB's sound engineers, working at Kings Street, Castle Hill and Junction 10. and each one went on to work for big-name acts. By way of a few random examples, Big Mick actually worked with the Redbeards from Texas (in fact, he was the only one with a real beard), and he makes sure that Metallica never sound tinny. It's Roy's job, of course, to make sure that Robert Plant and Seasick Steve are pleasing to the ear, and Dave is responsible for those romantic crooners, Slipknot.

This is an extract from John Weston's visitors' book, dated 18/1/74, by Simon Nicol, of the Richard & Linda Thompson band:

> *On my way to find this place from my native Huntingdonshire, armed only with the directions 'JB's, King Street'. I traversed said thoroughfare some 2 or 300 times, causing who knows how much confusion to the traffic and a possible bomb scare amongst the late-night shoppers in Tesco. Eventually I abandoned the car for fear of running out of fuel and took to Shanks's pony, asking in turn two taxi drivers and an unshaven, incoherent Irish newspaper vendor whose speech had for some time become affected by a lifetime of emitting hoarse cries of 'Hep Step Peppep!' (he was meant to be saying Express and Star apparently) as the evening papers were dispatched from his plywood kiosk. I was fortunately able to divine directions to the police station. On my way there I was nearly run over on a pedestrian crossing by a man in a dirty 1965 Ford Zephyr, who left most of his back-wheel rubber on the road. Upon reaching the station and finding the enquiry desk, I was duly ignored by two sergeants, an inspector, and another bobby of the normal type. It was he who eventually enquired of me my business, but as soon as I stated it, Sergeant D31 came up with the necessary information.*

Chris Adams of String Driven Thing wrote:

> *Don't believe this guy. EVERYONE knows where JB's is!'.*

Richard Thompson, songwriter and guitarist, added to the visitors' book,

> *Wonderful food, nice clean beds and a good view of the seafront.*

The list of band appearances for 1975 is sadly incomplete, but we know that Jess Roden and Bronco returned, as did the ubiquitous Supercharge and Steve Gibbons. August saw the inaugural appearance of the super-slick Brummie band, City Boy, with their clever 10cc-like lyrics and vocal harmonies, married to a polished instrumental virtuosity that was reminiscent of Queen. The band had scored a top-20 hit with 'Moonlight', quickly followed by the massive hit '5705', which took them to a new level, paving the way for American tours, where they played alongside the likes of Thin Lizzy. Strangely, though Phil Lynott's band was a far bigger act in the UK, its role was to support City Boy in the States. Upon arriving in Britain, however, Thin Lizzy would immediately pull rank, meaning that City Boy reverted to being the support act! One wonders if this change of status also applied to the air travel, with City Boy flying out first class with Lynott and the boys in economy, and vice versa on the return flight, with buns being thrown back and forth during the in-flight meal.

September saw a touch of lunacy return to the club, with not only The Bonzo Dog Doo-Dah Band, but also the hilarious Alberto Y Lost Trios Paranoias.

Things were to get even better in 1976, but before we get to that, let's delve into the monetary side of things. What do you think a well-known rock band earned, back in the day?

Irish band, Skid Row's Noel Bridgeman. The band also featured top guitarist, Gary Moore, and drummer 'Brush' Shields. These Irish lads could play fast, and I mean fast. Check out the mentally speedy 'An Awful Lot of Woman' from 1971 on YouTube.

Robert Plant indulging in a sneaky bit of product placement.

The ever-cool Mr Gibbons in front of the famous stencilled logo.

☞ *Richard and Linda Thompson (Fairport Convention) resist the overwhelming temptation to stick their fingers in their ears.*

☞ *Times were hard back then. Sam Jukes and friend wait patiently for Chris Lea to pass the bottle round.*

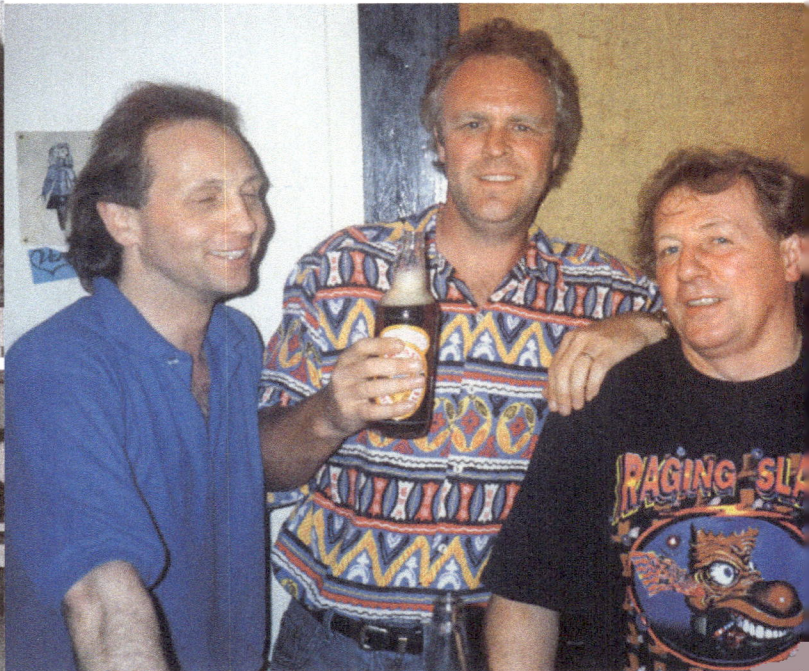

The receipt stub showing Jasper Carrott's extortionate fee of £25. The signature alone is probably worth that nowadays.

Money, Madness and Memorabilia

"We're only in It for the Money"
(album title)

Frank Zappa and the Mothers of Invention

In this final chapter of those dedicated to the first five years, we explore just how different the 1970s were to the present day, in terms of clothes, money, and musical tastes. We will also throw into the mix a few choice anecdotes that are still queuing up in the wings, waiting patiently to be heard, and expose a few embarrassing photographs that should really have been kept in a suitcase in the attic (or destroyed to preserve people's self-respect and dignity).

When Sam finally retired from running JB's, thankfully, he kept quite a few boxes of memorabilia, to remind himself of the club that had been his life and his raison d'être for 41 years. For this, we should all be eternally grateful, because the old receipt books, posters, printed gig guides, etc., proved invaluable when compiling this book. Not only that, they are – and this is no exaggeration – important pieces of rock and roll memorabilia. There were five or six old-fashioned receipt books – the stubby blue 'Challenge Duplicate Book' ones, if you remember them, with a loose piece of carbon paper inside and numbered pages, and also several small pocket diaries, in which Sam recorded the names of the bands due to play at the club.

Having been chosen to write this story, I was handed a good many items from the committee members, and also sent email attachments containing old newspaper articles. I printed everything out and kept it in a large, old red box that Roy Williams gave me, for safekeeping. If I am honest, the prospect of sifting through six old receipt books did not exactly set me alight, but I knew it had to be done. The first one I picked up was dated by Sam on the first page. It said 'JB's club, King Street, Dudley, 24.11.72, so I knew it was an early one. The first receipt page said 'Clear Blue Sky, £25.00'. This was a band that I had not heard of, but even so, the fee seemed extremely cheap. I had obviously forgotten just how much the cost of things had rocketed since then. I turned the page and found Chicken Shack. They had received £100. A small note above the fee said 'Catacombs'. Perhaps this gig had been staged there for some reason. Now,

I was curious. I felt as if I were viewing an important old document, rather than a humble receipt book, and I swear that I felt the hairs on my neck stand to attention at the prospect of what I was likely to find. I flicked through the pages, and, voila! I found The Sensational Alex Harvey Band, who had been paid the less-than-sensational sum of £40. This was intriguing, and seemed to shed light on how bands were judged at that time, the irony being that Alex Harvey would go on to command huge sums, yet some of the bands that went nowhere and never achieved fame seemed to be commanding better fees in 1972. Next up was The Pigsty Hill Light Orchestra (worth checking out on YouTube) who were paid the paltry sum of £35, even though there was a charabanc full of them! They probably attended the same School of Economics that the members of Little Acre were at.

The receipt book just kept getting better and better. I found Medicine Head, who were on Top of the Pops in 1973 with their single 'One and One is One', which made it to number 3 in the top 20. The two-piece outfit scooped a massive £100 from Sam's struggling wallet at the time – not bad to share between just two band members, when one considers that Pigsty Hill probably ended up with around a quid each. Sonny Phobes (whoever he was – I typed his name into Google and ended up with websites about Sony phones!) only succeeded in screwing Sam for just over 12 quid, but a few pages later (and this was the one that really excited me), Jasper Carrott – comedian, Brummie superstar, co-owner of the rights to Who Wants to be a Millionaire, the hit TV quiz show – was paid the princely sum of £25.

Johnny Bryant's new band, Salty Dog, was awarded the magnificent sum of £120 (some nepotism going on there, surely?), and a few days later, no less that Richard and Linda Thompson (or Linda Peters as she was back then) were offered a meagre £35. For those who are not aware, these two became folk superstars. Richard founded Fairport Convention, and has since had his songs covered by the likes of Bonnie Raitt, David Gilmour, Elvis Costello, The Corrs, Sandy Denny, Martin Carthy, Graham Parker, The Pointer Sisters, Los Lobos, Loudon Wainwright the Third, and many more. Richard was appointed an OBE in 2011, and also an honorary doctorate by Aberdeen University. Not bad for £35, one would have to admit. Maybe he was also given a percentage of the door takings.

Understandably, I was now hooked on old receipt books. I found Brinsley Schwarz (£100), Trapeze with Glenn Hughes (£119.25) no, I'm sorry, I have to pause there – that sum of money is ridiculous, Tony Capstick (£25), the Average White Band; wait for it – £45! Stealers Wheel (£69), Jasper again (still £25 – Jasper's signature to acknowledge payment is now worth that much!), and Salty Dog return, but this time for just £20. Why the drastic pay drop from their previous £120? Were they that awful the first time? The Average White Band appeared again in March '73, and was awarded an increase which raised their fee to £74, and then immediately after that, heavy-metal gods, Judas Priest, deafened everyone for – no, this can't be correct – £20 plus £2 VAT!

Bronco, Travis (not the other, more recent Travis, sadly), Terry Reid, Capability Brown (the band, not the gardener), String Driven Thing, Gypsy, Gary Moore, Paul Carrack's Ace, Steve Gibbons and Back Door, a very good jazz-rock outfit that toured with Emerson, Lake and Palmer, all came and went several times, and none of them seemed to make more than £100 – most making far less. Nick Lowe and Brinsley Schwarz seemed to be virtually living at the club, with around seven or eight appearances in one year. They may have been paid peanuts, but they certainly kept coming back for more of them. And this was just the first receipt book, remember. It may be jumping ahead, but by the time JB's was situated at its final venue on Castle Hill, tribute bands, some of them pretending to be the bands that played at King Street in 1973, were commanding sums of £1,600, and on the 15th May, 2010, The Wonder Stuff were charging a whopping £5,000. Wheatus, riding high in the USA with a number 1 hit on their hands, arrived at JB's after negotiating a £7,000 fee. Of that night, more later!

While we are talking money, let us remind ourselves what it cost to have a night out at King Street in the early '70s. Back then, punters were charged 10p for a half of draught Guinness, or 20p per pint. A port and lemon would also set you back 10p. The entrance fee for the disco evenings before the decimal changeover was 1/6d (can anyone out there work out what that is in decimal currency?), and, depending on the status of the band, the price ranged from free to a pound on average, with good, but not so well-known outfits, entertaining us for around 50p. Incidentally, if you younger readers get confused by the fancy version of the letter 'L' (£) being used for the pound symbol and a 'd' used for a penny, it comes from the days of Roman rule, when we used the lira and dinar. Don't say this book isn't educational! 1971 saw Britain switch to decimal currency, so after the changeover, it became 'p' for penny, but we held onto the '£' sign!

And now – as those ageing comedians currently staging come-back concerts in order to supplement their pension schemes would say – for something completely different. *A few more stories!*

☞ *Hamish Stuart, fronting the Average White Band. And have you spotted the wonderful drum skin cartoon?*

☞ *JB's favourites, String Driven Thing. You wouldn't want to bump into him on a dark night in the Deep South would you?*

Capability Brown. Bands name themselves after virtually everything and anything. This lot chose a Victorian gardener, for reasons best known to themselves, while Jethro Tull was named after a bloke that invented the seed drill. ☞

CAPABILITY BROWN

The King Street bar, with, from left to right: Sam Jukes, Jim Lea, Big Dave Hodgetts, Angie Lea, Ros Stephens and Dermott Stephens.

An atmospheric old picture of the King Street bar. Interestingly, the folks on the right seem to be from a different time zone to the folks on the left. Spooky!

☝ Brian 'Elvis' Lee (occasional doo:man) has left the building, watched by Dermott Stephens.

☝ Some people get a nice watch for their birthday, others, a new sweater. Sam got a roly poly stripagram.

☞ Far right: The lovely Glenis Smythe, JB's barmaid and Little Acre member, now enjoying the good life Down Under.

☞ The inimitable (and who'd want to) Roz Hardwick wearing shades at night.

☝ Sam and Big Dave at one of the many New Years' Eve fancy dress evenings. Dave appears to be wearing a fake beard and lumberjack outfit over his real beard and lumberjack outfit. Sam seems to be attempting to eat a tomato through his nose.

BACK DOOR

Colin Hodgkinson   Tony Hicks   Ron Aspery

Colin Blunstone insisting that Johnny Bryant takes off his new Indian kaftan immediately.

Strange but True

Stories from King Street

◆ On the 7th December, 1973, members of Back Door, the jazz-rock band mentioned earlier, arrived at the club, walked through the front double doors, and found themselves confounded by the width of the inner door, leading to the main room. Frustratingly, it prevented one of their very large PA speakers from being carried into the room – this being the time just before JB's installed its own permanent PA system. Sam did a bit of hurried measuring, and assured the band that, if he removed the doors, the speaker would just about go through the gap, and this they duly did. Whether or not it was down to laziness or some other, more practical reason, the doors were never replaced. Nothing more was said until one wag realized that Back Door couldn't get through the front door, so they asked Sam to remove the front door in order to let Back Door in, because they didn't actually have a back door. Well, you get the idea!

✳ Many bands that played JB's rehearsed in nearby Wednesbury, at the church near to the big island, where the large Centro bus terminal is situated. The church owned a building, perhaps once an old school like JB's, which had several adjacent rooms that were ideal for bands, as they were far enough away from civilization to prevent neighbours from being deafened. This was actually a very real concern, as Judas Priest often rehearsed there. The rooms were presided over by the vicar (Holy Joe, as he was christened by the musicians), who was almost certainly the most disagreeable clergyman in the UK, and that is saying something. He was so ill-mannered and brusque, he made the late Ian Paisley look like Father Dougal McGuire, of the TV show Father Ted. A band would arrange with him to book a room, and at some point during the evening, he would show up, interrupt the rehearsal without apology and demand his money, with menaces. Then, by all accounts, he would repair to the local pub and spend his ill-gotten gains on alcohol. When the band members called it a night, they would often pop into the boozer for a quick one, only to find this man of the cloth quietly plastered in the corner.

♣ *The no drugs policy, which has already been mentioned, was enforced by Jimmy the Con, even though he was partial to the odd smoke himself. This didn't seem to prevent John Weston and Larry Oakley, now respectable, clean-living middle-aged men, of course, from wanting to try LSD for the first time, just to see what would happen. Having taken the pill at the club during a Gypsy gig, suddenly John began to see sounds as colours, a condition known as synaesthesia, or more accurately, chromesthesia, when related specifically to colour and sound, as John's experience was. To his amazement, the notes that Gypsy played flowed out from the stage in multicoloured lines. He also noticed a strange red aura around those in the room that he knew had also taken the drug, but blue auras around those that hadn't. He explains that this had not only happened to him, but with many people who had taken LSD, and it was supposedly why The Beatles had created the Blue Meanies characters in their Yellow Submarine animated film. Having somehow got himself home, Larry lay naked on his bed playing Joni Mitchell loudly, until his dad came in, demanding to know what on earth was going on. Meanwhile, in John's garden, the Christmas trees had morphed into space rockets and were whizzing into the night sky. Then, once the trees had all gone, prehistoric animals seemed to be infesting the garden and shrinking in size like something from Alice in Wonderland, before a giant frog with blood-red eyes arrived. Meanwhile, blissfully unaware of any of this, Leicester band, Gypsy went down well as always, and later went on to play the Isle of Wight Festival. Since his first encounter with LSD, Larry can no longer listen to Gypsy, or John to the Sergeant Peppers album, without breaking into a cold sweat and screaming, 'Don't let the frog get me!'*

◆ **Having already fingered Thin Lizzy as the culprits of the 15th October 1971 Stolen Whiskey Saga, we draw your attention to other serious crimes of the '70s, by people you'd think would know better. We hope that the Historical Unsolved Crimes Division of the West Midlands Police is listening.**

◆ **JB's King Street boasted several sturdy rustic tables made from the cross sections of trees. There were two less after Terry Reid played there on Saturday 9th June, 1972. This talented kleptomaniac also borrowed one of the Pirelli calendars, and Sam wants it back, purely for artistic reasons of course.**

✳ *When Supercharge played one of their many gigs at the club, Sam hid their fee in the fridge until such time that he had to hand it over. He figured that no one would think to look in the freezer compartment. He employed the same flawed logic when he left his own wallet in the cooker at home, suspecting that his wife, Sue, would never dream of venturing near the thing. Unfortunately, Albie Donnelly had happened to look in the fridge for whatever reason – ice cubes maybe – and spied the cash, which, out of devilment, he duly pocketed. At the end of the evening, he brazenly approached Sam and asked for his gig money, but Sam had already spotted Albie taking the frozen wedge and noted where he'd stashed it. He promptly stole it back and paid Albie with it, making a mental note to keep it in his Y-fronts next time.*

✴ **When Johnny Bryant's band supported ex-Zombies singer, Colin Blunstone, writer of the classics, 'Say You Don't Mind' and 'She's Not There', Blunstone's manager walked into Johnny's band's dressing room and informed him that he couldn't wear his nice embroidered Indian top (in fairness, they were fashionable at that time), because Colin was wearing one just like it. And they say that girls are catty.**

✦ **When Vinegar Joe played JB's, the women seemed to be fixated on Robert Palmer, whereas the men were deeply fascinated by Elkie Brooks' Mickey-Mouse-design knickers,** which made many appearances, thanks to her unbuttoned denim skirt. Oh, and the band sounded good too, apparently.

⭐ **During the British heavy metal revival, spearheaded by the likes of Saxon and their ilk, a band was pounding out its set at JB's, to a room of about 50 disinterested people. Dinko Dyson, a local character, was at the bar with his back to the band and not taking much notice. The band's lead singer called out to the audience, 'I know there are not many of you here tonight, but I want you to pretend you're 5,000!' Dink's voice suddenly cut through the stony silence that followed. 'Yo pretend yo'm a fuckin' band, an' we'll pretend we'm 5,000 folks.' RIP Dinko.**

✩ *Little Acre, featuring, amongst a cast of thousands, Johnny Bryant and Johnny Higgs, played a gig in Talgarth, Wales. Band member, George Northall, was a recent convert to the Hare Krishna movement, and came across as a peaceful soul, but when an unexpected fight broke out and one of the band was subsequently hit by a flying bottle, George seemed to instantly forget his religious calling and began to demolish the troublemakers like ninepins.*

⭐ Mike Hamblett, owner of the Robin 2 rock club in Bilston, was once the drummer of Sub Zero, who played at JB's several times. When King Street was vacated he purchased a number of 11-inch-square beams that had once been a part of the club, and had them sawn down into planks, which he used in the renovation of his 200-year-old cottage. He often admires them, and they remind him of all the famous bands that once played there!

♣ *Ace played regularly at JB's, and their gigs were always laid-back affairs. Paul Carrack would have an old beaten-up Persian rug on stage, usually with an old Labrador dog lying on it, seemingly unperturbed by the noise all around. Maybe it was deaf. If it wasn't at the start, it certainly was by the end. Paul would wear one of those beaded Moroccan-style flat caps, and sing, 'How long, has this been going*

on?' month after month. Usually, some wag at the back of the room by the dartboard would shout, 'Too fucking long!'

✚ JB's had no shortage of characters. One lumbering gentle giant of a man by the name of Dave, with a face like a Shar Pei dog, would enthusiastically bellow for 'MORE!' when a band had finished its last song, but he pronounced it 'MOO-ER!', in traditional Black Country fashion, so loudly that those around him became permanently deaf. This sparked an outbreak of copycat behaviour, and quite soon many of the regular patrons began shouting it too. Quite what visiting out-of-town bands made of it is not on record. There was a middle-aged couple who came every week, but always looked as if they'd mistakenly turned up at the wrong venue. They resembled and dressed like

The lovely Elkie Brooks flashes her Mickey Mouse undies.

George and Mildred, and seemed much more suited to Quarry Bank Labour Club. Another regular, a shy-looking introspective type, stick thin with floppy hair, 'Should have gone to Specsavers' glasses and an impressive collection of teenage zits, would bring along his paperback, always a foot thick, and sit by the dartboard quietly reading and not speaking to anyone all evening. Motörhead or Trapeze could have been playing (and often were) at around a million decibels, but he seemed oblivious. Curious onlookers often wondered quite why he felt the need to come to the club at all. Surely, they argued, he'd have been just as happy in his bedroom, lit by a bare 40-watt bulb. Anyway, we have put our finest minds to work on this one, and we can reveal that our shy bookworm was and still is Ben Stacey, who now works for the council and still haunts the Lamp and Cowshed. We trust he has improved with age.

◆ *Jimmy the Con was asked to be best man at Lyn Fitzpatrick's and Kevin 'Rosko' Fisher's wedding, much to the consternation of the bride's God-fearing Catholic aunts. It wasn't just the expletive-riddled best man's speech that upset them, it was also the gentleman's morning coat with the sleeves ripped off.*

✳ One evening, during a particularly loud and boisterous band's performance, a long-haired biker-type stood bashing his empty Newcastle Brown bottle on the corner of one of the club's wooden tables (see earlier section on 'Terry Reid, table, theft of'). Several times he was advised by all around him that this foolhardy act might well end in tears – advice he chose to ignore. Then, seconds later, in a scene reminiscent of that rather sinister Stephen King film, Carrie, horrified customers saw a fine jet of blood arc across the room, spraying everyone and everything in its wake. Conservatively, it travelled some ten feet, like the water jet from one of those Super Soaker water pistols that were all the rage years ago. The screams of the customers almost drowned out the power chords

emanating from the stage, and the hapless biker suddenly looked paler than a bottle of milk. Luckily, there were folks who knew just what to do in such circumstances, and he was quickly bundled off to hospital. We hope he is still with us!

♣ *A band arrived at JB's one evening, driven by a pair of excitable roadies. They invited a few of the JB's staff to take a look inside the back of their Luton van, explaining that the band (name deleted for legal reasons) had played at the BBC in London earlier that day, and kept a souvenir to remind them of their visit. The JB's staff members were somewhat taken aback to discover a rather menacing-looking dalek peering out from behind a Marshall 100-watt cabinet, and pointing its deadly ray gun in their direction.*

☆ Sam Jukes was watching TV one evening – a Rwanda famine-appeal documentary as it happens – when the camera focussed on a small child of no more than 8 or 9 years of age, staring back at him with those pitiful, huge brown eyes that can melt our hearts. The little boy was wearing a black JB's T-shirt.

★ Viv Stanshall, singer with The Bonzo Dog Doo-Dah Band, was as crazy and eccentric as one would expect. During one performance, he had taped a Marigold rubber glove around his head and inserted one of the fingers into his ear – a look that he kept for most of the evening. It was only after a considerable amount of time had elapsed that the audience realized that he was in fact taking the mickey out of traditional folk singers. Later, at the bar, Viv asked John Weston for ice to drop into his drink, but straight-faced, John replied that he did not have the recipe at hand for making the stuff. Vivian, apparently, did not find this hilarious.

⬩ The Fight, a local punk band, actually wrote a song called 'JB's' in honour of the club, which can be heard on YouTube. Upon discovering this little nugget, one of the band members was approached and asked to supply a little more background on the song, so that The Fight could be given a small paragraph in the book, and she responded with all the enthusiasm that a turkey has for Christmas. This book is apparently good enough for Robert Plant, as well as The Wonder Stuff, The Mighty Lemon Drops, Blur, Steve Gibbons, Ned's Atomic Dustbin, et al. to contribute to, but not, apparently, for The Fight. Ho-hum!

★ **Like many rock clubs, JB's was often troubled by drug dealers. They knew that Jimmy the Con would soon throw them out of the club if they dared enter, but this did not deter them from hanging around in the car park, trying to peddle their wares to the JB's customers. Fearful that this could result in the police closing the club down, Sam decided on a pre-emptive strike, and invited the Dudley Drug Squad to organize surveillance, courtesy of Pathfinder boss, Percy the magistrate. One evening, Dudley's boys in blue were staked out on the top floor of Pathfinder, filming the comings and goings below, when the West Bromwich police suddenly arrived and raided the club. Sam invited the West Bromwich inspector to pop outside with him for a minute, and pointing to the top floor of Pathfinder, informed the senior bobby to smile because he and Sam were both on candid camera. According to Sam, the West Brom lads beat one of the hastiest retreats in police history.**

★ The Maisonettes used JB's stage as the backdrop for their hit single 'Heartache Avenue', when they appeared on The Tube. Lol Mason, former member of City Boy (hit single – '5705'), was also a talented scriptwriter, and his father, Edward J. Mason, wrote Dick Barton Special Agent, and The Archers, for many years. Mark Tibenham, the keyboard and guitar player, also had a famous father, Philip Tibenham, the Panorama presenter. Drummer Nick Parry, sadly, did not have a famous father. The single 'Heartache Avenue', which reached number 7 in the charts, had two female backing singers, one of whom was Carla Mendonça, who went on to become a TV comedienne, starring in Bottom

with Rik Mayall, Harry Enfield and Chums, French and Saunders and Alas Smith and Jones. However, Mendonça and friend could not commit to the various live appearances, so Lol recruited two Dudley girls who looked the part, but sadly didn't sound it. From then on, the girls, Denise Ward and Elaine Williams, were forced to mime to Mendonça's original vocal on Top of the Pops. Graduate Records' boss, the late and greatly missed David Virr, was keen to replace them, especially when one of them, not knowing who he was, called him a posh twat.

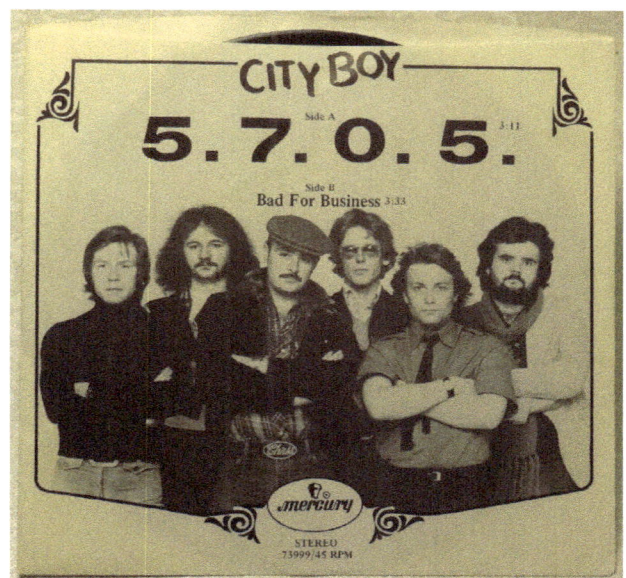

★ City Boy, who played at JB's at the time of their massive hit single '5705', had a drummer by the name of Roy Ward, who was also a very good singer, and it was he who supplied the main vocals on that single. He was asked to record 'The Lion Sleeps Tonight' for a manufactured band by the name of Tight Fit, the members of which, like Denise and Elaine, were chosen for their looks and not their voices. Consequently, Roy's vocals could be heard pouring forth from the lips of a chap with a matinee idol's looks and a Tarzan loincloth, each week for what seemed like an eternity, on Top of the Pops. After a recording session at Zella Studios, the lads from City Boy were relaxing in a nearby Harborne pub, when a woman selected 'The Lion Sleeps Tonight' on the jukebox. Roy

73

Gypsy in the JB's boardroom, seconds after Sam explained that their fee was only going to be £75.

Antipodean theatrical rockers, Split Enz, who came, saw, and soon went.

spontaneously began to sing along with his own vocals, which caused the startled woman to comment that his voice was remarkably similar to the Tarzan chap's on TOTP. 'That's because it was really me singing it!' explained Roy, proudly. 'Bollocks,' said the woman. 'Do you think I was fucking born yesterday?' Had it not been for the huge royalty cheques, Roy would have been crushed.

☆ Two young Americans had seen an article in an American magazine on Robert Plant, which mentioned that he often frequented a tiny rock club by the name of JB's, in a West Midlands town called Dudley. Star-struck, they spent every cent they had in the world, and travelled all the way from the USA in the vain hope that they might see him there. Heartbroken when they discovered that he wasn't actually at the club when they arrived (how naïve are these Americans anyway?), Roy Williams kindly took them to Robert's farm to meet him. Robert then paid their airfares back to the USA, as they were completely broke. Apparently, they sent the money back to him, which he wasn't expecting!

✳ **The original JB's stage backdrop, based on the Nantucket Sleighride album sleeve by rock band Mountain, was painted by barman and occasional DJ, Les Bates. It was later replaced by Shaun Payne's Knave of Hearts design, and finally by the famous black and white stencilled logo.**

✴ *...and for ten points, can you name the connection between snooker, Italian ice cream and JB's club? Yes of course! It's Maria Catalano, a member of the Sicilian ice cream vans dynasty from Darby End, Netherton, near Dudley. Maria was a JB's King Street regular all through the 70s, until she left to work at a holiday camp down South, where she met her husband-to-be. They eventually married, had a baby boy, who was born at Wordsley Hospital, and later moved to London. The boy grew up to be very famous indeed, so if your pub quizmaster asks which five-times snooker world champion was born near Dudley, the*

answer is of course, Ronnie O'Sullivan!

✴ If you are a fan of spooky coincidences, you might like this one. Several of the JB's committee would occasionally visit the Middle Earth club in Covent Garden, London, in the early days, to see bands such as Pink Floyd, The Bonzo Dog Doo-Dah Band, Fairport Convention, The Byrds, Captain Beefheart and the like, with a view to setting up a similar establishment back in Dudley. The DJ and promoter who ran the club was a gentleman by the name of Jeff Dexter (ring any bells? Remember the manager of America with the annoying clicker?). And can you guess where this London club was situated? Yes, that's right – King Street.

✳ The award for 'The Band that Came and Went' was won by Antipodean theatrical rockers, Split Enz (who later morphed into superstars – Crowded House). At 3.30pm, their roadies arrived at the club and instantly began moaning that the stage was far too small, and, incredibly, the mirrors in the dressing room weren't good enough! In an effort to placate them, Sam told them, 'Look lads, there's the bar, if you need a drink, there's the stage, and there's the door, if you're not satisfied.' They chose the door. Later, at 5.30pm, the actual band members arrived, and couldn't help noticing that the stage was bare, a bit like Old Mother Hubbard's kitchen cupboard. Sam explained what the roadies had said, and, in fairness, the band members were all for giving it a go, or at least, they said they were. They left immediately in search of their crew, and were not seen again. Runner-up for this award was Scottish rockers, Simple Minds, whose members thought the place was just too shabby for them. What is it about these colonials?

UB40

UNEMPLOYMENT BENEFIT ATTENDANCE CARD

Surname (block capitals)   Initials   NI Number   CODOT No.

M

Post Office

1 IMPORTANT NOTICE ABOUT CLAIMING BENEFIT

You should make your claims for unemployment benefit at the Benefit Office each week on the days and at the times shown in the box on the right. Produce this card on each occasion.

If you fail to claim in any week on the day specified you risk losing benefit and you could be disqualified for all the days between your last claim and the day you next claim.

If you do miss claiming benefit on the day specified go to the Benefit Office on the very next day you can (but not on Saturday or Sunday). Do not wait until the specified day in the following week.

This notice ceases to apply when you start work or claim another benefit. If you again become unemployed you should claim benefit on the first day of unemployment.

MON
TUES
WEDS
THU
FRI

Signing box

Surname   Initials   NI Number   chkd by & date

2 CLAIM FOR OUTSTANDING BENEFIT

If there is outstanding benefit in respect of days for which you have already claimed, payment will be made by post to your home address **on return of this card with part 3 completed**. If there are days between the last day on which you claimed benefit at the Benefit Office and the date on which you started work (or claimed another benefit) **complete the declaration below**.

"I HAVE READ AND UNDERSTAND the leaflet 'Responsibility of Claimants' issued

I CLAIM BENEFIT for the following dates

SIGNING OFF

AND DECLARE that on those days I was unemployed and did no work; I was able and willing to do any suitable work but was unable to get any; the circumstances of my dependants were as last stated." (If there was a change cross out this last item).

Signature   date

DO NOT SIGN UNTIL THE LAST DAY FOR WHICH YOU WISH TO CLAIM BENEFIT.

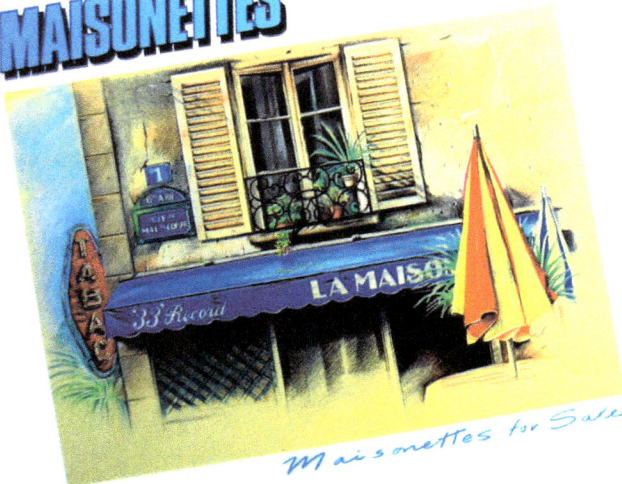

MAISONETTES

Maisonettes for Sale

Geoff Tristram with two of the record sleeves he designed for David Virr of 'Graduate'.

✣ **UB40, soon to be catapulted to stardom, courtesy of their squillion-selling album Signing Off, played JB's on Thursday the 1st of May, 1980. I (Geoff Tristram, professional artist and author of this very book, no less), designed their album sleeve for the princely sum of £110. When it went platinum, I was informed that the sleeve designer was entitled to a framed platinum disc. Excitedly, I accepted, but was duly informed that it would cost me £150 plus VAT for the privilege. On principle, I refused, citing the example that Marlon Brando didn't have to pay for his Oscars whenever he won one.**

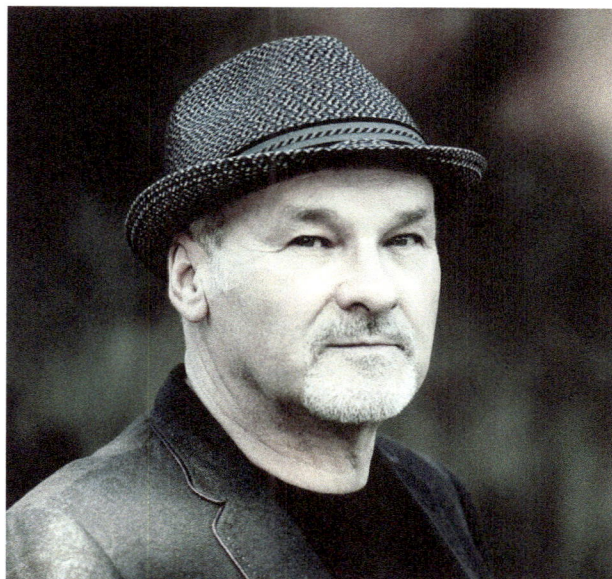

✸ Larry Homer recalls an evening in the Graduate Records recording studios with local punk outfit, Virus. Tim, the drummer (whom Larry describes as looking like one of The Bash Street Kids), bored senseless because Larry was busy recording vocal tracks, found a lump hammer that had been left in the studio after a recent DIY job, and began playing around with it. Then, apropos of nothing, he whacked himself forcibly in the middle of the brow with the blunt instrument, an action which had broadly the same effect that a stun gun has on a cow awaiting slaughter. Once the drummer had mercifully recovered enough to communicate, Larry asked why he had done it. Tim replied groggily, 'I wanted to see if it hurt.'

◆ *If we can be forgiven for interfering with the chronology of this book by fast-forwarding to 17th October 1986 – just for a minute – we will reward you with the following gem. The Dudley police raided the club and insisted, for some strange reason, on counting the beef burgers in the kitchen. A week later, they came back, counted the burgers again, and then left. To this day, no one has the slightest inkling as to why they did this. As if this wasn't bizarre enough, Sam assures us that the band on stage that evening was Betty Bondage. Could it really be that the police had created an excuse to raid the club, just so that they could get an eyeful of what they erroneously believed to be a kinky, gimp-masked and handcuffed stripper?*

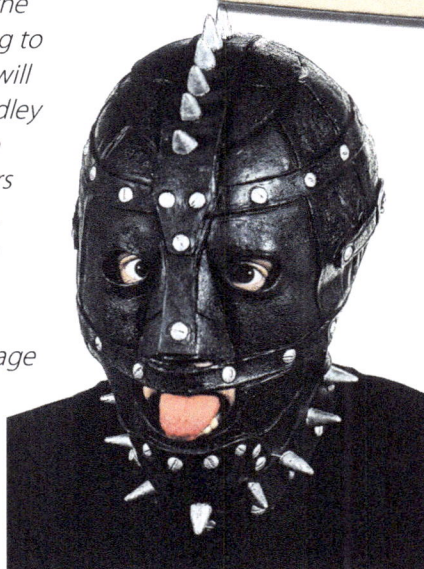

*Just in case you were wondering – yes, Paul Carrack is **still** going on!*

1975

Jess Roden (pictured left) returned to delight us with more of his soulful songs in early February, followed by Brett Marvin and The Thunderbolts. Those who are not familiar with the output of this blues rock band might nevertheless be aware of the band's then keyboard player, John Lewis, who changed his name to the more memorable Jona Lewie, an artiste who went on to have hits with 'You'll Always Find Me in the Kitchen at Parties' (used in a high-profile TV advertisement, amongst other things) and 'Stop the Cavalry', his poignant little ditty about World War One.

The 21st of February welcomed a band by the name of Kilburn and the High Roads, featuring Ian Dury, who eventually fronted the well-known and much-loved Blockheads. That evening, Dury had to be helped onto the stage by Jimmy the Con due to his polio-affected leg. Once settled behind the microphone, he grinned at the assembled multitude, and for no apparent reason, loudly uttered the word 'Semprini', a pointless, random detail that has remained with me ever since, as these things do. A witty songwriter, raconteur and trained fine artist (he was friendly with

the likes of Sir Peter Blake, creator of the iconic Sergeant Peppers album sleeve), Dury and his tight backing band belted out songs that laid the foundations for future hits such as 'Hit Me With Your Rhythm Stick', 'Billericay Dickie', 'Reasons to be Cheerful', and 'Sex & Drugs & Rock & Roll'. Cult Black Country comedians of that time, Ted and Harry, a less-than-subtle reworking of Derek and Clive but with Cradley Heath accents, recorded a fairly obscene little song in honour of Dury, the gist of which is printed below.

> "*Beer and fags and sausage rolls, are all my brain and body need,*
> *Beer and fags and sausage rolls, are very good indeed!*"

Taken from Ted and Harry live! (with apologies to Ian Dury and The Blockheads). Any of you who still own an original copy of this recording, on cassette only, with free condom, should treasure it. Nowadays, they are extremely hard to come by. Even Ted and Harry don't possess one!

The 7th of March 1975 meant it was time for Back Door, and those gifted with a good memory will remember that it was this band that was responsible for removing the front doors at JB's in order to get its huge PA system into the main room. On the 16th of May, JB's pulled off something of a coup, having managed to persuade the legendary (not a word to be used too lightly) Sonny Terry and Brownie McGhee, two of the original American Bluesmen, to visit the club. McGhee, like Ian Dury, had been affected by polio as a child. He played guitar, and at the age of 22 he became a travelling musician. He met Terry, a harmonica player, in 1939, and when he moved to New York in 1942, he teamed up with his old friend. The two became an instant success. From then on, they toured relentlessly, often for 11 months of every year. The 1960s blues revival boosted their fame and gave them a new lease of life, and as a consequence of this, we saw them turn up at a small Black Country club, singing, amongst many other songs, the classic, 'Baby Please Don't Go'.

Ian Dury before he became a 'Blockhead'.

There was a very real feeling in the club that evening that the audience was watching something of historical importance – something that would soon be gone forever. Here were two relatively elderly gentlemen who were there when the roots of rock and roll were planted, and the crowd was privileged to be able to witness it all first-hand. Four years later, Sonny Terry and Brownie McGhee appeared in Steve Martin's classic comedy, The Jerk, so dig it out and take another look!

Jona Lewie finds himself in the living room for a change!

☞

Sonny Terry and Brownie McGee bring a touch of Beale Street blues to Dudley.

1976 – 1980

"Come mothers and fathers
Throughout the land
And don't criticize
What you can't understand
Your sons and your daughters
Are beyond your command
Your old road is rapidly agein'
Please get out of the new one
If you can't lend your hand
For the times they are a-changin'"

Bob Dylan

In 1963, The Beatles burst onto the music scene like a breath of fresh air, igniting the imaginations of all the youngsters who had, until then, been fed a diet of balladeers, crooning their way through Tin Pan Alley's formulaic hit factory output. Moon rhymed with June, and sweethearts cuddled at drive-in movies. If that didn't appeal, there were always the maudlin country and western ballads about broken-hearted lovers tragically dying in car crashes, or faithful old dogs breathing their last. Sinatra and Co. were wonderful, of course, but they meant nothing to your average 15-year-old Black Country youth. Neither

did Burl Ives, Perry Como, and those of that ilk. Rock and Roll had been around a while, but at that time it was far too American, and spoke of exclusively American things – kids met under boardwalks (what exactly are they?), drank soda pop (likewise), and went boppin' at the 'High School Hop'. This was all lumped under the heading of 'Music for the Parents and Grand-parents' – the ones who thought 'Two-Way Family Favourites' was essential listening each Sunday, accompanied by the smell of Pledge furniture polish and Sunday lunch being boiled senseless.

Then, one sunny, memorable day in the mid-60s, it was as if someone had washed out the radio with a high-pressure hose, as 'She Loves You' blasted out of the newly-purged speakers for the first time. At last, the new breed of British youths had something they could understand – something home-grown and exclusively for them.

Ten years later, and a lot had happened in the interim. Amongst other things, progressive rock had arrived, and gatefold record sleeves had become works of art that came with more reading matter inside them than the Dudley & District Yellow Pages.

As will always be the case, the new generation of young kids regarded all this as something for their parents. They didn't get Rick Wakeman (understandable) in his sequinned cape and long girly hair, standing amidst umpteen keyboards, playing hundreds of twiddly pseudo-classical notes while Jon Anderson warbled, choirboy-like, about Starship Troopers and Topographic Oceans. To them, this was just another version of Perry Como, but this time wearing a superhero cape. Then (can you see history repeating itself here, folks?), in 1976, someone turned on their radio and had their ears melted by 'Anarchy in the UK', but this time, it wasn't so much a breath of fresh air as someone setting off a fire extinguisher at the vicar's tea party. The song achieved the same basic effect as 'She Loves You', but the marketing boys had added a twist (if you'll excuse The Beatles pun), and that was public outrage. Not your old-fashioned outrage caused by Elvis swivelling his sexy, leather-clad hips around, but real, Daily-Mail-style outrage. It was the end of civilization as we knew it, apparently. Provocative hip-swivelling was one thing, but these people were wearing Nazi insignia and spitting all over the place. Surely, this was scraping the bottom of an already disgusting barrel.

It was all packaged as a youth revolution, but be aware, these things seldom are. Somewhere in a dark, secret operations room, someone is plotting the next big thing, and you can bet your bottom dollar that he isn't 16 years of age and spotty. He is a manipulative marketing man with a plan to make serious amounts of money out of the youth market. Won't get fooled again? Oh yes you will, about once every ten years.

Just as Tin Pan Alley, the music factory, and later, Stock Aitken Waterman (SAW), churned out tunes aimed at the new generation, so did Malcolm McLaren in the mid-1970s. He used an old and well-used recipe – loud rock music – but added quite a lot of spittle, bile, offensive language, the obligatory bizarre and unfamiliar new haircuts, bondage clothing and safety pins, and finished it off with a sprinkle of Nazi regalia, just to make sure that the older generation who had lived through the war got really pissed off. His objective was to alienate everyone who wasn't part of the new 'scene', and guess what? He succeeded. His main weapon of mass destruction was the aptly named Sex Pistols, who were, sorry to report, every bit as manufactured as The Monkees had been. It is worth

remembering that The Beatles were not. They were a natural, organic product – a rarity nowadays, it has to be said. They were four young likely lads who bumped into each other at school or college in Liverpool, and maybe this was the real secret of their success (oh, and having three geniuses in the band did help too). There were no marketing men in suits staging auditions with the intention of creating a musical version of Frankenstein's monster (think One Direction). The Beatles were the real deal. The manipulation and marketing inevitably followed, thanks to Brian Epstein, but all he was doing was fine-tuning an already wonderful raw product. There is a big difference.

So now, the new message was anti-government, anti-royalty, anti-everything. Nihilistic anarchy with bondage accessories. Gatefold record sleeves were out, replaced by simple, crude, makeshift, home-made, stencilled and blackmail-note-inspired, cheap, Day-Glo sleeves. The punks hated all that pretentious progressive-rock gatefold tosh with the 50-page full-colour brochures inside. The trouble was, the punk albums still cost exactly as much as the Yes and Genesis albums did. You paid the same and got far less for your money. Won't get fooled again? You just did! We always do!

And the live performances had to reflect the image of this new punk wave. Out went 'the twist', and screaming prepubescent girls; out went introspective navel-gazing, and smoking weed whilst waving a lighter in the air, and in came spitting (which genius thought of that one?) and pogoing.

Sam and Co. could sense the wind changing, and they had three choices. They could close down and give up, carry on with their heads in the sand, or they could go with the flow and welcome in the new arrivals, alongside their existing regular bands. A mixture of simple expediency combined with the JB's ethos of nurturing all forms of music led to the only sensible decision. The times, they were a-changing, and JB's would change with them.

All this talk of marketing men and manipulation might sound deeply cynical, but anyone who has lived through several musical fashions will know that each had their fair share of unspeakable dross, but more importantly, each era also gave us some remarkable songs to add to the 'classics' pile. The Sex Pistols may have been a manufactured band, just like the Monkees

The Stranglers, the only band ever to be 'hooked' off stage for being so awful.

Howard Williamson's photograph of a JB's punk, circa '76.

EDDIE AND THE HOT RODS

Dave Higgs   **Barrie Masters**   **Steve Nicol**   **Paul Gray**

Eddie and the boys doing anything what they want to do.

A youthful Joe Jackson stepping out on stage at JB's.

Elvis played a blinder but refused to play an encore.

Ultravox who, whilst gigging in Vienna later that year performed their new single, 'Dudley'.

(the latter created by the USA because it was deeply jealous of our Beatles), but that said, 'I'm a Believer', 'Daydream Believer', and 'Pleasant Valley Sunday' are great pop songs, just as 'God Save The Queen' and 'Anarchy In The UK' are undoubtedly great punk-rock songs, and that, folks, is all that truly matters when all is said and done, and the dust has settled. One just hopes that the last two songs were not penned to order by a middle-aged gent wearing a cravat, in Music Room 246 of some vast hit factory in the Home Counties. Unlikely, admittedly, but nowadays you never know.

The first punk band to visit JB's was, of course, the Sex Pistols, masquerading as The Spots (The Sex Pistols on Tour Secretly), but the first to actually play there, according to the surviving records, was The Stranglers. They were, Sam remembers, the worst ever band to play JB's. They certainly hold the award for the only band in the JB's club's long and proud history that was paid-off, asked to stop playing and go away instantly, in short jerky movements. Sam recalls that they were hopeless, unrehearsed, foul-mouthed and spitting all over the place. This, it has to be said, was not an auspicious beginning for the new punk movement. Eight weeks later, however, they sold out at Barbarella's in Birmingham. The Stranglers were undoubtedly shocking, but in their defence, this was the era before JB's installed a good in-house PA system, when bands would bring their own gear, and apparently, only half of The Stranglers' PA system was working, which contributed to their awful sound, and subsequently the band's frustration, which manifested itself as a swearing and spitting fest. Not an excuse, by any means, but anyone who has played a gig with faulty equipment will know how soul-destroying it can be. And there endeth the evidence for the Defence, Your Honour, courtesy of Dermott (the aforementioned JB's disc jockey), who knows and cares about these things.

Gradually, over the next few years, the punk bands amassed a following at the club, and eventually Fridays were unofficially earmarked as Punk Night, with appearances by The Vibrators, The Defects, Conflict, The Adicts, Cockney Rejects, Broken Bones, Rubella Ballet, and home-grown talent such as Virus, The Sect, Subterfuge, and Indecent Assault. Rob Jones, bassist with Subterfuge, would go on to become 'The Bass Thing' in The Wonder Stuff. Meanwhile, Indecent Assault are happily still going strong today (see photograph), and recently played the Rebellion festival

in Blackpool. As ever, exotic creatures covered in safety pins and outrageous pink Mohicans now mixed and mingled with all kinds of other youth cults (there was even a JB's Mod Club at one stage), and in the true spirit of the place, all of them rubbed along together in harmony.

Jean Vincent, the wittily named and fabulous female singer, who was at the time fronting Jean Vincent and The Nightcaps (the original Gene Vincent suffered with a limp and so did she, hence the pseudonym), remembers seeing a full-on punk eject a very smartly dressed gentleman from the club because of his boorish and antisocial behaviour. He explained to her afterwards that JB's was a place that made him welcome, and he was damned if anyone was going to mess things up for him. Remarkably, it transpired that the offending gentleman was none other than the punk's brother. Here was a club that could have justifiably adopted the motto 'vive la différence' alongside its logo – it was so cosmopolitan and all-inclusive. The only thing that was frowned upon was spitting. This antisocial, inexplicable by-product of the punk scene certainly manifested itself at JB's on occasion, but it was a brave, or else very foolish punk, that would do such a thing in the same room as the formidable Jimmy the Con.

The punk phenomenon settled down and took its place alongside all the other forms of modern popular music that were being showcased at the club, and within a few years a more commercial – some would say watered-down – derivative would emerge, which was labelled 'new wave', or 'power pop'. The music was still high-energy, but the dress code had softened a little, with old school ties taking the place of safety pins, and spiky hair replacing the Mohican. Most important though, was the fact that the songs had mellowed somewhat, and had become more catchy and melodic. The often repellent punk attitude had given way to a more socially acceptable look and sound, but this new wave of bands still had the raw energy that almost harked back to The Beatles in their early days in Hamburg. Examples of this genre are bands such as Elvis Costello and the Attractions, Blondie, and Joe Jackson, who were belting out 3-minute songs with attitude.

Of course, the bands that peddled other forms of music were still putting in regular appearances at the club, and there would always be a place for them. February 1976 saw Neil Innes (formerly of The Bonzo Dog Doo-Dah Band) perform there, and later The Beatles spoof outfit, The Rutles), followed once more by City Boy. Shortly after that came a double-header with prog-rock bands Still and Cleardays (the latter featuring the author of this very book, who also later became a guitarist for Still), and late in May came Frankie Miller ('A Fool in Love', 'Darlin''etc.), the man they often call the Scottish Paul Rodgers, whether he liked it or not. Canadian rocker Pat Travers and the George Hatcher Band followed.

Eddie and the Hot Rods, a high-energy live band that was originally lumped in with the punk movement but evolved into one of the power-pop outfits mentioned earlier, played the club in September. They enjoyed considerable success with the rather vacuous youth anthem 'Do anything You Wanna Do' – under their new, snappier name, The Rods – which reached number 9 in the British charts. On the 2nd of October, The Pretenders took to the stage, fronted by Chrissie Hynde, and thankfully, someone in the audience had the foresight to bring a camera that evening – not a common sight at the club, regrettably – to capture Chrissie in all her glory.

Little Acre, the club's home-grown band, played one of their many gigs on the 16th of November, and shortly after that – hold onto your hats and dig out your waterproofs – came The Stranglers again, presumably forgiven for their previous attempt at entertaining the Dudley crowd. The year ended with Chapman and Whitney's Streetwalkers, better known as the men behind legendary progressive-rock band, Family. They duly treated the crowd to classics such as 'Rollin' and Tumblin'' and 'The Weaver's Answer'. They'd have surely been lynched if they hadn't.

On reflection, 1977 was a golden year in terms of bands that would later become very famous indeed. The year began well enough with heavy rockers Magnum, but it was the weekend of the 22nd/23rd of April that saw arguably two of the most famous bands to play at JB's, other than Robert Plant, of course. Not that anyone realized it at the time. Squeeze comprised Chris Difford on guitar, Glenn Tilbrook on vocals and guitar, Jools Holland on keyboards, Harri Kakoulli on bass, and Gibson Lavis on drums, though this line-up changed fairly regularly. Their impressive list of hit

singles included 'Take Me I'm Yours', 'Cool for Cats', 'Up the Junction', 'Another Nail in My Heart', and 'Pulling Mussels (from the shell)'. A few years after this JB's performance, Holland left the band and was replaced by Paul Carrack.

Cherry Vanilla and The Police were just like any other band back then, flogging their way around what were fondly referred to as the 'toilet venues', trying to establish a following. Cherry Vanilla was a New York actress who had appeared in Andy Warhol's films, and also worked for David Bowie as his publicist. She formed a band with her boyfriend and Gordon Sumner, and moved to London as part of the new punk / new wave scene. Sumner's own band, The Police, featured Stewart Copeland on drums and Andy Summers on guitar. The Police agreed to lend Cherry Vanilla their equipment for £15 per night, and in return she would allow them to be the support band! It was this arrangement that JB's was treated to. By all accounts the show was okay, if nothing special, and one young lady, whose name has been erased from the history books to protect her reputation, persuaded a youthful Gordon Sumner, or 'Sting' as he understandably preferred to be called, to sign her breasts with a felt-tipped pen. The more conservative Susan Jukes had her neck signed instead.

Spring 1977 seemed to be an extra-fertile time for bands that were destined for fame. XTC played at the club on the 6th of May, followed by Ultravox on the 13th (starring little Midge Ure), who received the princely sum of £50 for their efforts. Then, Midge's future partner in Band Aid, the unstoppable force of nature that is Bob Geldof, arrived with his band The Boomtown Rats in tow on Friday the 8th of July. Sam had originally asked him to do the Monday, but Bob didn't like Mondays, apparently.

Top of the Pops rock and rollers, Darts, played at the club on the 16th of July, a night that was as memorable for an off-stage incident as it was for the music. Apparently, members of the band had taken it upon themselves to spray-paint the word 'DARTS' in huge letters on the newly painted JB's dressing-room wall. 'Big' Dave Hodgetts, who had spent ages renovating the room, retaliated by spraying the letters JB's on the back doors of the band's new van. La vendetta è un piatto che va mangiato freddo. Get a passing Italian to translate it for you. It's an old Mafia expression. Fast-forward to the 27th of August and those in the know were flocking to the club to see and hear what was widely regarded as 'The Next Big Thing'. Step forward Elvis Costello and the Attractions, who played a fast-paced, exciting (if short) set, and then put a damper on the whole evening by steadfastly refusing to do an encore, in spite of the highly enthusiastic cacophony of wolf whistles and applause the band received. Such audience alienation is quite unforgivable. Anyone would think old Elvis was Van Morrison.

Next up was the newly formed Tom Robinson Band, playing their inaugural gig, which was somewhat marred by the sight of Jimmy the Con dealing with a troublemaker in the crowd, right at the front by the stage. Tom, appalled by the fracas, appealed for calm, and that came soon enough, once the offending punter was swiftly removed. Once order was restored to its throne, the band played a tight little set of memorable songs that included '2-4-6-8 Motorway', their big hit single at the time, and a song that was to be their follow-up single – (Sing if You're) 'Glad to be Gay', which they somehow managed to get virtually all of the crowd to sing along to, regardless of their sexual preferences. The violence that erupted early on wasn't the best introduction to the usually friendly folk of Dudley, and it is more than probable that Tom and the lads couldn't wait to get onto the M1, and back to what they regarded as civilization, singing a reprise of their motorway song as they trucked on through the night.

The year ended with appearances by Sad Café, whose single 'Every Day Hurts' reached number 3 in the charts, later on in 1979. Wilko Johnson brought his unique blend of high-energy rhythm and blues, deranged serial-killer facial expressions, and darting power walk to the cramped JB's stage in mid-November, and finally came Chris Spedding, whose job it was to finish off a vintage year in style.

You may be forgiven if you know little of Spedding, because his solo career was at best, sporadic, with only one notable single to show for it, namely, the largely forgettable 'Motor Bikin''. However, as a session guitarist, he has worked for the likes of Paul McCartney, Roger Daltrey, Nick Mason of Pink Floyd, Bryan Ferry, Brian Eno, Katie Melua, Free's Andy Fraser, Harry Nilsson and Cream's Jack Bruce. He also provided

the guitar parts for the Sex Pistols' wonderful anthem, 'Pretty Vacant', but all this pales to insignificance when compared to his finest hour. Chris Spedding most notably played on Mike Batt's Wombles' records, and can be seen on vintage Top of the Pops videos dressed as Wellington Womble, with his Gibson Flying V slung around his furry little neck. It doesn't get much better than that, folks!

1978 saw yet another couple of unknown acts arrive at JB's, which subsequently went on to achieve worldwide fame. On a cold, half-empty evening in March, an American singer by the name of Johnny Cougar (his real name was probably Gordon something or other) came on stage to a smattering of polite applause. There were probably only 30 or 40 people in the club at the time, so in fairness, it was the best they could manage. He then proceeded to treat his sparse audience to one of the tightest, slickest shows some of them had seen for a long time, and took the opportunity to air his new single, 'I Need A Lover', which was to do rather well for him. Cougar was a typical streetwise New York character with a Springsteen attitude and a band to die for – the kind of band Bruno Mars wouldn't have said no to. It was just a shame that more people hadn't turned up to witness the show. For those not familiar with John Cougar Mellencamp's output (the somewhat strange surname was added later in his career), he went on to sell 40 million albums. He was nominated for 13 Grammy Awards, had 22 top-40 hits in the USA, and he was inducted into the American Rock and Roll Hall of Fame on the 10th of March 2008. Not bad for a man who once entertained a handful of people in Dudley on a freezing-cold March evening.

Johnny Cougar returned to JB's in June, and was guaranteed a full house, once the word had spread. The following Saturday, a bunch of lads with Northern accents arrived, and had a lot to live up to after the previous Saturday's gig. They needn't have worried, however. Dire Straits were special. Even in those formative years, the audience knew they were watching something that was a cut above. Sam was so impressed that he decided to have a little chat to Mark Knopfler after the gig, while the meagre fee was changing hands. He told Knopfler that, in his not-so-humble opinion, he and his band were set to go places, and offered to manage them. Knopfler thanked him, but explained that they had recently taken on a

Guitar ace Chris Spedding.

© Jean Luc Ourlin www.flickr.com/photos/jlacpo

FRANKIE MILLER FULL HOUSE

Our very own Sweet Jean Vincent.

INDECENT ASSAULT

Local punks Indecent Assault.

CHS 2501

THE SPECIALS

SOCK IT TO THEM J.B.
DO NOTHING

Johnny Cougar played to a handful of people at JB's before going on to achieve international fame.

THE POLICE

NEW OR

manager by the name of Ed Bicknell. Not long after their JB's gig, the band's single, 'Sultans of Swing', hit the UK charts, followed by 'Lady Writer', 'Romeo and Juliet', 'Tunnel of Love', 'Money for Nothing', 'Walk of Life', and many more. The band's album, Brothers in Arms, sold over 30 million copies and was the very first album to sell a million copies on compact disc. Dire Straits went on to become one of the world's most successful bands, with worldwide album sales of over 120 million. They won Grammy Awards, Brit Awards (including Best British Band), MTV Video Music Awards, and they spent more than 1,100 weeks on the UK albums chart, which meant that they were ranked 5th of all time. Quite how all these heady statistics affected Sam Jukes is not known, but one imagines that, on dark, rainy autumnal days, he occasionally pops down to his soundproofed garden shed and screams at the top of his voice, before composing himself, and returning to the house for a nice cup of tea.

Later that year, Dr. Feelgood made a welcome return, followed by Led Zeppelin superstar Robert Plant, with The Honey Drippers. Here was a man who was idolized all around the world, a man who was used to stadia that held 50,000 people, and a performer who travelled by private jet, singing at a club that could hold 200 people, if a few agreed to hang from the rafters or Velcro themselves to a wall. It is a testament not only to Plant's good character and personality, but also to the high esteem that the club was held in, that he was willing to do this.

December welcomed the return of City Boy (who managed to fit in gigs at JB's in between conquering America), Streetband (fronted by none other than Paul Young, with their daft joke single, 'Toast'), and finally, just in time for the Christmas festivities, Supercharge.

1979 needed something special to happen, if it were to hold its own against the previous year, which, even by JB's standards, was a corker. Joe Jackson answered the call on Saturday the 3rd of February, with a typically well-polished show that featured his huge hit, 'Is She really Going Out with Him?'

Jackson's songs also included the atmospheric 'Stepping Out', and 'It's Different for Girls'. Thanks to an outstanding body of work, ranging from post-punk and new wave to sophisticated jazz-rock collaborations, he was nominated for five Grammy Awards. He was also, and presumably still is, a fan of real ale and a vociferous

campaigner against the smoking ban. JB's, and the Lamp Tavern just down the road, must have been heaven for him then, but with all those pea-souper fogs we all had to endure every evening at JB's, that sharp suit he used to wear would surely have needed a dry-clean after every performance.

No sooner had Joe and Co. packed up their smoky old van and departed, that legendary post-punk outfit, The Undertones, arrived from Derry, Northern Ireland, featuring the one and only Feargal Sharkey, a man who looked as if he was wearing his face inside out, with a voice that any sheep would have killed for. For those lucky souls who were there that night, surely the sound of 'Teenage Kicks' shaking the walls of a tiny, old school hall, full to bursting point with sweating, pogoing sardines, must be a golden memory. As if all this wasn't enough, the next band due to appear was Scottish rockers, Simple Minds, but having arrived at the club and deemed it too small and shabby, they promptly left. Their loss. You can't always judge a book by its cover, as they say, and a slightly shabby, old, empty building would bear no comparison to how it looked and felt once the crowd arrived. That said, this cruel rejection must have hurt Sam's feelings, not to mention his bank balance, especially after the Split Enz debacle.

June saw The Pretenders return, presumably so that Chrissie Hynde could sample another of Sue Jukes' curries, and the following Saturday... well, JB's welcomed a band by the name of The Tourists, namely Dave Stewart and Annie Lennox, not knowing that in a few short years, the pair, who were 'an item' at the time but not for much longer, would blossom into one of the biggest acts in Britain, with some 75 million record sales worldwide. The Tourists achieved a hit single with a remake of Dusty Springfield's 'I Only Want to Be with You', but as the couple's later incarnation, the Eurythmics, they would have hits with songs including 'Sweet Dreams (are made of this)', 'Love is a Stranger', 'Right By Your Side', 'Would I Lie To You?', 'There Must Be An Angel', and 'Here Comes the Rain Again'. Nor did it end there. Stewart enjoyed a solo career after the Eurythmics, but Lennox's career reached stratospheric heights, with many more hit singles, four Grammy Awards, a Billboard Century Award, a Golden Globe, and an Academy Award for Best Original Song. Oh yes, and an OBE for her tireless charity work. No one would be foolish enough to state that JB's was responsible

☞ *The one and only Chrissie Hynde strutting her stuff in Dudley.*
Inset: A young, clean-cut Robert Smith of The Cure.

☞ *The Tourists, Dave Stewart and Annie Lennox.*

© Gered Mankowitz.

for all this, but without little rock clubs, none of the famous bands mentioned in these pages could have progressed, experimented, expressed themselves, or earned the money to finance their dreams. Maybe the very few who could not be bothered to respond when asked to contribute to this book should ponder this argument and duly apologize! Either that or else sack the manager who forgot to tell them about it, mentioning no names... Oh okay, I will – nice guy Mr

Carrack, of all people! And on a much lighter note, the naughty Tourists let off a fire extinguisher in their dressing room and made an awful mess. Tut tut! Shame on you Annie and Dave. I bet you don't behave that way now you're an OBE, Annie!

By now, punk had diversified. Certainly, the hardcore bands continued as before, but the new wave had arrived, with its usual deviations and subcultures. Two Tone was a ska revival, spearheaded by Jerry Dammers and The Specials, with lots of other Coventry-based bands leading up the rear, and it was The Specials that made the relatively short trip from Coventry to Dudley on the 28th of July. The band also featured Terry Hall, who would go on to fame and fortune with Fun Boy Three. Hall, if you recall, was the frontman who constantly reminded us that he had a PhD, but added that it meant nothing to him. His mother must have been proud though, don't you think?

Ska was fast becoming the musical choice for the skinhead and mod fraternity, which quickly merged with all the other exotic species that could be seen living in harmony at the JB's zoo. The Specials' hits included 'Ghost Town' and 'Free Nelson Mandela', and their splinter band, Fun Boy Three, enjoyed considerable success with hits such as 'The Lunatics Have Taken Over The Asylum', and the rather classy 'Our Lips Are Sealed', as well as collaborations with Bananarama, such as 'Really Saying Something' and 'It Ain't What You Do It's The Way That You Do It'.

Immediately after The Specials came The Quads, another punk/mod outfit, with their single 'There Must Be Thousands', which John Peel called 'the single of the decade'. The Merton Parkas followed, another mod-revival act, which obviously meant that the influence of Paul Weller's band, The Jam (which had released its first single in 1977), was being felt.

Just as the punks were welcomed as long as they behaved, so were the mods. Maybe if JB's had opened another club in Brighton in the '60s, and Jimmy the Con had been shipped in to take care of security, all those nasty mods and rockers fights could have been avoided.

Punk bounced back in September in the form of The Ruts, who achieved a top-10 hit with 'Babylon's Burning', and in October, Ricky Cool and the Icebergs returned with their particular brand of rock and roll, sprinkled with tongue-in-cheek humour. It is interesting to speculate on how Ricky metamorphosed from host of the JB's folk nights, into G.I. crew-cut-sporting, camp cowboy-shirt-wearing, sax and harmonica playing, wisecracking frontman. One can only imagine that he felt he'd get more girlfriends that way than by wearing a duffle coat, but whatever the reason, the result was worth every penny. Not only were Ricky's excellent, tight-as-a-drum musicians the perfect, ready-made backing band for singers such as Robert Plant, whenever he was moonlighting from Led Zep, but they were great to watch in their own right. Over the years, Ricky has

resurfaced with various reincarnations, which include The Rialtos, The Hoola Boola Boys, and the In Crowd, all of whom have been vastly entertaining. Cut from the same cloth as saxophone-based jazz/rock bands such as Supercharge and the sublime Mike Sanchez in his various guises, Ricky was a stalwart of the JB's scene, and continues to dazzle today. Also, if we can be shallow and superficial just for a moment, his haircut must be the Eighth Wonder of the World.

The year ended with an appearance by The Fall (which was another of John Peel's favourites), The Circles, a mod-revival band who recorded on Dudley's up-and-coming Graduate Records label, and, it almost goes without saying, Supercharge, to welcome in the New Year.

It had been an incredible decade for JB's, in terms of the quality of bands it had attracted, drawn from all kinds of musical genres. If Sam could have levied a penny in tax from those bands for every album sold, after their JB's débuts, today he would be cruising the streets of Dudley in a convertible Bentley. Sadly, that was not to be, and he and his staff, by and large, remained unpaid volunteers.

It seems fitting, having mentioned the volunteers once more, to dedicate the following section of the book to their stories, and also to include a few personal reminiscences from everyday punters. Some sections are written in their own words, and others have been rewritten to spruce them up a little (don't they teach spelling in school nowadays?). Some are pages long, whilst others are pithy one-liners delivered via the 'JB's Dudley – Back of the Pathfinder' Facebook site (boasting 1,500-plus members). Whatever format these stories and reminiscences take, they are all are informative, poignant, fascinating, or funny. The best are all four. They are the literary equivalent of a bite-sized chunk, so enjoy them with a nice cup of tea and a biscuit or two, and once you're done, we'll deal with the 1980s.

KING STREET DUDLEY
REAR OF PATHFINDER

JB's

TONIGHT, GOOD FRIDAY
CLOSED
SATURDAY 17th
2 GROUPS
CLEAR DAYS AND STILL
Admission 60p
MEMBERS ONLY

Telephone Dudley 53597

Ricky Cool with his trademark tenor sax, seen here with The Big Town Playboys.

On October the 21st, 1976, tragedy struck the club. **Possessed**, featuring Indian-born Vernon Pereira (ex-Band of Joy, where he played alongside Robert Plant and John Bonham), Mick Reeves, Terry Davies and Phil Brittle, were returning home from a gig in Carlisle, when their van careered off the road. The accident was responsible for the deaths of Pereira, Reeves and Davies, and others in the van were seriously injured. As the awful news spread around the club the following day, there was a palpable sense of grief and shock, made worse by the fact that the band had been at JB's the evening before the crash, laughing and joking with other local bands and telling them all about their forthcoming Welsh trip. It is only fitting that we take the opportunity to remember them, and also imagine what they may have gone on to achieve, had their lives not been so tragically cut short.

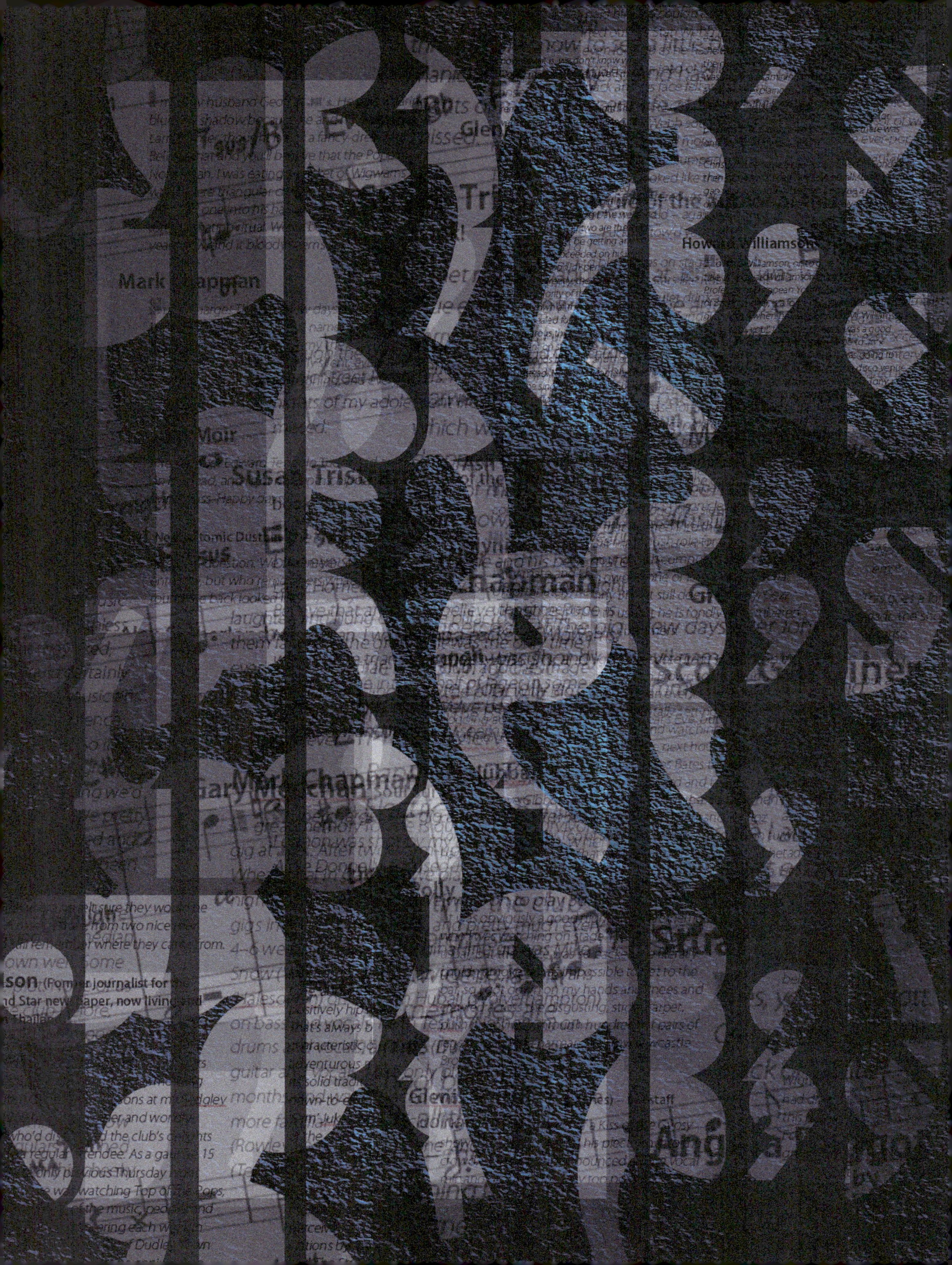

The Pathfinder Chronicles

Simon Davies

I am glad I started this Facebook group, even if it was several years after the club closed and many years after the move to Castle Hill. It is good that Sam's club lives on in the memories of so many of you. Let's face it, there are now more members here than would have fitted into the new club (as was), never mind the old one!

Chris Lea

Chris Lea is now retired and living in a lovely house in Belbroughton, Worcestershire. As a youth he was obsessed with not only seeing bands, but also recording the events in his Old Swinford Hospital School exercise books, in his best schoolboy handwriting. If any of his old school masters are still alive, they might like to take issue with Master Lea about wasting valuable resources – books that by rights should have been full of his geography or physics homework, maybe, and not endless lists containing comments such as:

Van der Graaf Generator, Genesis and Blodwyn Pig, Birmingham Town Hall, 4th January 1972. £1.50p. Excellent show.

Mind you, those lists, compiled with a lovely, almost trainspotter-like enthusiasm back in the '70s, are now probably classed as important historical documents, just like Sam's old receipt books. Chris frequented JB's from around 1972. His friend, Steve Street, had persuaded him to visit the club with him, and the first gig he saw was Colin Blunstone, the ex-Zombies singer who had enjoyed hits with 'She's Not There', 'Say You Don't Mind', and 'I Don't Believe In Miracles', amongst others. Chris remembers that it cost him 30 pence to get in, but in reality, he probably just looked it up in one of his school exercise books.

Colin Blunstone asks if anyone has seen his girlfriend, but sadly, she's not there!

From that night on, he was hooked, and frequented the place with such regularity that he was press-ganged into working behind the bar. Anyone who was seen hanging around and not doing much was inevitably given the king's shilling – or Sam's tanner in this instance – and put to work. One memory that won't go away, even if he wanted it to, was the night in 1974 when someone let off a stink bomb in the crowded club. The result, Chris says, was nothing short of catastrophic. The stench was unbearably awful. Gezz Tobin, the unfortunate disc jockey that evening, made an announcement to the retching masses beneath him, which went something like:

"We don't know who it is, we don't know what it is, but if we could mass-produce it, we'd make a fortune!"

Chris also remembers vividly the night The Stranglers were paid-off and sent packing. Sam immediately instructed Big Dave to hand back the entrance fee to all of the disgruntled punters, and this he did, until he came across two punk lads who argued that the band were 'great', and they'd been enjoying the unrehearsed cacophony, the swearing, and the spitting that had emanated from the stage. Big Dave weighed this and replied, 'Great! So you two are the only ones in the room who won't be getting any money back then!' and proceeded on his way, like a latter-day Robin Hood, dispensing coins to all and sundry. Apparently, the band had so alienated the vast majority of the audience that water was being thrown at them in retaliation. Hugh Cornwell appealed for the crowd to stop, as this was a dangerous thing to do with all the electrical equipment on stage. The JB's audience gave this a few seconds thought, and then began throwing food instead. Not so squeamish, Chris reminds us, was the singer in the band Chelsea, Gene October, who stood centre stage and refused to budge, no matter what was chucked at him, and was routinely coated in spittle, so by the end of the night he glistened like a moonlit snail. William Broad, the guitarist with the band, later to reinvent himself as Billy Idol, was probably less keen on being covered in vile bodily fluids.

Chris remembers that DJ Dermott Stephens would usually handle the Friday night shift, with Gezz Tobin taking the Saturdays. At first, punk was widely rejected by the regulars, but Dermott persevered, and gradually the crowd got used to it. From then on, Friday night was punk night. A vivid memory for Chris was watching the American band, Wayne County & the Electric Chairs, in 1977. In the mid-80s, the band released a catchy little single entitled 'Fuck Off' on puke-coloured vinyl, and by the time Wayne next appeared at the club he had treated himself to a sex change and wished to be known as Jayne County. Chris recalls a giant, blonde person with enormous breasts, terrorizing the occupants of the women's loos. After the gig was over and all the customers had long since gone home, Jayne was spotted examining the dartboard, having apparently explained to Chris's friend, Howard Williamson, that she'd never seen one before. She was subsequently taught to play darts (or

perhaps that should read 'play dart' as there was only one) by Howard at 3am.

Chris, who became a surveyor, moved to London, then came back again, and eventually took a gap year in Australia. He later became a property developer, which explains why he lives in a nice house.

Howard Williamson

Howard Williamson, or, to give him his correct title, Dr Howard Williamson CBE FRSA FHEA, Professor of European Youth Policy (University of South Wales), is a force of nature. Back in the olden days, when he was just plain Mr Williamson, or even 'oi, you!' to some, Howard was a good friend of Chris Lea, but refused to go to JB's because he wrongly presumed it was going to be similar to Tiffany's in Blackheath, a disco venue where the DJs had verbal diarrhoea, à la Tony Blackburn. He also imagined that the tunes they spoke all over were by the likes of Paper Lace and their demonic accomplices. After much persuasion, Howard was finally dragged to the club in 1979, kicking and screaming, just in time to see The Tourists. From that night onwards, he too was hooked. Howard had recently finished his university course in Cardiff and was now living in Birmingham. Like Chris, he was spotted lurking with intent, consequently commandeered for bar work, and came to love the edgy punk nights. He became a regular for around ten years after that, and his keen interest in photography – he was one of the few people in those days who took a professional camera into the club – resulted in Howard taking thousands of shots of bands, fashions, and audience members, that are now invaluable as pieces of rock history. He became a fan of the band New Model Army, and began to take photographs of them, and for them, with his Olympus OM-4 titanium camera. To raise himself above the heaving crowd, Howard would often be hoisted into the air by the band's fans, so that he could get a clearer view. He vividly remembers

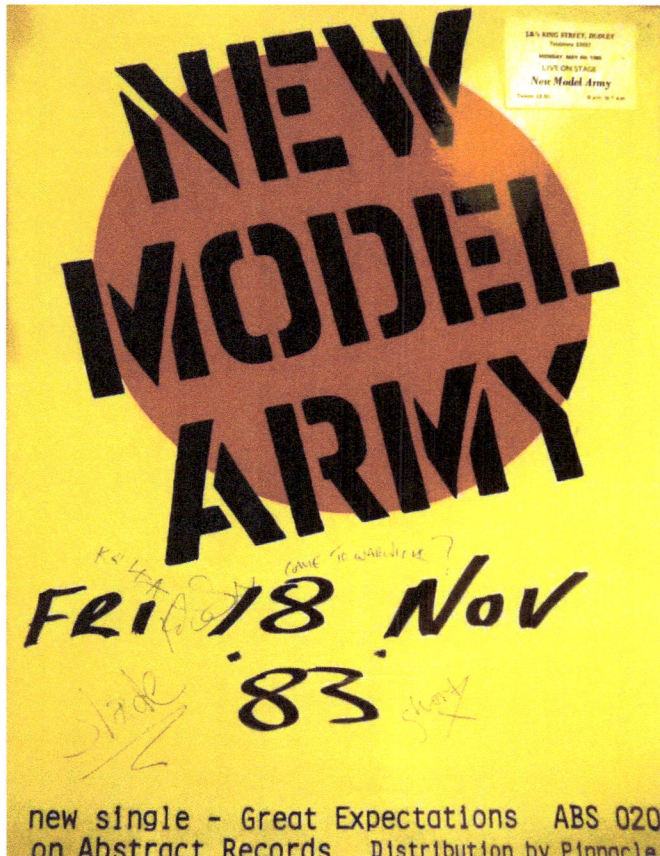

the band having a predilection for wooden clogs, which were purchased from Hebden Bridge Clog Factory! Howard travelled to and from JB's by motorbike, but would often be invited to stay over after gigs, leave his bike inside the club and sleep at Sam's. The next day, he would complete his cleaning chores at the club, collect the bike and ride back to Brum.

Howard, at that time, was a research officer for Oxford University. He lived in Birmingham from 1979 to 1983, and then moved between Cardiff (where he worked at the university), and Birmingham where he ran a youth centre. This continued until around the late 1990s, when he and his wife separated. He then moved permanently to South Wales and was unfortunately no longer able to visit JB's.

Howard was appointed as Professor of European Youth Policy, which meant that he was – and still is – constantly travelling the world, advising various bodies, colleges and governments. At one meeting, in Whitehall, Westminster, a senior civil servant from a government committee approached him, after eyeing him up and down for several minutes. Howard presumed that this might just be because of his appearance (he still looks more like a guitarist in a rock band than a professor), but then the civil servant spoke to him.

"Excuse me, Dr Williamson,' the man said, 'but didn't you work behind the bar at JB's?"

On another occasion, at the University of South Wales, Howard, who was busy preparing for his inaugural professorial lecture, met up with his new vice chancellor, Julie Lydon (no relation to Johnny Rotten) so that she could get to know a little more about him. As they chatted, Howard detected the merest hint of a Black Country accent. Incredibly, it emerged that she too had been a JB's regular, which meant that Dr Howard had almost certainly served her with drinks at some stage.

Howard recalls that JB's legend, Jimmy the Con, would often invite people back to his flat in Kates Hill, Dudley, for debauched dope and booze sessions after his shift at the club had ended. On Saturday mornings, a very timid milkman would call to collect his money, and Jim would open the door to him, stark naked, and insist that the milkman follow him through the flat, stepping over other naked, unconscious bodies, en route to the place where the cash was kept.

A constant problem for the bar staff, Chris and Howard agreed, was trying to decipher what the customer was gamely trying to order over the ear-splitting noise coming from the stage. One particularly amusing example of this perennial problem was when a man by the name of Steve Mills asked for two bottles of Mackeson. Howard stared at him blankly. Steve Mills repeated at the top of his voice, 'Two bottles of Mackeson!' Howard again stared imploringly at him. 'TWO FUCKING BOTTLES OF MACKESON!' he bellowed. Finally, Howard had managed to get the gist. He reached under the counter and handed him two boxes of matches. Apparently, Steve Mills' face was a picture.

This snippet of conversation was also overhead one evening at King Street. Female club member (becoming seriously maudlin upon hearing the traditional closing song of the night, the famous Santana instrumental):
"I'm going to have 'Samba Pa Ti' at my funeral." Her friend: **"Salmon Paté? Is that nice then?"**

Howard's final contribution, before we allow him to get back to advising his governments on the youth of today and how to get them out of bed before lunchtime, involves the record decks at JB's. Having treated the club to a pair of spanking new decks for DJs Dermott and Gezz to play with, Sam presented Howard with the old pair, which were still perfectly serviceable (these weren't those awful deathtrap ones from the Coneygre Youth Club days by the way – they were a very good quality, professional set). Howard was then able to donate them to his youth club in Birmingham, where he felt sure they would be treasured. A nice gesture, from two nice men who could still remember where they came from.

Robin Wilson (Former journalist for the Express and Star newspaper, now living and working in Thailand)

My first experiences of JB's were second-hand – intriguing accounts of Thursday nights at the 'Blues Club', told during Friday morning O-Level British Constitution lessons at my Sedgley school in 1969 by Rob, an older and worldly-wise pupil who'd discovered the club's delights and became a regular attendee. As a gauche 15 year-old whose only previous Thursday night musical adventure was watching Top of the Pops, Rob's whispered tales of the music, people, and ambience he was encountering each week in the incongruous surroundings of Dudley Town Football Club left me agog, as he conjured up exotic visions of a mythical rock utopia.

Our Friday morning lessons eventually became more of a JB's debrief than a study of the country's governmental system. I never did accompany Rob on his Thursday nights at JB's; that was a bridge too far for me at the time. In fact, it was a couple of years before I plucked up the courage to venture into licensed premises of any sort on my own. But the seeds had been sown, and they were soon nurtured by the JB's advertisements for weird and wonderful sounding bands that began appearing each Thursday in the centre spread of the Express and Star's classified ads section.

I can't recall the first time I actually went to JB's; it must have been a couple of years later on one of the Thursday nights at its new premises in the old Victorian building sheltered in the shadow of the Pathfinder clothing emporium, at the windswept top of King Street. This JB's was handily situated near popular 'pre-club' town-centre pubs like the Lamp Tavern, the Gipsies Tent Inn, The Crown, The Old Priory, and the Coach and Horses, which together with the club's unusual (for those times) Newcastle Brown Ale became traditional elements of a JB's night.

My earliest memory of being there is watching a 'progressive' group of kaftan-clad hippies thrashing out a Hawkwind-style cacophony, in front of a psychedelic-bubble screen projection. In retrospect they were pretty dire, but at that time, about 1971/72, the whole thing seemed positively hip for a small Black Country town. That's always been the unique attraction and characteristic of JB's – an ability to showcase adventurous musical experiences while retaining its solid traditional, local roots. Much of that down-to-earth outlook can be attributed to Colin 'Sam' Jukes, whose hard-working management of the club over the years saw him handling both the egos of musicians and occasional lairy attitudes of punters in the same even-handed Black Country style. It was also reflected in the studied indifference meted out to bands perceived to be displaying attitudes above their stations by astute JB's audiences. Both The Police and The Stranglers ended up on the wrong end of JB's crowds in the early days of their careers during the late 1970s. And when the Sex Pistols arrived one Friday night at the height of their popularity for a quick drink before a gig in Wolverhampton, they were more or less ignored.

Even Robert Plant experienced this audience reaction when he played there with his Honey Drippers band in 1981; what should have been a warm homecoming for a local hero got off to an uneasy start when a Black Country voice shouted 'Get that fucking scarf off' to him, during a pause at the end of the first number, and a sense of belligerence among the crowd gained momentum as the set went on. As with some JB's audience reactions, this seemed to be a case of local fans bringing a star back down to earth, but Plant to his credit took it in his stride and probably half expected it anyway. As grudging applause rang out at the end of the set, he simply said 'Thank you, it's been an education', and walked off. His dignified exit was in sharp contrast to that of Hugh Cornwell of The Stranglers some years

JB's CLUB

Presents

THE HONEY DRIPPERS

FEATURING
Robby Blunt, Andy Sylvester, Jim Hickman, Robert Plant & Keith Evans, Ricky Cool, Kevin O'Neil

MONDAY 23rd JUNE
From 8.00 - 10.30
Price £2.00

A quaint old Honey Drippers ticket, presumably designed by Liberace.

earlier, when he unwisely ended his band's badlyreceived performance (and they were extremely poor) by saying in his cockney accent: 'You lot up here; you don't know nuffin' about music.' One incensed audience member (the late Dinky Dyson, I believe) stormed to the front of the stage, poked his finger in Cornwell's face and bellowed, 'Nor yo doe, maert – goo an' fuck off wum!

Dinky and his mates were among those responsible for the famous JB's cry of 'Mooer' accorded to favoured bands at the end of their sets to request encores. That cry became a badge of honour to many of the bands who appeared on the club's battered stage through the years. Any negative band receptions were more than outweighed by the many acts that JB's warmed to and welcomed back on numerous occasions for storming nights of entertainment – Steve Marriott, Supercharge, Ruby Turner, Steve Gibbons, Ricky Cool and his various outfits, local heroes Little Acre, the E Numbers, The DT's, The Corner Boys, The Trevor Burton Band, and The Enid, to name just a few. JB's also had a knack of booking bands with members who had been in much bigger and famous bands; many of the club's band listings had bracketed references to those headline outfits. I recall seeing a band called Punishment of Luxury which had Chick Churchill of Ten Years After in its line-up, and remember what a thrill it was to chat to a musician I'd only previously seen in the Woodstock film, and from about half a mile away on stage at the 1970 Isle of Wight Festival.

My JB's journey, which started at the beginning of the 1970s, continued throughout that decade, albeit slightly disrupted during three early years when I was away at college. An early highlight

Mott The Hoople dress down for their photo shoot.

was a Christmas Eve concert at Dudley Town Hall, either 1971 or 1972, featuring folk singer Bill Caddick, local band Bronco, and Mott The Hoople; quite an event at the time. My abiding memory of that night is of Ian Hunter's reaction when a council jobsworth snapped on all the house lights at midnight in the middle of Mott The Hoople's set. He was a flamboyant sight – playing a guitar with a four-leaf clover body and wearing mirrored shades. As the lights lit up the hall and his band shuddered to a calamitous halt, he pointed skywards and yelled: 'Turn them fucking lights off!' And they did.

The homeliness of JB's was also a feature that made it unique: the simple club logo and basic membership cards; the scruffy metal front door that clattered and scraped against the floor when it was opened; quaint, A4 Xerox printouts of weekly band listings stacked up on the door counter; the moist floor sticky with an accumulation of spilled beer from hundreds of epic nights; the bare brick walls; a handwritten bar sign for pork scratchings that read 'Bits of Pig'; the well-worn stage with its black-and-white club-logo backdrop; the elevated DJ booth christened 'The Loft', and, of course, the folk who were in there week in and week out.

No cast of JB's larger-than-life characters would be complete without Jimmy the Con, the club's bouncer and – to some punters – a somewhat malevolent presence in the early years. In those days he used to shatter the homely good-time atmosphere built up during the night by going round collecting glasses when the lights went up, telling everyone: 'We've had your money – now fuck off.' But with the benefit of hindsight it's pretty obvious that this was simply Jimmy's typically forthright Black Country demeanour, and certainly nobody was ever offended.

There were many other characters: the big bloke who looked like Lee Marvin who also collected glasses at the end of the night; the biker with a white rat on his shoulder; Big Dave Hodgetts on the door and the bar, whose quick-fire repartee belied his lumbering figure; Sam's wife Sue with her refreshingly disparaging opinions of bands – no matter how big they were; the young, long-

haired greaser with 'No Sleep Till Kidderminster' on the back of his leather jacket; middle-aged suburban couple Bob and Margaret Ridley who were there every Monday night; local worthies with names like Tick, Bazza, Fidget and Mossa; and Charlie, with his short blond hair and gold-rimmed glasses, who always wore a collar and tie underneath a neat woollen cardigan (he looked like a trainee accountant and may well have been one, but he was the biggest Link Wray and Wilko Johnson fan I ever met).

My favourite Big Dave story is from the mid '70s. My mate Nev was a big fan of Stan Webb and was eagerly looking forward to seeing him play at JB's on a Sunday night. All week long he was banging on about it and when we finally got to the club that Sunday he was in a high state of excitement. Big Dave was slumped over the door counter unenthusiastically taking cash from punters. As Nev paid him, he couldn't contain himself, and blurted out 'It's Stan Webb tonight!' Big Dave didn't even look up as he handed back the change, but replied 'Ar, a load of bollocks.' Nev was taken aback and his face fell as we went inside. As it turned out, it was a crap gig; the band was all over the place, Stan Webb sounded out of tune and Nev became more and more downcast. When we left Big Dave was still slumped over the door counter in what looked like the same position as when we had entered. As we trooped despondently past him he said – again without even looking up – 'Fucking tow'd yer, day I?'

As well as hosting big names on stage, the club was also a place to glimpse stars like Robert Plant and Trevor Burton having a quiet drink at the bar. Later on in the early '80s when Mondays were rockabilly nights, Plant's daughter caused a stir by becoming a regular attendee, although no one seemed able to pluck up the courage to make any advances towards her. The club's bar in those days was also home base for the members of local band Little Acre – exotic-looking rock characters who returned to their Black Country roots replete with hilarious tales from gigs at venues the length and breadth of the country.

At that time the bar was along one side of the room with a hatch that opened into the dressing room.

On early week nights when no bands were on, the dressing room became a sort of snug bar – another Black Country trait – for favoured friends of the staff. It was the position of choice for Bob and Margaret Ridley every Monday night, a place where they could lean on the hatch and chat to Sam and Sue, creating a homely atmosphere more akin to a traditional Black Country boozer than a rock club.

There were some great nights in the early to mid '70s, and a few stand out. Canadian rocker Pat Travers used to end his show by having three audience members on stage for an air guitar contest with cardboard guitars; Richard and Linda Thompson played their gig with the audience sitting cross-legged on the floor; and fellow ex-Fairport Convention member Dave Swarbrick – a pixie-like figure – brought his band Whippersnapper for a great Saturday night gig and spent ages chatting afterwards in the passage outside the dressing room. In those days every Saturday night ended with the playing of a strange track by a band called Pavlov's Dog, featuring an allegedly male singer who warbled in a very feminine way – perhaps a precursor of what was to come some years later. The ever-popular Thursday nights always ended with Santana's 'Samba Pa Ti' as the lights came on. Even today I can't listen to that track without hearing a disappointed Black Country voice saying 'Fuck it, I'll get me coot.' A popular tradition was the New Year's Eve fancy-dress parties which became legendary fixtures on the JB's calendar – no bands, just non-stop music, drink, and festive celebration. Later on in the decade I'd started work as a journalist on my first newspaper and I used JB's as a resource for a weekly music page. The easy access to acts was a godsend. I had fantastic interviews with Tom Robinson, who appeared just as '2-4-6-8 Motorway' was topping the charts, as well as a somewhat bewildered Annie Lennox who appeared with Dave Stewart in their early band The Tourists one Friday night.

When punk reared its head in the later '70s, JB's began to host a new generation of bands and fans. Those strange creatures I had seen during the day knocking about town with Day-Glo Mohicans, tartan kilts and safety-pinned leggings were now up at the bar, and their music was the top feature of the club. It says a lot for the place that every style of music and fan was welcomed and accommodated at JB's. There was no animosity between anyone (not that I saw anyway), although some of the old guard, myself included, looked askance at all the pogoing and spitting.

From being a largely underground phenomenon, JB's gained a measure of mainstream notoriety when Channel 4's The Tube show was filmed there in the early 1980s with host Jools Holland, who fondly recalled playing at the club in his earlier Squeeze days.

Steve Marriott played at the club two or three times in the early '80s, with his band Packet of Three. On one of those Saturday night gigs he was about half an hour late starting and the packed crowd was getting restless. When he finally bounded on stage he announced in his cheeky cockney accent: 'Sorry I'm late – I got held up. He's a c**t, that Dick Turpin.'

With punk, neo-punk, new wave, and all the other styles of the moment being highlighted, Sunday nights at JB's in those days were reserved for more traditional blues and soul acts and they became my favourite club nights. My diaries from that time are filled with the revolving cast of mostly local bands who played then – the E Numbers, the Redbeards from Texas, Melvyn's Marauders, The Trevor Burton Band, The DT's, The Resistors, the Red Lemon Electric Blues Band, Steve Gibbons, etc. I had moved abroad to work by the time the club had relocated to its new Castle Hill premises, and only visited that JB's once or twice in later years during trips home. My JB's memories are all of nights and Sunday lunchtimes in the old, converted 'rear of Pathfinder' school building, and I'm grateful for that. As well as all the bands there, I even saw – or thought I did – the reputed ghost of the building. Early one evening I caught a shadowy movement out of the corner of my eye at the end of the corridor near the front door, which seemed to be going into the main hall. I hadn't been drinking and there was something odd about it, but nothing was there when I went to look. Other old members have related similar stories.

Whoever that restless spirit is, he or she must be wondering where all the youthful, musical energy and camaraderie of those days have gone. Perhaps, trapped in a time warp, this restless spirit has the ability to relive it all. What an experience that would be.

Paul Marsh The Mighty Lemon Drops

Does anyone remember that guy who used to smoke a pipe with a man's face on it, and the little man on his pipe was smoking a pipe too?

Dermott Stephens – JB's DJ

Yes, there were two middle-aged blokes that arrived together. They travelled from Northampton every week, which is miles away from Dudley, and we always called them Pipe and Hat, as the second chap was never seen without his little trilby.

Adrian Saunders

Brilliant times! I remember the highlights being local bands, Ye Fungus, Happy Death Men, Credit To The Nation and Ned's Atomic Dustbin. From further afield, The Mission, Skyclad, and Blur. Happy days!

Scott Gardiner

I'm pretty sure I went there a few times! There is video evidence of me stage-diving at a Mercenary Tree Freaks gig. Not sure if I dreamt this, but I'm sure I attended a karaoke session on a Monday night on a couple of occasions.

Stuart Tonks

Yes, you did, Scott. I remember me, you and little Craig doing a terrible version of Michael Jackson's 'Black or White'!

Angela Baggot

The King Street venue? You couldn't beat it. To me, that was JB's!

Lei Woodhouse

My first ever gig was Gaye Bykers On Acid. The last was Sultans of Ping FC.

Rat Ned's Atomic Dustbin

Here's a question. We all remember the entrance, but who remembers what the exit round the back looked like?

Alex Sutherland

If you mean the steps behind the fire doors, yes, I remember them, but I'm not going into detail. Just ask my ex-wife.

Ash Loydon

I lost something on those back stairs many years ago.

Nicola Louise Hale

I may have been taken round the rear entrance once or twice.

Mark Steed

I went to look at the old place last night, just for nostalgia's sake! It's now rendered, extended, and creamy-yellowy coloured, with a small conservatory!

Glenn Tranter The Injectors, Jacobites, etc.

The first band was The Only Ones, June 1978. The last was probably The Dogs D'Amour. Highlights? Magazine, The Long Ryders, The Specials, Destroy All Monsters, The Cure, The Undertones, The Boys, Starjets, The Records, The Tourists, Gang of Four, Jimmy Norton's Explosion featuring Glen Matlock, Steve New, Danny Kustow and the drummer, Budgie, Tenpole Tudor, and The Pirates. Honorary mentions: Pinpoint, The Lurkers, The Members, The Yachts, Fischer-Z, The Invaders, Punishment of Luxury, Merton Parkas, Orchestral Manoeuvres in the Dark, The Pleasers, Chicken Shack, The Honey Drippers, Supercharge, and lots more that I can't recall. A truly special club and it was a privilege to have it on our doorstep.

Ash Loydon

I still have the scars from when the toilet collapsed.

Glynis Gammon now living in New Zealand

My mate and I had tickets to see Steve Marriott. Unfortunately, he didn't turn up, as that was the night he died, which was a very reasonable excuse. However, before we were made aware of that, I was standing by the bar and not really taking much notice of what was going on around me. There was a guy standing next to me with blond hair and a leather jacket. I got the drinks and returned to my mate, who was all of a fluster. 'Didn't you see who you were just standing next to?' she asked, excitedly. I turned and looked back, and realized that it was Robert Plant!

Steve Gibbons

JB's had been up and running for quite some time before our first appearance there in 1973, by which time it had a well-earned reputation for being a good place to play. When we first arrived I was very impressed. This was a real music club, with a good stage at one end of the room, a good bar at the other, and a professional sound system with the genial Roy Williams at the controls. Add to this a proper dressing room and with a dartboard too, what more could a band want?

The club had a great rock and roll aura and that familiar aroma of the night before; it seemed to permeate the carpet, the wood, and the walls, but it wasn't bad, it was the smell of good times, a working smell – in a word, its funk. And then there was the one-man mob that was Jimmy the Con, built like the proverbial brick shithouse and effin' proud of it too. He was probably self-appointed and provided all the security that the club ever needed, on his own. Musically, he was very well informed; he loved it, and got it for free every night, of course. I think the young Johnny Bryant was very much involved with the launching of this happy ship, and for the many years thereafter, Colin Jukes, aka Sam, was its solid and trusty captain. I was proud to have walked its boards.

Mark Chapman

I went from 1971 to 1991. I started at The Talbot in Colley Gate, then the Lamp, and into the club for 9pm. The days when you could get bladdered or a fiver and get a taxi home. JB's was a music venue with a very discerning and often ruthless audience. The clientele knew what they liked, and if you didn't fit the bill, they would certainly let you know. I saw some very talented musicians indeed leave the stage there to a stony silence, just because they were not a 'JB's band. So it was one Thursday night in the late '70s that a group of us went up for the regular disco, something we'd been doing for a few years by that time. We pretty much knew which records would be played and who we would meet; a regular pattern had been set, one much enjoyed by the punters. Except this night something changed. This night there was to be no

The King of Cool. JB's stalwart and all-round nice chap, Steve Gibbons.

disco; we were having a comedian instead. The news did not go down well. Some muttered that Sam had lost the plot. None of us had ever seen a comedian in the club before, especially on a Thursday night, and the mood darkened when we found out who it was. It was to be children's comedian, Ian 'Sludge' Lees.

Ian was a regular on Saturday morning TV show Tiswas, something many JB's regulars watched without fail. We were all familiar with this cheeky chappie dressed in a Liquorice Allsorts suit, and were very much annoyed that our routine was to be interrupted by a kids' entertainer. There was a grim atmosphere, and Mr Lees took to the stage to behold a room full of scowling faces.

But Ian had more than one string to his bow. He may well have been a children's entertainer, but he was also well able to cater for an adult audience, as we soon discovered. Within a few minutes, the scowls turned into wide grins, and then to unrestrained laughter as Sludge fired off one adult gag after another. I was fortunate to be standing by the bar, which at that time still ran down the side of the club, and which provided much needed support. Others held on to whatever they could, including each other, as Mr Lees set about demolishing the audience. As well as the sound of repeated deep belly laughter from Big Dave behind the bar, my abiding memory is of two large, bearded bikers nearby, clinging to a pillar, mouths fully open and tears running down their faces, but not a sound coming from them. Their faces contorted beyond recognition, they had reached a level beyond laughter, and hung on to the pillar to prevent them falling to the ground. It was the only time I ever saw a comedian in the club, and the image of the two bikers clinging to the pillar with Big Dave laughing his head off in the background will remain forever.

Susan Tristram
wife of the author of this book!

I met my husband Geoff at JB's. He was wearing blue eye shadow because he and his best mate, Larry Homer (pictured right), thought it was a fancy-dress night. Believe that and you'll believe that the Pope is Norwegian. I was eating a packet of Wigwams, which were triangular cheesy biscuits, and I dropped one into his half of lager in some strange form of mating ritual. We've been together for 40 years now, and it bloody seems like it.

Mark Chapman

Supercharge! The gig a few days after John Lennon was shot by my evil namesake, when Albie Donnelly accused Jimmy the Con of being a woofter! The place fell eerily silent, every eye on the Con, until he started laughing, and everyone fell about with relief.

Gordon Moir

I remember Edward Tenpole Tudor had an arrow on his head, and I got my tooth chipped by a flying glass. Happy days!

☞ Tenpole Tudor and his band, Ninepole, Eightpole and Sevenpole Tudor.

Gary Meechan
Soul Survivors

A great memory for me is our first Soul Survivors gig at JB's. After two warm-up gigs at The Wheatsheaf in Oakham, we played a Sunday night – the first of many! We went on to play 300 gigs in our first 12 months, and pretty much every 4–6 weeks at JB's. The original line-up was Mike Snow (Wolverhampton) on trumpet, Keith Evans (Halesowen) on sax, Tim Huball

(Wolverhampton) on bass and vocals, Keith Testill (Netherton) on drums and vocals, and me (Dudley Wood) on guitar and vocals. Mike only played with us for 6 months, and was replaced with what became the more familiar line-up, including John Johnson (Rowley Regis) on trombone, and Rob Fenton (Telford) on trumpet.

Mat Power

I met my future wife on the dance floor. Sat with my feet stuffed into the radiators after traipsing through the snow to see a little band called the Manic Street Preachers. And had some of the best nights of my adolescent life at King Street. Sadly missed.

Sue White

I find it highly amusing that we have been asked to post our memories of JB's. I went from 1978 till it moved to Castle Hill, but most nights fade into a blur of great times, fun, and alcohol. I do remember being dressed as Andy Pandy and pogoing across the stage one New Year's Eve, but as for individual bands...

David Hubball

Seeing Steve Gibbons the week he was in the charts with 'Tulane', when he refused to go to London to record for Top of the Pops because he had a residency at JB's. That's dedication!

Polly Trice

It was obviously a good night – can't remember who I was watching on stage. I was thirsty, as usual, but the place was so packed we literally couldn't move. It was impossible to get to the bar, so I got down on my hands and knees and crawled across the disgusting, sticky carpet, pushing my way through hundreds of pairs of legs to reach the barman, and my Newcastle Brown!

Glenis Smythe (née Jones) – bar staff

I remember at the end of a Kiss of the Gypsy show the guitarist flicked his plectrum into the crowd, which promptly bounced off the vocal mic and dropped into my top pocket!

When Long John Baldry played at JB's, it was a really cold evening, and there were huge icicles hanging on the window ledges outside the club. Baldry asked for whiskey on the rocks but we'd run out of ice, so someone said, in true Black Country fashion, 'Ey, ode pal, goo aht theer and bost one of them icicles off the winders – that'll do the trick!' Baldry and his male 'assistant' were not overly impressed

Dermott Stephens

One soundcheck I particularly remember was the one by The Undertones in November 1978. Rather than a preview of one of the songs from the set, or treating us to the boring 'testing 1-2-1-2', they went straight into 'Pretty Vacant'! Hearing that with Feargal's distinctive vocals was absolutely amazing. I wish I'd had a cassette in the mixing desk at the time.

Roz Hardwick and Les Bates

In the 1960s, Bearwood girl, Roz Hardwick, could usually be found hanging around places such as the bierkeller at The King's Head pub, Frank Freeman's in Kidderminster, the Adelphi in West Bromwich, the rather exotically named Casa Bamboo café in less-than-exotic West Bromwich, or maybe the Mothers club in Erdington. In those days she was a typical hippy chick, listening to underground music (remember that term?), digging around in flea markets – such as Birmingham's famous Rag Market – for retro clothes, or pottering around in the Bus Stop shop and Crowther's boutique in Brum city centre. Either that or she and her friends made their own clothes. If the end result made them look a little more like Julie Driscoll (of Brian Auger and the Trinity, with their single 'Wheels on Fire'), well, that was just perfect. Roz was a livewire, a tad eccentric, and full of life and laughter. She still is. She explains that what she and her friends got up to, the way they dressed, and the music they liked, seemed perfectly normal to them, but in fact, they, in common with the old guard of JB's, were actually a minority cult. In reality, most people of her age were pretty strait-laced and belonged to the Radio 1 mainstream.

Roz had often bumped into Sam Jukes and Gezz Tobin at the aforementioned venues, and was duly informed by them that a brand-new club was opening in Dudley, right after the Isle of Wight Festival (the one that featured Bob Dylan)

had drawn to a close. She remembers visiting this formative club, then based at the Dudley Football Club ground, and watching their home-grown attempts to create a light show with great amusement. Two lads, she recalls, were fiddling around with a cut-glass fruit bowl full of liquid and shining lights through it. Having already covered Mick and Larry's exploits in the field of creative lighting earlier in this book, this incident sounds suspiciously like a description of one of their many unsuccessful early prototypes. Roz clearly remembers that JB's would often host what were, in effect, jumble stalls, where people could rummage for interesting clothing. In fact, she seems to possess a remarkably clear memory for one of the old-school JB's crowd, most of whom can barely remember anything with any degree of clarity, which caused untold difficulty to anyone compiling a book that purports to be accurate. Roz also remembers the time during Ted Heath's government, when the country was brought to its knees by power cuts and the Three-Day Week measure, during which time JB's never closed, and often relied on candles and lamps on the bar.

One of Roz's most significant observations is the importance of the various 'satellite' pubs and venues that revolved around JB's like planets around the sun. She cites the Gipsies Tent Inn, the Little Barrel, the Coach and Horses (locally known as The Vic), and the oft-mentioned Lamp Tavern, though there must have been others. These were important drinking dens which JB's punters used for a pre-gig pint or two, as it was very uncool indeed to turn up at the club too early, when no one else was there. The Gipsies Tent was run by two bizarre brothers, she recalls with glee, and was a completely eccentric place in those days. One brother kept a roll of old theatre tickets, which he used to tear off and hand to customers who had misbehaved. Being handed a ticket was akin to being given the black spot by blind Pew. It often meant a lifetime ban, and both siblings had very good memories about the folks they had barred, as Roz will testify. One evening she arrived at the pub accompanied by a gentleman named Big Jezz le Roy. As they entered the bar, a brother shouted out, 'You (Roz), come in, and you (Big Jezz), you're barred!' This, in spite of the fact that

Jezz had not shown his face in the pub for several years.

The two brothers, she informs us, never spoke to each other. This situation arose because one of them was engaged to be married, and one day, having borrowed his brother's car, he found his fiancée's gloves in there. From that day onwards, all conversation (except for sulkily mumbled essential comments concerning pub business) ceased. If trouble reared its ugly head, either Tweedledum or Tweedledee would shout, 'On the car park, gentlemen, please!' and the argument would transfer outdoors. One brother, Roz remembers, looked like a sailor on shore leave, whilst the other was more the dapper, cravat-wearing type. The brothers also had a deeply disturbing habit of keeping small Britvic fruit-juice bottles discarded by customers, and draining the sludge from the bottom of them into a new bottle until it was full of the foul leftovers. Then, when a hard-up punter asked them for 'a fruity one', he or she would be handed one of these concoctions for a few pence.

New Year's Eve at JB's was always fancy-dress night, and Roz was an enthusiastic fancy-dresser, as one might imagine. One evening, at a pre-gig session at the Lamp Tavern, she encountered JB's barman, Glynn Nash, dressed as a giant poodle. No, this was not a vision caused by the use of hallucinogenic drugs; the young man was indeed dressed as a poodle. He confided to Roz that he intended to subtly alter his attire when he got to the club, so that the bottom half of the costume was back to front, meaning that Glynn's penis (to refer to it by the correct anatomical term) was inside the poodle's hollow tail. Glynn's sinister plan was to invite attractive women to wag his tail for him, in the hope that he could then breed with them. It is not known whether his devilish plan succeeded or if any resulting offspring were registered with The Kennel Club.

Roz has also provided valuable information about the various DJs that inhabited The Loft, as their elevated section of the club was fondly known. Once Johnny Bryant stepped down, literally and metaphorically,

in the early '70s, Trevor Long did a short stint. Trevor later became sound engineer for Toyah Willcox, and tour manager for Duran Duran, Dexys Midnight Runners, Simply Red, and Haircut One Hundred, before disappearing down South for reasons far too complex to delve into here. Then came Gezz Tobin, who was, by all accounts, a gentle soul who was into American West-Coast music – a man who modelled himself on the great John Peel in terms of vocal delivery. He became the main DJ at the club until around 1976, when he had to move due to work commitments. Gezz was a very well-read individual who bought many of his albums from the Graduate Records second-hand store in Dudley, owned by David Virr, who eventually created his own label and signed the likes of UB40, and The Maisonettes. It was Gezz who instigated the playing of Santana's instrumental track 'Samba Pa Ti', to signal the end of the evening – time to go home. Incongruously, in spite of Gezz's genuine hippy credentials (he even named his two children after Tolkien's Lord of the Rings, and C. S. Lewis's Chronicles of Narnia – Arwen and Edmund, respectively), he apparently worked in some hush-hush role for the army, and was playing around with computers well before any of us even owned one or knew exactly what they did (Johnny Bryant still doesn't). Sadly, Gezz is no longer with us, but he is fondly remembered by many ex-JB's customers.

Trying to drag an anecdote from some people is akin to asking Gordon Brown to do stand-up, whereas spending an evening with Roz Hardwick is like accidentally setting fire to a large box of fireworks and watching them fizz, bang, and sparkle for the next hour, non-stop. Add ex-barman and DJ Les Bates to the mix, and the anecdotes come so hard and fast that it's a struggle to write them down, especially when one has no knowledge of shorthand. As Roz reels off names, incidents and places, this in turn stimulates Les's dormant memory cells, and he chips in with his wonderfully odd bits of trivia. He describes a character by the name of Fidget (Chris Ford), a hyperactive mod and music enthusiast who owned a Jeep that he somehow managed to crash into the Pathfinder's showroom window (the building immediately in front of JB's) so that he could 'borrow' a few suits. This, it transpires, is one of the people who fell into the river during those early Mystery Tour excursions. Then there was 'The Tray Basher', a punter who used an old beer tray to bash the top of his head in time to the music of whichever band was playing. And just when you think this is as weird as it gets, along comes another JB's regular, Peter Pinhead, who apparently tried to summon up demons at the infamous Kinver Edge party, where the accident-prone Gezz fell off the cliff and broke his hip. Now Roz, falling about laughing, is champing at the bit to tell us what happened on one of her birthdays, all those years ago. This same Gezz Tobin had kindly organized a narrowboat for Roz's party, and Jimmy the Con, not wishing to be outdone, took it upon himself to organize a guard of honour, namely a row of Hell's Angels. Proudly, Jim escorted her down the line, as a senior military man might escort the Queen as she inspected the troops. He then announced, 'Roz, you can have any one of these guys for your birthday. It's all arranged!' Roz, in a state of shock, mumbled, 'Er, Jim, thank you, but it's okay. I wouldn't know which one to choose.'

"No problem,' replied Jim. 'You can have all of 'em."

This goes a long way to explaining why Jim never made the shortlist for the host of TV's Surprise Surprise.

Les 'Master' Bates was not only a barman and DJ but also a keen amateur artist, which meant that he was often cajoled into decorating the club walls and doors in his spare time. It was he who was responsible for the yellow submarine in the ladies' loos, and the word 'Scheizenhausen (which he and a thousand others fondly imagine is the German word for shithouse) emblazoned on the door of the gents'. Laurence Llewelyn Bowen would surely turn in his grave if he were dead, but we must remember that this was the 1970s, and Sam's budget couldn't run to Laura Ashley.

Johnny Bryant

As a child I was always surrounded by music. Ma and Pa singing harmony at family parties, big brothers and sister playing rock & roll and bringing home 45s to play on the radiogram. The Beatles and mainstream pop music ensued and then when I must have been about 14 I remember hearing John Lee Hooker's 'Stomp Boogie' on the King label, which I think was initially released under the pseudonym of Texas Slim. I was dumbstruck. This was music from another planet! I was set on a musical journey that continues to this day.

To have an almost unfettered role in playing music that is palpable to all in a given space is a truly wonderful feeling, especially when some of the music is chosen by those gathered. The waffle exuded by the DJ is inconsequential, it's the music played LOUD. I remember people bringing me weird album tracks to play but, out of the bedroom, into the club, through a huge PA system, everything sounded better; gave you a bigger feeling. From Blind Willie Johnson to Moby Grape to Glen Miller to whomever – it's a personalized thing that hits you full on – it's yours to relish and hold. But wait! Can all of the music all of the time make all of the people happy? No, of course not, but I've witnessed 400 people in a small club in Dudley being so tuned in, so ecstatic that nothing else in the world really did matter.

The club was first and foremost a live-music venue, it was a loosely run semi-organic venture that snowballed, but because everyone involved believed in their own contribution it succeeded. No one ever became fazed by the words 'that's not possible'. We all simply got on with it (with a little sprinkling of help from the Lebanese community!). Vivid memories come flooding back – Sonny Terry and Brownie McGhee, Terry Reid, Stevie Marriott, Average White Band, me and Ritchie Hayward getting rolled up in the dartboard mat. Me, Big Dave and Brucie Wilson laughing until it physically hurt.

To have continued for 41 years is a testament to the devotion and hard work of Sam and Sue Jukes. Bless you both. Love and peace, JB.

Colin 'Sam' Dukes

On one typical busy evening at King Street, I was standing in reception minding my own business when I suddenly felt a huge weight around my

Prog rock heavies, Budgie. Behind them is a mountain of 'Trill' bird seed, their fee for the JB's gig. ☞

🖙 *JB's King Street as it looks today, an Indian social centre.*

neck. A voice behind me said, 'Sam, can you look after this while I go for a piss?' I looked down, and to my horror, he'd draped a massive snake around my shoulders – an anaconda or a python maybe, I'm not an expert. There was another biker character who'd regularly turn up with a pet rat on his shoulder. It would have been interesting had both punters decided to visit the club on the same night.

Dave Reeves

Black Country Nights Far Out
A small extract from a piece written to commemorate a JB's reunion in 2008

Dudley Town Football Club, Thursday Nights, Progressive Disco – the news went round the Zoo's Safari Lounge, faux Hollywood African chic, where nightly, out of boredom, you were as likely to get a caning with a bamboo pole that had been removed surreptitiously from the décor, as you were from the alcohol you couldn't afford to buy; where the leather from the seats of the chairs could be turned into a very stylish fringed shoulder bag (and was); where I got stabbed in the arse by Jez – Big Jez, Bad Jez, call him what you will. Jez – no malice, just a game (a bar game? A Rough bar game that involved something akin to wrestling, and a knife), a romp, a misjudgement – me not keeping still when the blade came near, the pool of blood, the attempt to staunch it in the toilets, the vertical journey to A&E in the back of a van, a friend's van, a band's van, stacked with PA and amp (very rock 'n'roll), and a warm, wet sanguine creeping down my leg; the nurses queuing to watch as the stitches went in; throwing the sopping red underpants out of the van window on the way home; missing some TV show I really wanted to see (some weekly ritual); being off work unable to walk, just shuffle; and Jez – Big Jez, Bad Jez – picking me up on his motorbike on Saturday to take me and my record box to DJ – me on the back of a Triumph Bonneville sat on a borrowed cushion.

So a new home was grown for Thursday nights, and then more nights: disco nights, band nights, folk nights... crowded into the small clubroom, bursting out for air. What bands did I see? Few – I was too short to get much of a view. Did I hear? I

don't remember, I went for the atmosphere; the ambience; the cheap alcohol; the stands.

Dave Reeves presents re.Lit, a live, monthly literature show on Internet radio station www.radiowildfire.com, transmitting in real time from 20.00–22.00 hrs on the first Monday of every month. Dave's book and CD, Black Country Dialectics, is now available from Offa's Press.

Roy Williams

Here are two of my favourite reminiscences from King Street. Having finished their main set and a couple of encores, Flaco Jimenz with Pete Rowen and his all Mexican Tex Mex Band, said they would play on in return for some more beers. Providing beer for the band was fine, but the club's licensing hours for the punters had come to an end that evening, so they could not be sold any more alcohol legally. The audience was informed that the band wanted to play on, but no alcohol would be available. Those that wanted to leave could do so and those that wanted to stay would be locked in (subject to health and safety rules) until the band stopped playing. A good hour or so later the band left the building to carry on playing at another lock-in at a pub just outside of town.

On another evening, a practical joker at the club, knowing Sam's penchant for cigars, purchased a pack of exploding ones from a local joke shop and presented him with them. Sadly, Sam did not take the bait, and instead placed them behind the bar for later on. The cigars were completely forgotten about for months, until Bob Ridley, a fairly elderly gentleman who was the JB's insurance broker, came to discuss policies. Ever the genial host, Sam offered Bob a cigar, only to discover that he had just lit up the last one in his packet. He then remembered the pack his friend had given him, behind the bar, and gave Bob one of those instead. Minutes later, the cigar exploded, nearly causing the broker to keel over with a heart attack. One wonders if he was insured against such an eventuality.

(May I add that I have struggled to type this particular anecdote, as I am rather prone to extreme giggling fits. GT)

Tales from The Loft

Into the 1980s

With JB's longest-standing disc jockey, Dermott Stephens

"I don't wanna rock, DJ
But you're making me feel so nice
When's it gonna stop, DJ?
Cos you're keeping me up all night"

Robbie Williams

Dermott Stephens was, and still is, a tall, curly-haired man with a gentle Somerset accent. After living in Taunton and working in his spare time as a DJ, he moved to the Midlands in 1974 to attend a college in Birmingham, which is where he first heard about JB's club. He duly went along to check the place out, and ended up being the resident DJ there for a remarkable 30 years. In fact, next to Sam Jukes, he was the longest-serving committee member at the club – a fact that undoubtedly makes him very proud indeed. There are, as we have already mentioned elsewhere, three basic types of disc jockey. The tedious, overly verbose, middle-of-the-road radio presenter, the incompetent amateur at the discotheque who speaks through a cheap, fuzzy-sounding microphone over at least half of the record they're spinning, and finally, saving the best till last, the learned music presenter who is keen to explore different genres and expose the music of exciting new talent to his or her flock. Thankfully, Dermott was in the latter category. Comparisons are inevitably odious, but both Gezz Tobin and Dermott were very much in the John Peel camp. Their laconic, cheese-free, spartan vocal delivery, coupled with their sincere desire to shut up altogether when the record began, made them ideal for JB's, a club that insisted that its DJs didn't sound like DJs.

If we can briefly backtrack to the mid-70s for a moment, Dermott arrived just as the club was evolving and reinventing itself, as it did constantly during its remarkable 41-year history. The old guard – people such as Sid, his twin brother John, Larry, and Johnny Bryant – were less involved than they had been due to family and work commitments, meaning that Sam was now seeing lots of new faces

Jesus Miguel Sanchez with one of his Big Town Playboys.

New Model Army, who were rather fond of wearing clogs, apparently.

NEW MODEL ARMY

at the club, not only in his audiences, but in his staff, and this was probably a good thing. It kept the club fresh and in a constant state of flux, in parallel with the music scene, which was also ever-changing. Gezz Tobin was still working the decks, as were Roy Williams, Graham Hucknall, Big Dave, and Les Bates. Generally, the decision as to which DJ worked on what night was organized in a very ad hoc sort of way between themselves, depending on who could make it or who fancied it. There were never any arguments about money, or hogging the shifts, because no one got paid anyway.

Dermott was, by his own admission, more 'left-field' and experimental than his colleagues. The thrill for him was to explore new music and expose the JB's audiences to it. As with anything new, sometimes they liked it, and sometimes they didn't, and they often made him aware of their displeasure in the typically direct Dudley way. Dermott liked garage punk such as MC5 and The Stooges, American West-Coast psychedelia such as Jefferson Airplane and Quicksilver Messenger Service, plus mainstream acts such as The Beatles and The Byrds. He also played a lot of folk music, proving that his musical tastes were truly eclectic. Some of the old-school bands at that time, he recalls, were failing to attract large audiences, but it was obvious that the pre-punk acts – Dr. Feelgood, Eddie and the Hot Rods, Ian Dury, The Hammersmith Gorillas, The Count Bishops and Joe Strummer's 101'ers – were all being well received, and spearheading the revolution against the older, traditional blues and rock bands. When Dermott first heard 'Anarchy in the UK', his world changed. He couldn't get enough of it. He began to play a lot of punk music, which, at first, was not terribly well received by the majority of his listeners. As ever, it was the shock of the new, and comparable to the first time that Paris exhibited work by the Fauvist Art movement (from fauve, French for 'wild beast'). The drawing was crude, the colours brash, and the workmanship non-existent, at least in the eyes of some of the art critics of the time. One eminent critic called their inaugural exhibition, at the Salon d'Automne of 1905, 'A pot of garish colour flung into the face of the public', such was his outrage, but once the dust had settled, Matisse, Derain, and friends were able to join the ranks of the mainstream, just like those who had initially caused outrage before them, throughout history. Popular music has often begun its life as very unpopular music. It was ever thus.

Dermott ignored the calls for his execution and continued to introduce his audiences to bands such as the Ramones, The Damned, the Buzzcocks, The Jam, Siouxsie and the Banshees, and Magazine, and gradually, the crowds accepted it. Just as fresh staff members replaced the old committee, new music fans replaced the older ones, who had gradually slipped away quietly to bring up families or start new lives elsewhere. The occasional cull, the naturalists tell us, is needed to keep the species healthy, and the same goes for music clubs. Most importantly, Sam embraced the changes, and this was how he was able to survive and thrive.

One incredibly fruitful and intuitive move was the introduction of local bands playing midweek for free. Dermott and Sam championed the Wednesday night gigs, because it gave fledgling acts the opportunity to play in front of a crowd, and to take advantage of a good-quality PA system. This led to a cross-fertilization of musicians and ideas, which played a huge part in the forming of local bands that often went on to achieve considerable recognition. It was, in effect, the JB's apprenticeship scheme! Again, there is a marked similarity with the world of art. Back in the 1970s, art colleges were run pretty much in the same way that schools were run, with students all sharing a classroom, and working within sight of each other. This inevitably led to ideas being shared, with students wandering around in their tea breaks to observe what their colleagues were doing, picking up tips, ideas and techniques, and transferring them to their own work. Nowadays, sadly, art students meet for an hour to receive their brief, and then disappear to who knows where – a seedy bedsit perhaps – until the following week, when they hand in their project, which has been created in total isolation. These students have no human contact, other than episodes of Neighbours or Home and Away, maybe, which don't really constitute 'human contact'. There is no camaraderie, no feeling of togetherness, no classroom banter,

Local heavy rockers Diamond Head.

SUNDAY 25TH MARCH
ACOUSTIC DIAMOND HEAD

A very young 'Edge' (above) with the equally young Larry Mullen Jnr. and Bono, (right) back in the days before U2's world domination.

GRAD 4

A side OPENING UP
B side BILLY

Both Written by THE CIRCLES

Produced by David Virr
Ⓟ & Ⓒ 1979 Graduate Music
1, Union Street, Dudley, West Midlands DY2 8PG Telephone Dudley (0384) 59048

The Stray Cats. One of the many memorable bands at JB's.

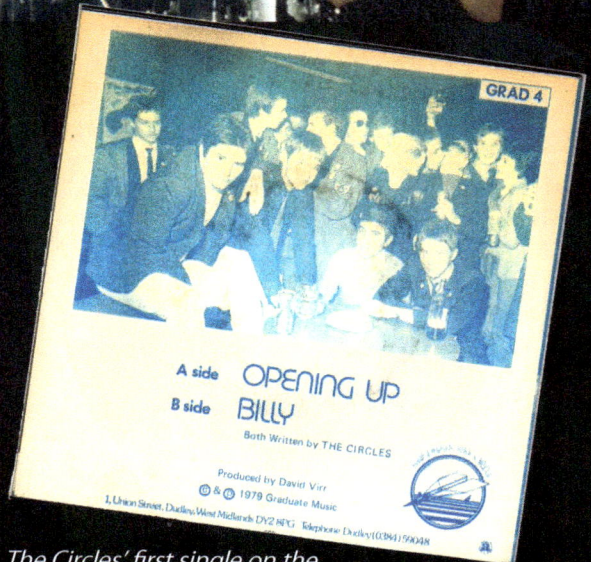

The Circles' first single on the Graduate label.

nothing. Result – the work they turn out is often dismal. What JB's offered on Wednesdays was that much-needed classroom environment.

JB's spawned many bands throughout its long and proud history. New wave and punk bands such as Virus, 999, The Boys, The Radiators from Space, Radio Stars, Pop Will Eat Itself, The Wonder Stuff, The Mighty Lemon Drops, Last Gang, Goats Don't Shave, and many, many more, met, socialized and played together at JB's. Bass players left to join rival bands, and bands joined forces to create new bands. The club was a melting pot, a creative hub for so many people, and it was a free service. A perfect example of this morphing of one band into another was The Injectors. The band disintegrated, but then became The Circles, a mod-revival band that signed to Graduate Records and released its first single, 'Opening Up'. The record's cover photo was actually taken outside JB's, and Dermott even penned the B-side, 'Billy'. And you just thought he played records!

Punk had truly arrived, and, whilst no one could say that it was the saviour of the club, it had nevertheless given JB's the kick up the arse it needed. The post-punk movement followed, and in Dermott's opinion, brought with it the most productive period in the club's history, with gigs by Elvis Costello, The Specials, UB40, the Stray Cats (universally recognized as one of the best JB's gigs in a long time), Echo and the Bunnymen, The Cure, The Teardrop Explodes, Orchestral Manoeuvres in the Dark, The Fall, and Irish future rock giants, U2, starring a youthful Bono before his dark glasses were welded permanently in place. This era was the musical pinnacle for Dermott, who had now begun to work five nights a week. Graham, meanwhile, had suffered a very nasty accident which sidelined him, and Les still contributed, but to a lesser degree, so it was down to Dermott to keep the show on the road. A bootleg of The Fall live at JB's was produced during that period, and the ubiquitous DJ was even featured on it, introducing the band.

1980 also saw many of the older acts making regular appearances, artistes such as Ruby Turner, Steve Gibbons, Ricky Cool and the Icebergs, and of course, the evergreens Supercharge, but it was the new wave that dominated the gigs list. The Coventry ska influence continued to flourish, with a first appearance by Bad Manners. Diamond Head supplied heavy rock for the bikers, while pin-up boy Andy Lloyd and his smartly suited and booted mod band, The Wedge, showed us how to write 3-minute hit singles and make the young girls go all unnecessary at the same time. Weapon of Peace and future superstars UB40 gave us reggae, which had always allied itself with punk. A year later, the New Romantics were rearing their coiffured heads, and it was interesting to note that local hero Andy Lloyd's band had also received a makeover. They were no longer The Wedge, but The Bloomsbury Set, and a Graduate Records' outfit. Shortly after their JB's gig they released 'Hanging Around with the Big Boys', which entered the UK charts, and they were invited to support Duran Duran on a British tour. New Model Army made two appearances in fairly quick succession, as did The Enid, a prog-rock band to pacify the old-school punters. UK Subs, one of the earliest proper punk bands, provided a bit of raucous entertainment for the pogo enthusiasts, and the aforementioned Wayne County played at the club on the 2nd of September, followed by his new alter ego, Jayne County in December. What he lost and gained in the interim does not bear thinking about.

In 1984, The Vibrators arrived to treat the crowd to some vintage punk, and returned later in the year for a bit more. Rather incongruously, band member John Ellis later recorded with Peter Gabriel, as well as Peter Hammill of Van der Graaf Generator, which must have seemed to some dyed-in-the-wool punk fans like fraternizing with the enemy! Ellis later joined The Stranglers on a full-time basis. Other highlights include more appearances by The Enid, New Model Army, The Redbeards from Texas, and Steve Marriott – ex-member of The Small Faces and Humble Pie. Strangely, popular country-star Raymond Froggatt played the club three times in as many weeks around June, suggesting that he either needed the money or was asked back by popular demand (or most likely both). It was around this time that Sam introduced a blues night on Sundays to keep the traditionalists happy, so now the club was open five nights a week on average. It was like the Folies Bergère – it never closed!

Just when you thought that New Model Army would have had enough of the place, they popped up again in November, wearing their nice, new wooden clogs, followed by the always popular Dr. Feelgood. December saw Mike Sanchez fill the entire stage with his presence, and for those who are not au fait with him, here follows a small appreciation of the great man.

Jesus Miguel Sanchez was born in London of Spanish parents, but moved to Worcestershire at the age of eleven – Bewdley, to be precise, and London's loss was our gain. Sanchez was greatly influenced by one of his high-school teachers, one Richard Rodgers, better known as Ricky Cool. There goes that incredible cross-pollination thing happening again. The West Midlands' musical fraternity was – and is – so inbred! Robert Plant (here we go again) introduced Sanchez to a few useful people, and lo and behold, the Big Town Playboys were born, which for several years featured Ricky Cool, Sanchez's old teacher, on tenor saxophone and vocals. Soon, all manner of famous musicians were beginning to notice Sanchez's talents as a pianist and charismatic frontman, and before long his band was backing Robert Plant.

Sanchez met Gary Brooker of Procol Harum, who then introduced him to Eric Clapton, Andy Fairweather-Low and Albert Lee (boy, this lad could network!). This led to Mike playing on the soundtrack of the Paul Newman / Tom Cruise film, The Color of Money (and before you point out the typo, 'color' is spelt the American way, as it's an American film!). The Playboys disbanded in 1999 after playing at many high-profile concerts, namely Eric Clapton's Royal Albert Hall events, and various gigs with Jeff Beck. Sanchez later joined Bill Wyman's Rhythm Kings, supplementing his income with many solo appearances.

1985 welcomed Steve Marriott once more, followed by The Spencer Davis Group. Earlier in this book, we featured the ancient receipt pads that Sam had kept for posterity, and it's interesting to refer to these, just occasionally, as we wend our way through the years, to see how things had changed, financially speaking. Spencer Davis, featuring the great Steve Winwood, charged the princely sum of £600, while Steve Marriott only wanted (or should that be only received?) £350. Dr. Feelgood succeeded in wrenching £285 from Sam's iron wallet, which is still far better than Eddie and the Hotrods and Wreckless Eric could manage, getting £200 and £150 respectively. We will revisit this theme again later on in the book, and the difference in fees may shock you. Meanwhile, let's look at a couple of Dudley businesses that were vital to the club's well-being, and vice versa.

☞ Steve Marriott (ex Small Faces and Humble Pie) at one of his many JB's gigs.

☞ Wreckless Eric, still going the 'Whole Wide World' at the age of 60!

www.wrecklesseric.com

Active Restraint, who
morphed into the
Mighty Lemon Drops.

David Newton of the Mighty Lemon Drops.

Les Bates, occasional DJ, and the
man responsible for some of the wall
decoration at King Street.

The Mighty Lemon Drops in action,
above and right.

The 1980s were also memorable for the creation of a surreal character by the name of Frank Sidebottom. Frank was basically a human body topped by a huge round head with massive eyes. He was created by comedian and musician Chris Sievey, and enjoyed a considerable amount of fame and TV exposure in the 1980s. Jon Ronson, one of the musicians who played in Frank's 'Oh Blimey Big Band', has written several books, notably Frank, which has recently been made into a Hollywood film. For those with good memories, Frank's band actually played at JB's.

What follows is an extract from 'Frank' by Jon Ronson, who also wrote the film screenplay with Peter Straughan:.

And now our Frank film – directed by Lenny Abrahamson and starring Michael Fassbender, Maggie Gyllenhaal and Domhnall Gleeson, is going to be premiered at the Sundance Film Festival. As I prepare to go to it, I remember something Chris once said to me. It was late one night, and we were in the van, reminiscing about a show we'd played a few weeks earlier at JB's nightclub in Dudley. It was very poorly attended. There can't have been more than 15 people in the audience. One of them produced a ball, the audience split into teams and, ignoring us, played a game. In the van, Chris smiled wistfully.

"That Dudley gig," he said.

"Ah ha?" I said.

"Best show we ever played!" he said.

This is an edited extract from Frank: The True Story that Inspired the Movie, published by Picador. 'Frank' premiered at the Sundance Film Festival and opened in cinemas nationwide, in May 2014.

Inset photo of Chris Seivey by Gemma Woods.

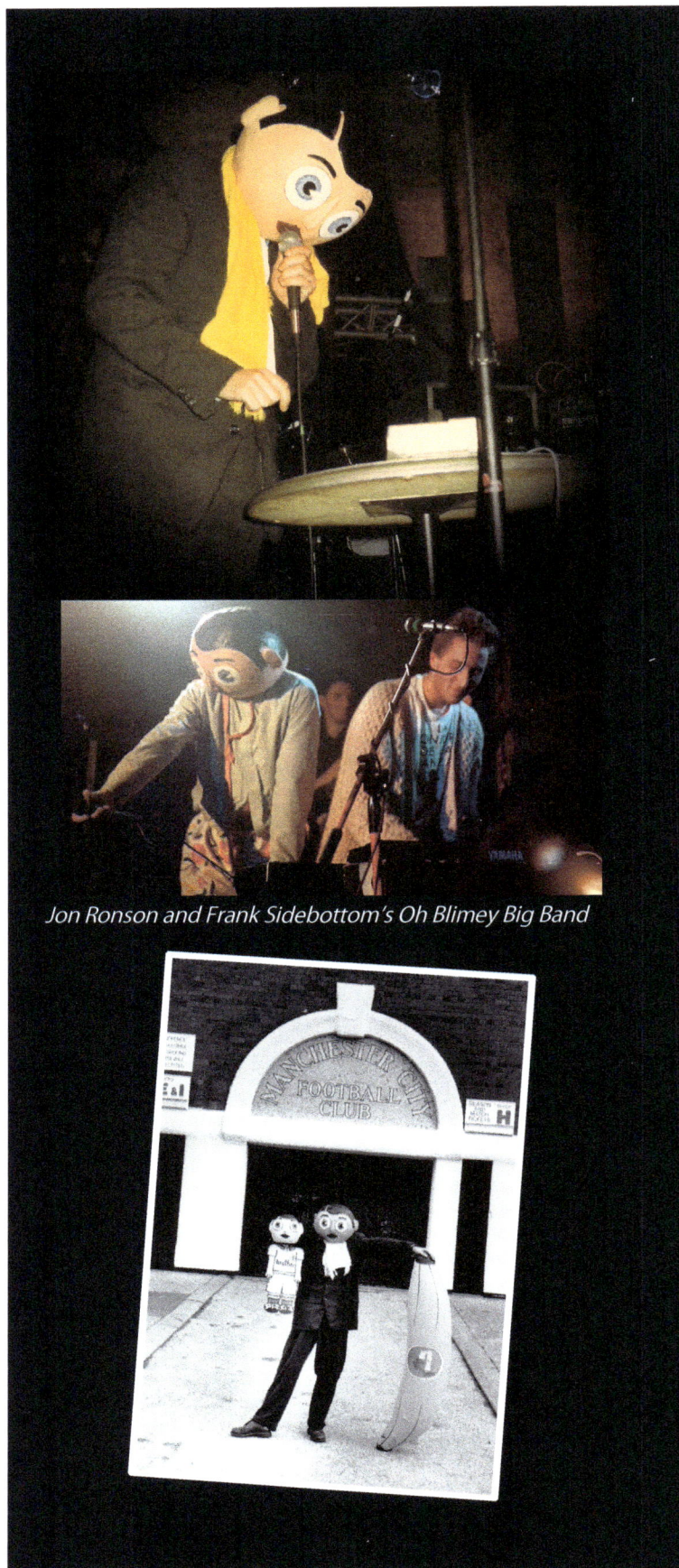

Jon Ronson and Frank Sidebottom's Oh Blimey Big Band

Jim Hickman, the Honey Drippers and Little Acre bass player.

Dangerous Girls.

Paul Gilbert, virtuoso guitarist from Mr Big.

The late Howard Rushton.

Second Nature.

The Honey Turtles.

Mark Moran, The Prehistoric Pets.

The Look.

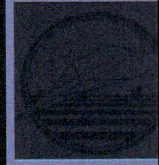

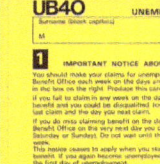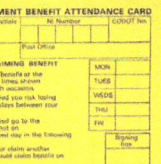
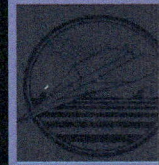

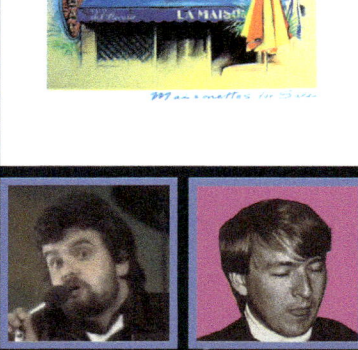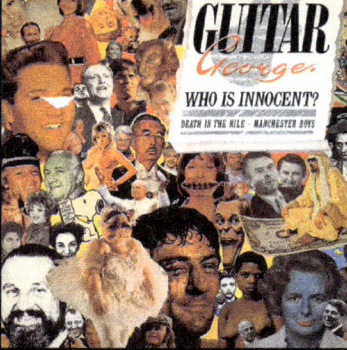

Graduate Records

David Virr was quite posh, by Dudley standards at least, if we can say that without insulting both parties! He lived in rural Worcestershire, and at the time was married to the equally posh Susan Virr. From 1969, while Sam, Sid, J.B. and Co. were toiling down the road at Coneygre Youth Club and setting up the football-club operation, David was running a second-hand record shop in Dudley, near to St Thomas's Church (locally known as 'Top Church', as opposed to the 'Bottom Church', St Edmund's), and often supplied the various JB's disc spinners with records. After a while, he expanded his business, and at one point he was managing six small record stores around the Midlands. After listening to John Peel's radio shows (that man again!),

David decided that he would like to create his own independent record label. His first signings barely managed to make an impact on the indie charts, but his luck changed dramatically with UB40, which became the most commercially successful reggae band in the world. Suddenly, David and Susan's lifestyle changed. They were able to afford a very nice Georgian house in Britannia Square, Worcester, and a smart Georgian office block in Wolverhampton Street, which was to be their new company's headquarters. Now, all of a sudden, Dudley, a small market town, boasted not only a top live-music venue, but also a top independent record label. Even better, the two were able to help each other in many ways.

Having tried to keep a reasonably low profile throughout the writing of this book, I (Geoff Tristram, in case you've forgotten me already) now have to briefly include myself in the JB's story. In the late 1970s I was looking for a new art studio in Dudley, having outgrown a tiny place that I rented above a hearing-aid shop, of all places, in Tower Street. David had more than enough room at his palatial new headquarters, so we entered into a marriage of convenience. I was given cheap studio space, and David had a professional artist on tap, for whenever he needed a record sleeve or poster designed in a hurry. Even better, we got on like a house on fire. David was an affable chap with blond, floppy hair and a huge grin, and we were both notorious gigglers, so it was a marriage made in heaven. I remember that most days, we would spend our time together laughing our heads off, albeit whilst working ourselves to death, David especially. He was driving so many miles each week that one day he fell asleep at the wheel, crashed through a motorway barrier and hit a tree, where he lay unconscious for hours, his brow split wide open.

I also got on very well with his tall, willowy, upper-crust wife, Susan, and in spite of their vastly different backgrounds, so too did my Netherton-born, working-class, Black Country wife, Susan (it seemed everyone of a certain age was christened Susan in those days). Suddenly we found ourselves being invited to frightfully posh dinner parties in rural Worcestershire, and even the odd holiday in Cannes! I remember David buying Susan (my Susan) and me a half of lager each at the Intercontinental Carlton Hotel, the most prestigious place to stay during the Cannes Film Festival, and visibly blanching when he received the bill. Meanwhile, back in Dudley, we continued to work hard, me on advertising illustrations, plus the odd album or single sleeve, and David – his floppy hair brushed down over his scarred brow (from the aforementioned car accident) – on creating his new recording empire. While living in the flat at the back of the offices, my best mate, Larry Homer, and his girlfriend, Anne Palmer (later to become Mrs Homer), ran David's small rehearsal and recording studio, situated in the basement. I distinctly remember local punks Virus using the place, but never having any cash to pay the fee for the use of the rehearsal facility. One night, Larry found a note pinned to the door, which read 'Sorry Lazz, we got no dosh again. Ay we c**ts!'

UB40 had changed David's fortunes and provided him with the much-needed funds to sign other acts, such as the Pink Umbrellas, Andy Lloyd's new band, The Bloomsbury Set, chart-toppers The Maisonettes (with Lol Mason of City Boy), Whizz for Atoms, Guitar George (mentioned in the lyrics of the Dire Straits single, 'Sultans of Swing'), Jezz Woodroffe (keyboard player for Ozzy Osbourne and Black Sabbath), Ruby Turner, Clifford T. Ward, Last Gang, China Doll, Virus

(of course), and the mod outfit, The Circles, plus several more whose names escape me. It was a very exciting and productive time for all concerned, with me churning out record sleeves – UB40's Signing Off and The Maisonettes debut album, Maisonettes for Sale, being the most high profile of them – and my new mate, David, tearing around the country in his old, white, high-mileage Mercedes Coupé for meetings with Richard Branson and the like. During that period I also designed the label logos for Graduate Records and its sub-label, Ready, Steady, Go!, the former of which has an interesting story attached to it. Having already sketched out some ten or so logos, none of which David particularly cared for, I petulantly folded one of them into a paper aeroplane and chucked it out of my studio window into Wolverhampton Street. As I watched it fly through the open window, I experienced a eureka moment. I quickly sketched the paper plane, and then drew a circle around it to make it look more like a logo. David popped in to see if I'd drawn any more ideas for him, saw my new scribble, and said 'I love it. That's the one!'

Having signed local bands such as Virus and The Circles, JB's played its part by giving them regular gigs, and this, in turn, sold more records. It was a classic win-win situation for all concerned. The club was even used as a venue for an episode of The Tube, presented by Paula Yates and Jools Holland, which featured a Robert Plant interview and The Maisonettes, who played live on the JB's stage, with its large logo proudly displayed behind them for all the world to see. Dermott, who was there at the time, does not remember the event with much fondness, due to the fact that he found one of the presenters to be a git (and I have more than somewhat cleaned up the actual description he gave of them!). This is a personal opinion, however, and does not represent the feelings of the others who were present!

At the grand opening of David and Susan's new headquarters, a band played live on the roof, in the style made famous by The Beatles. Waitresses served canapés and champagne, a certain guest, underestimating the power of the bubbly, drank too much and collapsed in the fireplace (mentioning no names... well, okay then, the well-known Dudley photographer and art lecturer, Tim Joplin), and out in the street, Jimmy the Con guarded the front door to prevent gatecrashers from entering. Finding Tim non compos mentis, Jim gathered him up and effortlessly slung him over his shoulder, before carting him off somewhere quiet to recuperate. Tim later woke up in a nearby freezing-cold churchyard, with memory loss and a terrible headache.

Sadly, David died in December 2006 of amyloidosis, which in layman's terms is a rogue protein that attacks the nervous system, the muscles, or the internal organs. In David's case, it was all three. It is an illness so rare that only a handful of people in Britain have suffered with it. His funeral was held at Great Witley Church, Worcestershire, and was attended by many of the musicians that he had helped along the way. He had parted company with Susan years before, only to marry another Susan (Coldicott), a keen equestrian, but the marriage didn't last very long. David was survived by his third wife, Tina, a delightful French lady with whom he shared a tranquil, simpler, and more contented life, in their small cottage in Shrawley, near Stourport, once the glory days were over. His three children – Alexander, Caroline, and Kieran (from his first two marriages) – and Tina still look after David's music-business affairs. In his later years he became interested in the spiritual side of life, and practised meditation. Tragically, just as he finally found real happiness, his life was cut short by his terrible illness.

I, and many others, miss him greatly. He was a lovely, funny man, and we had a wonderful, fun-filled time working and socializing together in Dudley, and elsewhere, during the 1980s.

The Virus reunion gig at JB's, featuring the supremely talented session guitarist, Dudley-born Dave Lowe.

☜ Bob Nash of Modern Music, Dudley (photograph courtesy of The Express and Star).

☞

Jack Mckechnie, renowned jazz guitarist with The Hedley Ward Trio..

Modern Music

If you drive down Castle Hill, Dudley, with the zoo on your left, see if you can spot the small shop on the far left of a row of businesses, just before the car park of the Station Hotel (where the likes of Laurel and Hardy, Split Enz, and all manner of entertainers have stayed over the years, usually when they were playing at the Hippodrome, or JB's!). The little shop near the hotel was, for many years, the most important place in the area if you were a musician.

It was called Modern Music, and it was owned by Jack Mckechnie – an old-school jazz guitarist and one-time member of the Hedley Ward Trio – and Bob Nash, a drummer and occasional clarinettist. This crowded little shop was where the visiting bands got their amps and microphones repaired, and where they purchased the strings, plectrums, drumsticks and all manner of bits and pieces that had fallen off their battered instruments due to a hard life on the road. It was also where they bought the latest effects pedal, or had their saxophone serviced, and most importantly, where they could chew the fat with fellow players, both amateur and professional. It didn't matter if you were one of a bunch of 15-year-old kids forming your first band, or

if you were Noddy Holder or Dave Hill, Modern Music was the place to go.

In common with all small independent music shops, it was a place of banter, and that particular brand of cruel sarcasm and wit that musicians seem to specialize in. John Bonham would always pop to the shop to buy hundreds of pairs of drumsticks to take on tour with him. He'd arrive on a huge Harley-Davidson motorbike, and would inevitably bash it into the wall when trying to park it. Modern Music also supplied speakers to the local mosques, which were used to call the faithful to prayer. Unfortunately, the mosque leaders were not the most technical of men, and were always banging on the door, demanding that Jack fixed their 'broken' PA systems immediately, even though there was never anything wrong with them. Jack would leave the speakers outside, plug them in to prove they were in working order, and let whichever muezzin had brought them in that day address his flock from the front doors of Modern Music, a truly bizarre sight, by all accounts. Alan Clee, a former employee of the shop, remembers The Who arriving one day to buy as many cheap Stratocaster copies as the shop could spare, so that Pete Townshend could smash them up at Stourbridge Town Hall that evening. And you thought he was smashing up the real Fender ones. We got fooled again!

Young lads with nothing pressing to do would sit on the many amps that cluttered the tiny shop floor, and show off their skills on Les Paul guitars (that they had no intention of ever buying) borrowed from the front window.

Meanwhile, in a back room full to bursting with spare parts, valves, speakers, and wires, Bob Nash, in his scruffy old green cardigan and large spectacles which were forever in need of a good clean, would be soldering away, while Jack stood behind the glass counter, making sure someone didn't borrow a Fender Telecaster and forget to pay for it. His youthful Saturday shop assistant, Dave Lowe, now a superbly talented session guitarist and composer, would inevitably be demonstrating a second-hand Gibson SG to an anorak who could just about play three chords, but knew all the right patter – a bit like the amateur photographers who can blind you with scientific camera knowledge but can't take a picture to save their lives. Dave would play so skilfully and so quickly, his hands were a blur. He didn't so much encourage beginners as put them off for life, and to add insult to injury, he was still wearing his Dudley Grammar School uniform at the time. On one particularly hectic Saturday, when Jack was suffering with one of his migraines but trying to soldier on (as opposed to Bob, who was trying to solder on), and Dave was treating a group of open-mouthed, dazzled wannabe rock stars to a bit of very loud Hendrix, Jack walked from behind the glass counter and, without

utterance, snipped Dave's curly guitar lead with a pair of scissors. The noise stopped abruptly. Jack said nothing, and returned behind the counter to sip his tea. It was that kind of shop.

The late Johnny Higgs was a regular visitor, but his intentions were not always pure. One dark night in the '70s, aided by an accomplice from his band of the time, he hurled a building brick through the window of Modern Music, and then relieved Jack and Bob of a very nice guitar. Jack, correctly suspecting the stammering singer of the crime, neatly parcelled up the brick in gift-wrapping paper, marched round to JB's and presented it to Higgs as a souvenir. There was a certain frostiness when Higgs needed new strings after that.

Jack sadly died and Bob retired, but the call of the small music-shop environment was too much for him. Stourbridge Music Centre, run by pianists Pete Cox and his son Matt (of the Space Hoppers), is almost a carbon copy of Modern Music, with exactly the same banter and sarcasm, but with quite a lot more room for cat-swinging purposes. Rather than see Bob bored, they offered him a job, which involved sitting in their own cluttered back room, still resplendent in his green cardigan and smeared 'Should've gone to Specsavers' glasses, soldering bits onto amps and guitars. Bob jumped at the opportunity, and worked there until a year or so ago, as happy as Larry, until he too went to the great music shop in the sky. It would be nice to imagine him reunited with his old mate Jack, and busy in one of Heaven's back rooms, restringing harps, servicing celestial trumpets, and so forth.

No book on JB's could ever be complete without a chapter on Modern Music. It is sorely missed by the countless musicians who frequented the place.

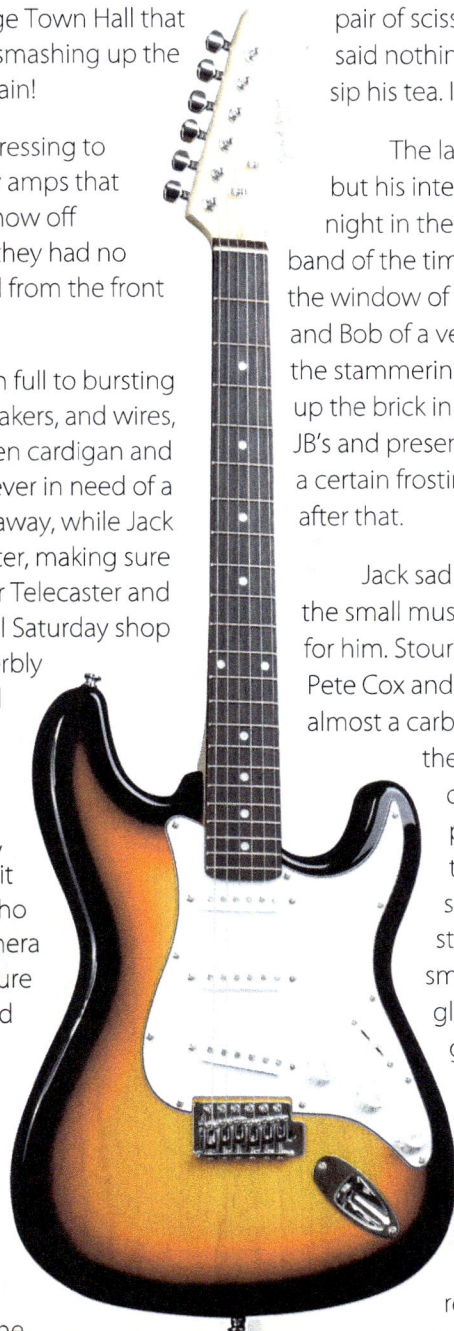

Hedley Ward Trio

Clint Mansell, formerly of Pop Will Eat Itself, and now a successful film score composer.

John Otway decides not to headbutt the microphone on this occasion.

The Mighty Lemon Drops.

From Eden, looking suitably camp.

Chris Farlowe and The Thunderbirds jet in from Tracy Island to entertain the people of Dudley.

Mark Moran of Prehistoric Pets, clowning around with the Goats Don't Shave boys.

The 1980s Continued

1986 highlights included Chris Farlowe and The Thunderbirds, The Adicts, and a first showing of The Mighty Lemon Drops, formed from the remains of Indecent Exposure. We have already spoken about the Lemons (who also enjoyed considerable success in the USA) in a fair amount of detail. In many ways, these acts were the start of yet another golden era, which seems all the more satisfying because the bands in question were largely conceived, nurtured, and grown in the hothouse nursery that was JB's.

The Wildflowers, one of Dermott's favourite local bands, played at JB's in April 1985, followed shortly afterwards by Goats Don't Shave, yet another locally grown talent. It was as if the JB's stable of bands was now ready to launch itself onto the world. A week later, and The Lemon Drops were back again by popular demand, and then it was the turn of Wild and Wandering (locally nicknamed 'Blind and the Blundering', due to their frequent inebriated performances) and From Eden, featuring Miles Hunt and Malcolm Treece, who, between them, quietly morphed into top bands, Pop Will Eat Itself, and The Wonder Stuff.

John Otway, occasional musical partner of Wild Willy Barrett, mesmerized the punters with his own brand of insanity in late April, treating them – if that's the right word – to his post-punk, half-spoken single, 'Really Free'. Debbie Bonham, the late, great John Bonham's daughter, a gutsy blues singer, appeared in May, and shortly afterwards, in June, the club welcomed the wife of one of music's true superstars, Angie Bowie. After her gig, Angie took the trouble to ring Jake 'Scoop' Elcock (Sam's best man at his wedding). who alongside Roy Williams, booked many of the bands at JB's, to tell him that her night at the club was one of the best and most enjoyable shows she had ever performed.

Later on, at the end of August, more homespun talent was unleashed in the guise of the Weeping Messerschmitts (see the following amusing article supplied by Dave Webb, about the last ever night at King Street and his souvenir carpet tile), and the newly formed Pop Will Eat Itself. The latter band, also known as 'The Poppies', was formed in Stourbridge (God's country) and went on to achieve considerable success. They released three well-received albums, and each of their singles charted progressively higher. The band toured extensively in the UK, Europe, and America, including appearances at the Reading Festival.

Their singer, Clint Mansell, has gone on to enjoy a hugely successful career as a film-music composer. When The Poppies disbanded in 1996, Darren Aronofsky – the American film director, producer, and screenwriter – hired Mansell to score his debut film. Mansell also scored Aronofsky's second film, Requiem for a Dream, which was well received, and the film's primary composition, 'Lux Aeterna', has been used in a variety of advertisements. Other films he wrote music for include The Fountain, which was nominated for a Golden Globe, Moon, Smokin' Aces, The Wrestler, and Black Swan. The trailer for The Lord of the Rings: The Two Towers was also written by Mansell. Not bad for a Stourbridge lad, only now he lives in Hollywood, of course. Is it possible to get Batham's Ales, Enville Ales, Banks's Beer, or KVE Pork Scratchings there, we ask? Alas, that is the price of fame. Sacrifices have to be made along the way.

Sid's trusty old gig lists reveal that The Poppies were asked back later in the year, along with the Wildflowers, Weeping Messerschmitts, The Mighty Lemon Drops, and Goats Don't Shave. The homespun bands were really taking off, but there was one more big act to come.

It's now 1987, and first out of the traps in January is The Wonder Stuff – that's if you ignore Billy Bowel and The Movements, a fun band cobbled together by the likes of Johnny Bryant and chums. The original line-up of The Wonder Stuff featured Miles Hunt on vocals and guitar, Malcolm Treece on guitar, Rob 'The Bass Thing' Jones on, well, bass, obviously, and Martin Gilks on drums. Sadly, both Jones and Gilks died early, in 1993 and 2006 respectively.

The Wonder Stuff formed in 1986, so this first JB's gig was a very early one. Their first album, The Eight Legged Groove Machine, was released in August 1988, followed by the wonderfully titled 'Groovers on Manoeuvres' UK tour. 'Don't Let Me Down, Gently' became their first top-20 hit, followed by the album Hup, and another UK tour. Ned's Atomic Dustbin, their JB's stable mates (of whom, more later), were given the support slot on a few of the tour dates. Martin Bell was enrolled to play violin and banjo,

with bassist Paul Clifford replacing Jones in 1990. In December, after receiving a Brit Award nomination, the group opted not to play at Wembley Arena, but instead, answering a fan's letter, they played at a school in South Elmsall!

The Wonder Stuff's third album, 'Never Loved Elvis', was completed in 1991, and the initial single from it was 'The Size of a Cow'. We should quickly clarify that the single itself wasn't the size of a cow, it was merely called that. This reached number 5 in the UK charts. An open-air gig at Walsall's Bescot Stadium saw around 18,000 fans turn up, and shortly afterwards the band embarked on a world tour, with the help of their new keyboard player, Peter Whittaker. A cover version of 'Dizzy', in conjunction with surrealist comedian Vic Reeves, stayed in the UK singles chart for two weeks, considerably raising the band's profile, which was consolidated by not only appearing on the popular USA chat show, the Late Show with David Letterman, but also by a headline slot at the Reading Festival. The Stourbridge branch of the JB's Mafia had finally arrived with a bang.

Other notable bands from 1987 include Fields of the Nephilim, a very influential goth outfit, and Eddie Floyd, from the USA, the renowned soul singer who wrote – amongst many other things – the soul classic 'Knock on Wood'. Once again, the home-grown boys were dominant, with Goats Don't Shave, Weeping Messerschmitts, and The Poppies making repeat appearances, capped by The Wonder Stuff, who played JB's an incredible four times that year.

Johnny Bryant and Big Dave Hodgetts.

'Big' Dave Hodgetts

Dave Hodgetts was a big bloke. That's why he was called 'Big' Dave Hodgetts. He looked like a Canadian lumberjack – the kind that wear red and black checked shirts and shapeless Levi's, and hang around bars with other lumberjacks, drinking beers and arm-wrestling. Dave was big of personality and big of heart, and he was funny. He also liked cars. Johnny Bryant swears that he purchased his first car, a Rover 90, when he was nine years old. It sounds mad and implausible, but he assures me it's true. Dave was the chap who won himself a car by wearing a top hat and carrying a tin of Andrews Liver Salts. You'll know this if you've been paying attention, because he's been mentioned a fair bit throughout the book already, and that alone tells us something. He also wanted to buy a tank, because he spotted that one was for sale in the Exchange and Mart. Johnny was keen to go 'halvers' on the tank, but was rightly concerned about where they could park it. 'Anywhere we fucking want!' was Dave's considered response.

Dave worked at JB's pretty much from the word go, helping out behind the bar, lifting heavy stuff, working on the door, whatever. He was also the last of the original gang to fly the nest. His appetite for fun, and, it has to be said, alcohol, was the stuff of legend. When Roy Williams bunked up with guitarist, Robbie Blunt at the Station Hotel in Sheffield, after one of Robert Plant's Honey Drippers' gigs, rather than suffer Dave's awful snoring, Dave drunkenly wandered off in search of another room to bed down in. The next morning, he couldn't be found anywhere. As anyone who has ever lost anything knows, the best plan is to look in places where things shouldn't logically be, once all the obvious places have been discounted. This they duly did, and came up trumps. Dave was sleeping it off in the Wendy house of the hotel's children's playroom. At least this was slightly more comfortable for him than the time they found him asleep in the hotel corridor,

right outside his room, because he was so drunk he couldn't work out how to operate the key. At another Honey Drippers' gig in Bristol, the barman foolishly told Dave to help himself to a drink or two from the bar optics. Dave drank freely from all of them, and then some, and ended up so legless that no one could manhandle his dead weight into the band's van.

Johnny also remembers with glee the time Dave and friends had been drinking at a club. The waiter counted some 250 empty Pils bottles on their table by the end of their session, which must have taken hours to cart away on those small trays they carry around! Shortly afterwards, Dave fell over and banged his head on the stage, knocking himself unconscious. Worried friends succeeded in lifting him up, only find a completely flattened 8-pack of beer underneath him.

Regrettably, Dave drifted away from the club after many years due to an awkward business decision. He took umbrage when Sam and Sue eventually formed a limited company and he was not included as a director. He thought he should have been, so he called it a day. He had also been working for Robert Plant as a general right-hand man, and could often be seen in Kinver High Street, on some errand or other. Then, gradually, people began to notice that Big Dave wasn't so big any more. He was losing weight rapidly, but sadly, this wasn't due to a fitness regime or a diet. It was caused by pancreatic cancer. Eventually, when his condition deteriorated, Dave was often hospitalized, and naturally feeling very low. Robert visited him often, as did Johnny, and paid for his friend to be treated privately, but it was clear that nothing seemed to be working. When Robert played at the O2 arena, he arranged for a private ambulance to ferry Dave to the concert and look after him. He was probably too ill to be let out for the night, but it was argued that the trip would do wonders for his flagging spirit. Dave was given a seat close to Roy Williams, who was sat behind the mixing console. At the end of the show, Robert shouted from the stage, 'How was it, Dave?' Dave raised his thumbs in appreciation. A couple of weeks later, he died.

His many friends and everyone who visited JB's during his time there will miss him. He was a true one-off, and just like Sam or Jimmy, the club wouldn't have been the same without him.

Thunder (www.birminghammail.co.uk)

Dogs D'Amour (www.flashtightpocket.blogspot.co.uk)

Ruby Turner (weekendnotes.co.uk)

Whitesnake (fanart.tv)

The Quireboys (www.mundomusica.es)

Bruce Dickinson (raulzito)

Rose of Avalanche (www.roseofavalanche.com)

JB's – Junction 10

*"Alone here in the kitchen
I feel there's something missing
I'd beg for some forgiveness
But begging's not my business
And she won't write a letter
Although I always tell her
And so it's my assumption
I'm really up the junction"*

Difford & Tilbrook, Squeeze

Around this time, Sam decided to start a PA-hire business. He formed a partnership with John Newey and Kevin Mobberley, and the result was Stage Audio Services (SAS), which supplied PA equipment, transport and sound engineers for all forms of entertainment. John Newey sadly died early in the company's history, but Sam and Kevin continued to develop the new business, which is still operating to this day, though Sam eventually left to concentrate on his club. It was his intention to set up a small chain of JB's music venues scattered around the Midlands, and to this end, he then joined forces with a friend, Alan Hodierne. A property in Bentley Road North, in

Darlaston, near Walsall, was duly purchased. It was situated close to Junction 10 of the M5, which is where the name of the venue originated from. The club opened on the 31st of August, 1988, with Ruby Turner, the well-known local soul singer, and the opening night was attended by an incredible 800 people. Junction 10 continued to be extremely popular, with acts such as Whitesnake, Thunder, The Rose of Avalanche, Bruce Dickinson, The Quire boys, and The Dogs d'Amour appearing there. Ironically, what Sam had feared would happen at King Street when Jimmy the Con briefly joined the Hell's Angels, actually happened at Junction 10 instead. The club became overtaken by a motorcycle gang and numerous episodes of troublesome behaviour followed, which naturally deterred the regular customers from attending. The problem became so bad that the club decided, albeit reluctantly, to close its doors for good, and a great live venue bit the dust prematurely. On the closing night, New Model Army entertained a crowd of 1,400 people, which perfectly illustrated what a wonderful venue Junction 10 could have been. It does beg the question, where were the police during all of this?

Dave Webb, of the Weeping Messerschmitts, with his magic carpet.

Dave Newton, of the Mighty Lemon Drops.

Pathfinder Chronicles Part 2

Back at safe, dependable old JB's in Dudley, 1988 was notable for Henry McCullough, guitarist with Joe Cocker and The Grease Band (and later Paul McCartney's Wings), followed by The Honey Turtles, another of Dermott's favourites, and yet another, vastly different reincarnation of Andy Lloyd, this time under the banner of Popman and the Raging Bull. Once a moddish, shiny-suit-wearing glamour boy, then a New Romantic, now Andy had reinvented himself as a cropped-haired reggae singer, alongside a black reggae musician with the unlikely name of 'Raging Bull'. The perennial Steve Gibbons and The Soul Survivors entertained the traditionalists, followed by The Redbeards from Texas, who hadn't really got beards and weren't from Texas – they were from Brum. Formed from the fabulous soul band fronted by gritty singer, Curtis Little, their main function was to fill in one night for a support act that failed to show. As a jokey homage to ZZ Top, members of Little's band dressed up as cowboys and played as support to their own soul band. Incredibly, as is wont to happen with all joke projects, they began to get bookings, and became a hot property in their own right.

The rest of the year pretty much consisted of repeat bookings for all the regular bands, and as such, is not particularly noteworthy, which doesn't mean it wasn't a good year. It was basically more of the same, good stuff. Then a new band, Ned's Atomic Dustbin, arrived in December, fronted by Jonn Penney, who was born, like all the best people, in Quarry Bank, West Mids, not to be confused with Quarry Bank, Liverpool, where Lennon and McCartney hailed from. He met bass player Mat Cheslin at the Thorns School and Community College in Quarry Bank, and formed The Neds (as we will call them for the sake of brevity) in 1988 whilst still a sixth-former. In the early '90s, The Neds achieved several hit singles including 'Happy', 'Kill Your Television', and 'Not Sleeping Around'. There were also three successful albums – God Fodder, Are You Normal?, and Brainbloodvolume. Sadly, the band split up in 1995, but a new band, Groundswell (not as catchy, admittedly, but easier to type), formed with The Neds' ex guitarist, Rat (do any of these lads have proper names, I wonder?), and released a few singles which didn't reach the fairly dizzy heights of The Neds.

Having taken a sabbatical, Penney completed a degree course and is now media officer for Wolverhampton Civic Hall. He also lectures part-time and writes a weekly column entitled 'Up Penneyscope' for the Express and Star newspaper. In 2000 he reformed The Neds in order to play the occasional gig here and there, and then, in 2008, The Neds' original line-up got together again for a concert at the London Astoria, followed by a home gig in Wolverhampton. Jonn's happiest memory was playing at Glastonbury, to a never-ending sea of people all singing along to words he'd scribbled down in his kitchen, sat on his own. Even better, The Neds were being supported by a little band by the name of Blur!

Jonn Penney

A few words from Jonn, especially written for this book

"*Ah, JB's! I remember having to hold the urinal up against the wall while making sure I peed to the left side of the crack in it so as not to get my feet wet. Also, lying on the carpet underneath the dartboard (because Newcastle Brown had rendered my legs useless), throwing darts into the board to see whether they stuck or dropped down to pierce random parts of my inebriated body. Stinking of beefburgers for days after visiting the place. Dermott (the DJ; the legend) always saying, 'One more time for Ned's Atomic Dustbin!' when we'd finished playing. Passing out on stage through heat exhaustion at our 'Kill Your TV' video shoot. Answering the phone at JB's all day long to tell customers I'd never heard of Ned's Atomic Dustbin, and adding, 'What a rubbish name!' And another thing, the crowd would hardly ever show excitement about the happening bands they saw until the next day at work or college, so the band would leave thinking they'd had a stinker of a gig. Marvellous!*"

1989 began brightly with American band, The Knack, who had a hit single with 'My Sharona', later on in 1995. The band returned to JB's not long afterwards in February. Meanwhile, Steve Marriott seemed to be living at the place, making yet another appearance, and on Saturday the 18th of February, spearheading the new 'Madchester' invasion that included bands such as Oasis, The Smiths and the

Happy Mondays, The Stone Roses arrived for the first time. The ever-popular Neds followed, and in March, Leeds goth rockers, The Rose of Avalanche, made their club debut. The mid-80s also saw the development of the goth culture in the club, in both fashion and music. Bands like The Sisters of Mercy, The Mission, The Southern Death Cult, Sex Gang Children, and Play Dead were constantly represented on the decks, if not live on stage. Both The Neds and The Stone Roses returned later in the year, along with Goats Don't Shave, John Otway, The Honey Turtles, and yes, you've guessed it, Steve Marriott.

Gavin Priest

was a JB's regular the late 80s, and played in a band called This November. I also worked in a local supermarket to help finance my rock and roll lifestyle. One evening, I had to stay late, restocking the biscuit aisle, and my favourite band, The Stone Roses, were playing at the club. I eventually caught a bus, arrived in Dudley and then ran, breathlessly, along King Street and down the slope, towards the front door, where I saw a hastily scribbled sign stating that the club was full. I was heartbroken. There was a minibus parked near the entrance, and the passenger window opened. I shrugged to the young lad inside, and began to walk back to the bus stop. He called me back and suggested that I go in with them. It was then that I recognized the band. It was The Stone Roses! They carried me into the club on their shoulders, past a smiling doorman, and set me down inside. I found my mates at the bar, who listened in disbelief as I recanted what had happened to me. What a magical night!

Jesus Jones made their inaugural visit in July, a band best remembered for several huge hits including 'Info Freako' and 'Right Here, Right Now', which was used extensively in TV advertisements.

Scottish indie band Primal Scream came in October, with The Rose of Avalanche returning with more gothic intensity in November. The '80s had ended on a high, but little did anyone know that dramatic changes were imminent, come the turbulent '90s. However, before we move to the new decade, here are a few more pearls of wisdom from the JB's faithful, courtesy of the 'JB's Dudley – Back of the Pathfinder Facebook site.

Dave Webb
The Railway Children, later known as Weeping Messerschmitts

JB's was always known as the place to play; the place to aspire to. Locally, it was the height of attainment for the home-grown bands to play a gig there. If you could get a paid JB's gig you had made the required level. Nationally, it had a reputation. Fridays and weekends were the target, but Sam also gave up-and-coming talent a chance to display their ability on midweek nights. Our band, The Railway Children, later known as Weeping Messerschmitts, performed at JB's in 1986, if my memory serves me correctly, and I had my eyes opened when I first stepped through those doors. Setting up early evening on a Friday, the place looked larger than I'd imagined, and when empty, it resembled a social club. Soundcheck done, I hid in the dressing room and strummed the guitar, waiting for our audience to arrive, as countless other bands before me had done, and flicked through the rather large photo album that was kept in there, which featured all the bigger, better bands that had graced the place previously. After a while the noise from the main room started to feed into the dressing room, so as a complete unknown I stepped out, just to have a look, and instantly wished that I hadn't. The first person I saw was a massive bloke, known, as I found out later, as 'Stonewall'. He was talking to the smallest punk-rocker girl I ever saw, who was barely sixteen. I saw blokes in smart suits, complete with shirt and tie; I saw a gang of rockers in black, well-worn leather with their chicks; blokes with just vests on (in December); girls dressed as mods; guys with Mohican hairstyles and no shirts; pretty girls in office attire; old men in the corner having a pint and searching for a box of dominoes; gaggles of girls sitting on the sticky dance floor; lads in small groups just chatting, laughing, and getting slowly pissed. Somewhat worryingly, I saw Hell's Angels patches on the back of sawn-off denim coats, and I saw hippies in flares, all sharing the same room. Then the butterflies began to flutter in my stomach. Why on earth did we accept this gig, I wondered? I went back into the dressing room that I'd thought of as a haven, but there was now a bunch of girls in there using the ridiculously situated payphone,

and this tiny room became evermore populated at the end of the evening when people queued to ring taxis. No mobiles in those days, remember! There was no place to hide. We had the word that we were on after 'Mexican Radio', one of DJ Dermott's regular tracks, and to be fair to him, he played the right kind of music to suit our own style. 'You're on now!' came the shout, and this meant that we had to shove our way through the crowd, packed tight in the passageway, right up to the edge of the stage, with guitars in hand, and no JB's security man to ease us through, nothing! Then I pass the jerk that twists the machine heads on my guitar and completely detunes it, and I laugh with him because I don't want to start a problem (plus, he's bigger than I am). Suddenly, I'm on stage and the apprehension kicks in. No need to worry! They are a very appreciative audience and knowledgeable too. Once you start playing and the first whistles and applause kicks in, you then begin to appreciate why this place was so special.

Barrie Birch

Jimmy the Con was on the door, and nobody messed with Jim. Two guys were fighting outside. The Con clocked them and nonchalantly took a piss against the wall. They stopped scrapping and ran off immediately. They knew Jim would knock 'em shitless when he'd finished relieving himself. Thursday nights were great. Newky Brown drunk from the bottle, with an extra one stuffed down your trousers bought just on 'last orders'. As 'Samba Pa Ti' played, Jim would shout, 'Come on you lot, we've had your money, now fuck off home.' I can never hear that Santana song without it transporting me straight back to JB's. I saw some great bands there. What would we have done without it?

Kath Pearson

I'm sad to say, like a lot of JB's regulars from back in the day, that I have now reached my late forties. However, I was a JB's regular from the age of about seventeen. I remember names such as the Little Angels, Blues 'n' Trouble, Ian the Goat (of Goats Don't Shave), and the E Numbers. I saw Thunder there, but as a massive

Led Zeppelin and Robert Plant fan, there was no better time than a low-key Planty gig. I'm afraid I can't remember the year of this particular one, but I think I would have been approximately twenty-six. Micky Merriman drank in my local, and knowing my love for Planty, he got me some tickets. Frankly, I got so hammered (each bar trip resulted in me commandeering three cans of Red Stripe, one in hand and one in each denim pocket – my trusty JB's tradition to avoid having to fight my way to the bar too often), that I couldn't even tell you what numbers Planty sang, but what I do clearly remember is knowing that when he left the stage to return to the green room, I had to follow him. On a march along the side corridor I went, and reaching the open door to the green room, I saw the terrifying vision that was The Con, stood squarely in the doorway. Fuelled by Red Stripe, my Dutch courage of choice, I put my hand on his substantial chest and pushed past him to get to Planty, who I spoke to, snogged (whether he wanted it or not), and got my 'Electric Magic' T-shirt signed, in that order. I've always thought since that if I had been a bloke he (or maybe Jimmy) would have nutted me! During the following week, Micky came into my local and handed me a Tesco carrier bag, inside which there was a good, close-up photograph of Planty on stage, with the JB's logo clearly behind him, and a Bob Dylan Bootleg Series T-shirt, which Planty had left in the green room. I still have the T-shirt to this day, and occasionally wear it around the house, and I also have the signed T-shirt, which is riffy. One sleeve is entirely covered in a beer stain, but obviously I'll never wash it. It is now framed, in its original filthy state, in my music room.

David Newton
The Mighty Lemon Drops

My first visit to JB's was in 1980. I was a young music fan from Wolverhampton and I had been aware of the club for a while, but I was 15 and still at school. At the time I was compiling a fanzine called S.O.S. with a mate, and had seen in NME that the Mo-Dettes were playing at JB's, but was concerned that I might not get in, being underage, so I wrote to the Mo-Dettes management and asked if they could put me on the guest list to interview the

band. They put me and my mate on the list, we did the interview, saw the show, and even had a couple of sneaky underage pints. That was it – I was hooked. The following week we went back again and from then on most of my Friday and Saturday nights were spent at JB's. In fact, by the mid-80s it would be Tuesday nights too, and even the occasional Sunday lunchtime after the footie team JB's Warriors had played! I had been in and out of bands since my early teenage years. One of my first bands, Active Restraint, played at JB's in 1982. A year or so later I played there again with the Wildflowers. However, it was my next band, The Mighty Lemon Drops, which made an impact. The Mighty Lemon Drops were a direct product of JB's. We met at JB's, watched bands at JB's, drank beer together at JB's, and hatched a plan to form a band together at JB's. We first played there on the 27th of August, 1985, and we would play there many more times during our existence. Even when we got quite popular and were playing larger venues, we would still play the occasional JB's show when we could. It is hard to put your finger on what was so great about the place. I think I liked the diversity of it. At JB's you would get an amazing mix of young punk kids, angular post-punk new-wave types, older ex-hippies, beer drinkers, folkies, bikers – you name it, it didn't matter. It really was the music that mattered. Tuesday nights were always fun. Spacemen 3 playing an amazing set of their hypnotic psychedelia to a pretty bemused Tuesday night crowd in 1986 springs to mind. They are now one of the most revered bands of that genre in the world. One of the greatest gigs I ever saw was an unsigned new band called Blur, in the summer of 1990. Glenn from the Sandkings tipped us off about them. Just brilliant! It was one of those JB's hot summer nights where you would congregate and drink on the patio – oops, I mean car park – just outside the club, to escape the heat and then go back inside to listen when the music started again. Pure magic. That was JB's! As for The Mighty Lemon Drops, we went on to do okay really. Our first independent EP in 1985, 'Like An Angel', stayed in the UK indie charts for over a year, and we signed to Chrysalis Records (UK) and Sire Records (owned by the Warner Music Group, USA) in 1986. Our first two albums, Happy Head (1986) and World Without End (1988), both entered the UK top 40 and were USA modern/alternative rock chart-toppers. Our third album, Laughter, fared even better in the USA, entering the Billboard charts in 1990. After extensive American touring and two further albums. Sound, and Ricochet, we called it a day at the end of 1992. I now live in Burbank, USA with my American wife, Becky.

Si Chadwick

An abiding memory of JB's is being out on a stag night with mates from work, most of whom were suited and booted (I was in regulation jeans and bike leathers). They were all set to go to some poxy nightclub. I told them I was going to JB's to see John Otway, whereupon the bridegroom said he was coming with me. Cue much pissing and moaning from the suits who said 'We can't go there dressed like this!' and I persuaded them that they would be welcomed and no one would take any notice of their attire, and I was proved right – we all had a great time, got a song dedicated to Tony (the bridegroom), and were made to feel at home. The same couldn't have been said if I'd turned up at the nightclub wearing my jeans and leather jacket! The highlight (or lowlight) of the evening was when I leant on the bar of the fire escape door, which duly opened, and I fell backwards through it à la 'Del Boy' Trotter, flat on my back clutching a bottle of Newcastle Brown... Happy daze!

Trevor Turley
Bass player with progressive-rock band, Still

The exit slope out of the club that took you up to King Street was very steep indeed, and a joy to navigate on foot, on a freezing-cold, snowy night, once the club had closed and you'd usually had too much beer. Many a night, we'd get almost to the top, only to slide right back down the hill to the club again, on our stomachs. Wearing Cuban-heeled boots did not help, but thank God for Afghan coats!

Alison Avon Powers Bar staff

Ask Sam about Robert Plant's birthday bash at the club. Rob only drank a certain, specific red wine (can't remember the brand, offhand), and some of the staff had inadvertently served it all to the regular customers. Sam and I had to dash to Tesco

to buy more. On the proposed last night of the King Street club, on New Year's Eve, we ended up with a lot of surplus beer, so we decided to open for another, absolutely final last night to shift it all. The trouble was, the beer disappeared far too quickly, so we were forced to go and buy a lot more, so as not to disappoint the customers! It would have been doubly funny had we then ended up with some left again, but thankfully, this time the punters managed to demolish it!

Dave Webb
Weeping Messerschmitts (the last night of JB's)

On the final night I was at JB's with friends and colleagues. It was a weird evening really – enjoyment and sadness rolled into one: the end of an era. Eventually, when Dermott played the last song, the room was as full as a room could be. The fire doors were open but no one wanted to be outside. The bar was closed but no one was without beer. The lights came on but no one moved. The music eventually stopped but they called for more. Nobody wanted to go home. Dermott obliged with 'Sit Down' by James, so those that could physically do so sat on the sticky, dirty, Velcro-type floor, created by years of spilled beer and other fluids that had matted together to enable inebriated folks to stand up straight, because their shoes were firmly glued to the spot. I saw that the people all around me loved those four walls, and it was beginning to sink in that they were part of a very special closing ceremony. Suddenly, fuelled by drink and a maudlin sentimentality for the old place, tears began to flow, and when Dermott played The Beatles' 'Let It Be', even the most hardened old rockers were choking up. I heard someone next to me say 'the new place can never be this good', and, of course, it wasn't. For some strange reason, on that last night, someone had left an old toolbox at the back of the stage. At the very end of the evening, happily pissed and uninhibited, I had a look to see what was in there, and I saw, amongst other things, a Stanley knife. I took it and quickly cut out a piece of carpet from the front centre of the stage, where every frontman/woman had stood in JB's' history. Five minutes later, I left with my piece of musical memorabilia. So many famous names and talented musicians have trodden on my bit of memorabilia. Including, I very proudly admit, me.

The 1990s

Size is not everything!

"Ch - ch - ch - ch - changes
(Turn and face the strange)
Ch - ch - changes "

David Bowie

Before you knew it, it was 1990, and at JB's, King Street, it was all business as usual, with many of the popular bands being rebooked, but a new band (to JB's at least), folk rockers the Levellers, arrived in February, quickly followed by The Neds yet again (goodness me, didn't those lads have homes to go to?). Mike Sanchez and his Big Town Playboys returned in March, and the ever-popular Steve Marriott followed in April. It was mentioned at the beginning of this book that many new bands became famous after they had played at JB's. It is also true that many famous bands revisited the club on the way back down the ladder. Marriott, for the handful who don't know, had achieved worldwide fame with The Small Faces and Humble Pie. His hits (with The Small Faces) included 'Itchycoo Park', 'All or Nothing', 'Lazy Sunday', 'Sha-La-La-La-

Lee', 'Whatcha Gonna Do About It', and many, many more, and at the risk of spouting clichés, for those of a certain age, these songs truly were the soundtrack of our lives. Virtually everyone can sing something that Steve Marriott wrote, and that in itself is a great compliment. By the time Marriott began visiting JB's, his best days were behind him, creatively speaking, but he was still a great draw. Sadly, time had taken its toll, and Marriott was drinking heavily and was reliant on drugs. His bandmates found him argumentative and difficult, and so did his loved ones. He was due to play at JB's again in April, but after a long and boozy flight home one night, during which, by all accounts, he had been in a foul mood, followed by a drunken last supper at a favourite restaurant, and an evening of bickering with his wife, Toni, he returned to his sixteenth-century cottage alone. At 6.30am, a motorist noticed that the cottage was ablaze and called the fire brigade, who could not rescue him in spite of their best efforts. News of Marriott's death sent shock waves around the club, which had come to regard him as one of its own, and was the talking point amongst the members for many weeks afterwards.

Life goes on, however, and just in time to take people's minds off the doom and gloom of Marriott's parting, along came a band which, until that point, had not actually ever been paid to play! In fact, the gig at JB's earned them their first ever wage packet, and in return, they treated the club to one of the most memorable gigs it had ever experienced. The band was Blur, and it's probably easier to allow bassist Alex James to take over the story. This extract from his excellent autobiography, Bit of a Blur, is by kind permission of Abacus Publishing (an imprint of Little, Brown Book Group).

"We were playing in Dudley, near Birmingham, at a venue called JB's. It was our first out-of-town headline slot. It was dark when we arrived because we'd got lost, as usual. We soundchecked and a friendly guy, who seemed too scruffy and nice to be in charge of anything, gave us a crate of Newcastle Brown Ale and showed us the dressing room. It was one of those ones with scrawling all over the walls and a couple of knackered but comfy sofas. We left the door open and sat in there necking the Newcastle Browns. Miraculously, the place started to fill up. Soon it was heaving. The guy came back with another crate of beer. We took it onstage with us. There was a huge cheer. These people had come to enjoy themselves. So had we.

Of all the shows we've ever played, this was the most memorable. They just got it, the audience, right there and then. They got the whole thing. Over the last few shows, we'd tightened everything up, rubbed off the edges and cut out the boring bits, but this was the first time we brought the house down. The audience invaded the stage. They went crazy, every last one of them. The dressing room was packed afterwards, and more crates of Newcastle Brown kept arriving. Someone said that I was the fastest bass player he'd ever seen. Graham was holding court with a couple of girls. They were gazing at him and laughing at everything he said. People wanted plectrums, people wanted photos, people wanted records signing, and all of a sudden we were giving our first autographs. It all happened in a flash, right there in Dudley. The friendly guy gave Jason a huge wedge of cash. We split it between us. There was ninety quid each, a fortune [interestingly, in the article that follows, Damon Albarn refers to the fee being £50]. Jason drove through the night to Colchester, where we

stayed, at Jason's folks. Colchester's not that far from Cambridge, which was our next gig. We went to bed insensible, and woke up invincible."

A lovely tribute from a lovely man, but who was that scruffy character he mentioned, we wonder? Sam reckons it was probably Big Dave, but this is probably a clever deception on Sam's part – a feeble attempt to blame someone else for his own sartorial shortcomings. It is a mystery that will probably never be solved, unless Alex still has the rubber band that held the wedge of money together. They say that DNA has come on in leaps and bounds since 1991. Hopefully, it can now be used to solve one of the most compelling rock and roll mysteries of all time.

Roy Williams, sound engineer for Seasick Steve and Robert Plant, occasional DJ at JB's, and one of the original committee, was recently in America, and bumped into Damon Albarn. He introduced himself, explaining that he was from JB's, and was greeted by a big, manly hug. It appears that Alex was not the only Blur member with a fondness for the old place. What follows is a small segment from a Black Country Bugle article, reproduced here by kind permission of the newspaper.

"Dudley JB's, that was the start of it,' Damon recalled. 'I think we made about fifty quid each, which was an enormous amount of money as we'd never been paid for a gig previously. But we made that because the way it worked then was, they'd give you a capacity, and if it went over that, then you got a share. And it went way over that. There were so many people in there that by the end, the stage was totally full of people, but the auditorium was still completely packed. I don't quite know how that worked out! I remember it was very hot and sweaty.
There was a buzz about it. For us, having never really played out of Essex and London, it was a magical experience, and that relationship has been maintained."

But that performance in the little building behind the old Pathfinder on King Street was vital to Blur for another reason, Damon said:

"Meeting Stuart Lowbridge and Darren Evans – also known as Smoggy. They're both from Wolverhampton – very much so. They hung about and followed us around a bit, and we just

The magnificent Blur, wondering what they could spend their first-ever pay packet on. Is Alex James' bass spinning around or is it a trick of the light?

A Blur poster from the time. Worryingly, it looks as if they are facing a firing squad. Either that or they're dressed as Ninja turtles.

1990 / 24784
© EMI RECORDS (UK) PHOTOGRAPHER: SIMON FOWLER

BLUR

FOOD

The original Manic Street Preachers line-up with Richey Edwards.

Roy Williams' photograph of Blur's Damon Albarn and Seasick Steve at the Bonnaroo Festival, Manchester, Nashville, USA. Seen here with one of their loyal Wolverhampton-based road crew, we think.

became really close friends. One thing led to another. I come up here from time to time, for weddings, birthdays, christenings. Those two especially, Stuart and Smoggy, are some of my closest friends. "

The Wolverhampton pair soon became part of the upcoming band's crew, and they're still at the centre of operations to this day, whenever Blur take to the road. When Damon looked to be in danger of breaking his neck on the wet stage of the Civic, it was Smoggy, keeping an eye on his old mate's welfare from the pit in front of the stage, who Damon turned to. The pair swapped shoes before the show could go on.

Blur returned to Dudley in 1993, a couple of years after that memorable first appearance, with two albums and a stream of hit singles under their belts. They were all set to entertain the students of Wolverhampton University's Dudley Campus with an open-air concert in the courtyard of Dudley Castle – but things didn't go to plan.

"We were going to play at the zoo," Damon remembered. "And that was quite disappointing. It was really bad that day, it was rained off. There was a deluge and the whole thing collapsed."

Blur were to return to the club two more times, following their inaugural gig. The Levellers, meanwhile, came back three times during 1990. The New Year's Eve slot fell to Hendrix-specialists, The Hamsters.

1991 saw a staple diet of local talent, bands such as the excellent Red Lemons, fronted by the legend that is Big Jim Merris, soul man Curtis Little, The Honey Turtles, Stan Webb, Debbie Bonham, Steve Gibbons, Trevor Burton, and The Mighty Lemon Drops, plus a welcome return for The Hamsters, but in terms of future big names, the highlight of the year was the appearance of a band from South Wales, the Manic Street Preachers, a year before their first album, Generation Terrorists, was released. A few years later, the band was winning every kind of award that existed – best band, best album, best live track, best contemporary song, best live act, best video, and for all we know, best sermon (Preachers, see? I shouldn't really have to spell it out), and best in class at Crufts.

Sadly, many of the old JB's gig sheets are incomplete, and will probably remain that way, but we know that December 1991 saw the arrival of Liverpool lads, Echo and The Bunnymen, who had been in existence since 1978. The band had recorded six albums by the time they hit JB's, and would go on to release six more by 2014. They also released an incredible 31 singles, including 'The Cutter' and 'The Killing Moon'.

The records for 1992 are extremely sparse, but we know that Doctor and the Medics (hit single, a remake of Norman Greenbaum's 'Spirit in the Sky') played at the club in February, along with the Steve Gibbons Band, who'd probably win the award for the most JB's appearances. Steve was a cool character in his early days, and he's every bit as cool today at the age of seventy-three. His first major band was The Uglys, followed by Balls, with Trevor Burton from The Move and Denny Laine from The Moody Blues. This was followed by Brummie band, Idle Race, which morphed into the Steve Gibbons Band. Ten albums and a lot of touring followed, with Gibbons releasing the hit single 'Tulane', which saw his ruggedly handsome, Terence-Stamp-like features beamed into our living rooms, courtesy of Top of the Pops.

Damon Albarn getting to grips with the Black Country dialect, 'ay 'ee.

Thankfully, the club's records for 1993 are slightly more complete, and show that JB's had not lost its knack of attracting big acts of the future. Radiohead came, saw, and conquered in January, but no one could have expected them to end up selling some 30 million albums. When they arrived in Dudley, they had just released their first album, Pablo Honey, but it was their third release, OK Computer, that saw them described as one of the best bands of their generation, with the album being called one of the most important of the decade.

In March, veteran Welsh rockers, Man, treated JB's to their unique mix of West-Coast psychedelia and progressive rock (that's West Coast, USA, not the west coast of Wales, by the way). Intriguingly, the rest of the year's details have been lost, except for three dates – two for an American band, Freak of Nature, a hard-rock outfit, and one for another American band, Sick Of It All, a hard-core punk band from the Queens district of New York. All of this sounds very much like business as usual, but things were about to change drastically at JB's.

☞ The Honey Turtles come out of their shells.

☞ Radiohead.

Lev
ell
ers

☞ An old Levellers poster from Sam's collection.

Ballyhoo
the best of
Echo & The Bunnymen

The Charlatans' flyer from the JB's era.
☞

the charlatans uk

© Anton Corbijn

severnclassics.com

'The unique 'Big' Jim Merris.
☞

Dudley Castle, built by Ansculf de Picquigny circa 1070, and below, the drawbridge and gateway of JB's, Castle Hill, built by Duke Sam of Coneygre, circa 1994.

The Castle Hill Years

"Daddy's takin' us to the zoo tomorrow
Zoo tomorrow, zoo tomorrow
Daddy's takin' us to the zoo tomorrow
And we can stay all day!
We're goin' to the zoo, zoo, zoo
How about you, you, you?
You can come too, too, too
We're goin' to the zoo, zoo, zoo"

Tom Paxton

Percy Hill, who owned Pathfinder, had passed the reins to his son, Dave, and one of the things he was responsible for was the collection of rent. Not only was he keen on collecting it, he also wanted to increase it. This now meant that it would have been a better bet to buy a property and pay a mortgage than to cough up rent money – which in effect was like throwing money down the nearest drain. For the first time in the club's lifetime, Sam and Co. began to seriously consider this option. The fact that the club had outgrown the King Street premises only helped to make their minds up. They had blossomed from a makeshift youth club discotheque into a venue that was attracting the cream of Britain's bands, and

often, when a bigger band appeared there, far more customers turned up than could be accommodated, and it made no sense whatsoever – financially speaking or from a goodwill standpoint – to turn them away. A rep who provided drinking glasses for the club had heard on the grapevine about a large nightclub venue that was about to come onto the market, and duly told Sam about it. Whilst searching around for a building to replace the football club, back in 1971, Sam had viewed an old disused church in Dudley, but at the time, had deemed it too large. In hindsight, he felt that it would have been a better venue than the Pathfinder address. Cromwell's, which was situated on Castle Hill, just down from the zoo and the Hippodrome Theatre (which by then had been closed down), could hold 800 or more customers in its main hall, as could the old church he had once viewed, but it also boasted a smaller room, which would be ideal for lesser-known bands, or perhaps discos. Upstairs was another huge room, should there be a need for it at any stage, and there was also a kitchen. The building was for sale at around £220,000, meaning that a mortgage would be, if anything, slightly cheaper than the rent they were currently paying to Percy and his son, back in King

The Hippodrome, an Art Deco theatre where the likes of Laurel and Hardy once performed. Should it stay or should it go?

The old Cromwell's nightclub, before Bryant and team moved in to begin the renovations.

Street. Cromwell's was elaborately fitted out, because it had been a nightclub where the clientele were expected to wear fairly smart attire, unlike JB's, where a Nirvana T-shirt and a pair of Levis, usually with a subtle hint of arse cleavage between the two (for both the males and females), was de rigueur. There were Tiffany lamps, polished wood, and enough brass to sink a ship, so firstly the place needed a bit of a facelift, only this was comparable to a beautiful, elegant woman asking the surgeon to make her look a bit rougher. The ceiling of the venue was a distinctive feature, being constructed from wood that was held up by wooden trusses. In fact, this structure, a Belfast Truss Roof, as it was known, was one of only a handful in the country. There was also a solid-wood floor, which made a nice change from the filthy, disease-ridden Velcro-like carpet that was usually found in seedier nightclubs, rock music venues and similar establishments.

Johnny Bryant, who is actually a very skilled pattern-maker and carpenter, was asked to renovate and oil the floor, and a stage was constructed that would suit the larger bands who were earmarked to appear at the place once the work was finished. The upstairs room was also renovated, and sublet to Leo's Fitness Academy, which ran judo classes and a gymnasium. Everything in the garden looked rosy, but sadly, Sam had chosen the worst possible time to set up a larger venue – not that he could have had an inkling at the time. The opening party got them off to a great start, but some had mixed feelings about the inaugural band being a tribute act. Having helped some of the biggest names in the music world on their ladder to fame and fortune, alas, things were changing. The supergroups were now playing massive concert venues that held many thousands of people, and suddenly, in the smaller halls such as Sam's, there was a void beginning to form that no one seemed to be filling, or at least, no one that had enough clout to entice an adequate number of punters to fill a large room by venturing out on a cold, rainy night. Instead of a new wave of talent arriving, musicians suddenly got lazy and decided to imitate the supergroups that were now charging megabucks to appear in huge cattle sheds, often so far away from the audience that they needed binoculars to see the bands. Tribute bands such as The Bootlegs Beatles, The Counterfeit Stones, and any one of a hundred Abba outfits, were becoming big enough draws in their own right to satisfy the concert-going public's needs in venues

the size of the new JB's, and at a fraction of the cost. Suddenly, they were all at it. Any pop star or band that had experienced even 15 minutes of fame, from Pink Floyd to The Sweet, now had a tribute band in tow, complete with a corny, pun-based name, sucking the lifeblood out of the real bands like leeches. It was almost as if they were intent on creating a musical parallel universe. Those who were present at The Robin rock club, near Merry Hill shopping centre (before the developers slapped an eviction notice on it, and then proceeded to do absolutely nothing with the land for years), on the night that the excellent China Crisis played there, may remember the band's acerbic comments, vis-à-vis tribute acts. Gary Daly, one of the two frontmen, told the audience that he had arrived at the club and been met by a corridor full of posters advertising a plethora of tribute bands, and had spotted the China Crisis poster in amongst them.

'For a minute, I thought we were just a China Crisis tribute act,' he confided to his audience, 'but then I realized we were the real fucking thing!'

The first band to play at JB's, Castle Hill, was Ballroom Glitz, a Sweet and 70's music tribute (isn't one Sweet more than enough, we ask?). Even so, Sam recalls that the place was full to its lovely Belfast rafters, with many more punters stuck outside. This was both gratifying and worrying. It did cross Sam's mind at that point, that even his brand-new venue wasn't quite big enough. He need not have fretted. The overcrowding was caused by the opening of a new club, rather than by Dudley's obsession with glam rock. Ballroom Glitz, incidentally, were paid £150 for their efforts, with the strangely named band Man Bone Envy getting a mere £50 the following day. October was a good month, thanks to Bruce Dickinson, airline pilot and ex-vocalist with Iron Maiden, followed by Shed Seven and Coventry ska band The Selecter, featuring Pauline Black.

November was also promising, with Nazareth (who were riding high with a cover of Joni Mitchell's 'This Flight Tonight'), Harlan the Jester, the Alex Harvey Band (or should we say The Sensational Alex Harvey Band, featuring guitarist, Zal Cleminson, who was that funny, Pierrot clown-type creature that stood to the right of Harvey), and finally, those Hendrix-loving Hamsters. The year finished well enough, with more original bands, including the Wildflowers and Corrosion

The youth of Dudley seem to be enjoying their nights at the castle.

A panoramic view of the Dudley Castle concert.

Terrorvision's Mark Yates.

Terrorvision's Tony Wright.

Jonn Penney, of Ned's Atomic Dustbin.

Miles Hunt shows off his new short haircut.

Dumpy keeps his rusty nuts in a fetching pair of Y fronts.

The Steve Gibbons Band's Bob Wilson.

The DTs, featuring Simon 'Honeyboy' Hickling.

Dave Carroll of The Steve Gibbons band in the shirt he made from his mom's old curtains.

Buster Bloodvessel shows the ladies why he's so popular.

Dr Howard Williamson, back in the day, with his trusty Olympus. A professor with dreadlocks? What's the world coming to?

Spike, of the Quireboys, in the Jack Sparrow fancy dress outfit his mom got him for Christmas.

Sam gets a cuddle from Lydia the Encyclopaedia, sorry, no, it's Beth!

Hannah, of Winter Storm.

of Conformity (catchy name) from the USA.

1995 continued in the same vein, with a repeat appearance by Dickinson, then Tyketto (another hard-rock ensemble from New York), Shihad, all the way from lovely New Zealand, The Hamsters, again, Bad Manners (featuring the large-tongued pretty boy, Buster Bloodvessel), Doctor and the Medics, and then – a tribute band that seems to have become a major act in its own right, The Australian Pink Floyd. The Selecter returned, but then it was straight back to the tribute boys, with the LA Doors, One Step Behind, and The Paul Weller Experience. It didn't end there. Limehouse Lizzy played the new JB's on the 2nd of December, which must have been quite a strange evening for the older members who remembered when the real Thin Lizzy took to the stage, back in the '70s. This seemed to open the tribute flood gates, with Bi Jovi, AB/CD, Fred Zeppelin, Jean Genie, and Beatlemania following in quick succession. All very frustrating for a club that prided itself on breaking exciting new acts and watching them flourish into major recording bands, with cabinets crammed with music awards and walls full of platinum discs. Nor were these imitators particularly cheap. The old receipt books reveal that Jean Genie, for example, cost Sam £1,000 in 1995, and One Step Behind, the Madness tribute, charged £1,100. Poor old Debbie Bonham, meanwhile, was only given £250, and she has a famous dad, for goodness' sake!

From then on, the tributes began to outnumber the original acts by five to one, and it is amusing to try to guess, just by their names, who they thought they were – Radar Love, Stratus Quo, Gary Gutter (surely not!), T.Rexstasy, Wonderwall, Maet Loaf, Free's Co, Free at Last, The Other Beatles, Stoned Again, Fred Zeppelin, Voulez Vous... The list goes on forever. It is refreshing to still be able to find the odd worthwhile original band amongst the gig lists for Castle Hill, but searching for them becomes more and more of a chore, like sieving through tons of mud to find a minute nugget of gold. 1996 nuggets included Tyketto, Shed Seven, and The Hamsters, with local quality provided by the excellent Stubble Brothers (starring that man Johnny Bryant, Paul Smith, Chris Jones, Colin Edmonds, and Rob Newall), a band boasting three exceptional singers, with a sound that was reminiscent of Crosby, Stills & Nash. Finally, Groundswell, featuring Jonn Penney and Gareth Pring, ex-members of The Neds, made their inaugural

appearance in December.

Before the local tribute bands hold a protest in Dudley High Street and start burning copies of this book, I must explain that their skills and expertise, not to mention their crowd-pleasing abilities, are not in question. I have the utmost respect for them in that regard (for example, John Mainwaring, frontman of Jean Genie, is uncannily similar to David Bowie, vocally), but one has to ask, where will it all end? For a start, pretending to be someone else is really rather creepy when you think about it. Elvis impersonators, take note. I also understand the idea of giving audiences a facsimile of their heroes to satisfy their cravings, especially if the artiste in question is deceased, which somewhat limits their live performances, or maybe if the ticket prices for a big-name band have become eye-wateringly expensive (The Rolling Stones spring to mind). The need to earn a living is another good excuse for dusting off the wigs and glittery jackets. However, quite soon, there will be no original acts left, and we will end up with a situation where The Australian Pink Floyd has its own tribute band, The Bilston Australian Pink Floyd, or maybe there could be a band called The Bootleg Bootleg Beatles. Before you know it, music will disappear up its own back passage, and then where will we be?

Thank goodness, then, for Enuff Z'Nuff from Illinois in November, and last but not least, Roger Chapman's Streetwalkers, who arrived in December. During 1997, it was also nice to see The Selecter again, old rockers Uriah Heep, UK Subs, and Dr. Feelgood, even though one might question why a tribute to Paul Weller got paid almost as much as Wilko Johnson and his boys (£1,000 to be precise). Sorry, I'll lay off the tribute acts now, I promise! At least they were easy to please, from Sam's point of view. They breezed in, set up, soundchecked, played, and breezed out, whereas the big names tended to bed in for the whole day, fiddling with this and that, and demanding evermore prima-donna-like riders in their contracts, on top of their sizeable fees. 'Johnny Guitar' must have 20 bottles of Jack Daniel's, 30 clean towels (not pink), 3 proper meals (no junk food or sandwiches with crisps), and the stage must be at least two and a half miles wide and have a Persian rug for the drummer, preferably from Persia, not Lee Longlands on Broad Street.

Club member, Gary Garfield, recalls seeing a gig

Sam proves he's still king of clubs

John Ogden meets Colin 'Sam' Jukes

COLIN Jukes was just 14 when his name first appeared in our columns, and it's popped up regularly ever since, so why everyone calls him Sam is a mystery – even to him.

The boss of what is surely Britain's longest-lived rock club – JB's, in Dudley – knows who to blame, though: his lifelong pal Sid Weston, who helped Sam through a cataclysmic life-change when his double-life, as a footballer and speedway rider, came to an agonising end at Cradley Heath.

"You expect injuries in both sports, but I got mine all in one go," says Sam, a sturdy champion of live rock music, and one of the West Midlands' most popular characters.

"I shattered my knee and broke my femur in three places, so that stopped the football and the speedway. When it comes to an abrupt end like that you feel your life's ended, but then you concentrate on getting back to physical soundness as best you can, and having a lot of mates who were into the music scene was a help."

His old school pal Sid, then in a rock band called Buzz Kane and The Citizens, suggested that he and Sam start up a disco,

Cheers – Colin 'Sam' Jukes and John Ogden take a break at the Dudley club

kick a ball as hard as he did in my whole life."

But Sam wasn't happy. "I stayed there a couple of years, but I got disillusioned

His rock and roll pals helped him recuperate, and soon he, Sid and JB were touring the colleges with their disco. Fed up

Ah, so that's where he got his nickname from! Sam interviewed by the Express and Star's John Ogden, who also played bongos with Little Acre and Trapeze, back in the day!

JB's 40th birthday party Seasick Steve poster.

Seasick Steve, flanked by John and Sid Weston, the only identical twins in England that don't look like each other.

by The Damned in 1997 – the 24th of March to be exact.

'Punks who had arrived from London didn't have the entrance money and were begging for pennies to get in. All night long, people were coming up and saying, "give us a swig of your beer, chief", because they were so broke. Then Captain Sensible came on and said: "Every one of you wankers has paid £7 to get in, so shut up and listen to us play." He must have had 50 beer cans bounce off him in 5 seconds flat – and he loved it!'

Here, another club member, Iain Black, recalls another memorable night from that period.

"I was working for a company that had an office in West Bromwich, and I was able to arrange a meeting there so that I could catch the Enuff Z'Nuff gig that night at Castle Hill. It was one of the first shows with the new line-up, featuring original members Donnie Vie (vocals, guitar) and Chip Z'Nuff (bass, vocals), and newer members Ricky Parent on drums and guitarist Johnny Monaco. I also hoped to hang out with the band afterwards, so I made a point of booking a room at the Station Hotel opposite, which was significant to me as Laurel and Hardy had stayed there during one of their famous UK tours! The romance was not to last when I checked in and was told to park my car under a security light if I didn't want it stolen, and then found an empty vodka bottle under my bed. The memorable thing about the gig was that for an extra £5 you could get a ticket to the band's after-show acoustic set. I was really here – drinking in this amazing venue with its wooden rafters in the main hall, and what looked to be another club area at the back, as well as the basement. When the band came on, Donnie was wearing a multicoloured jacket and there was a bit of drama when someone threw a drink in his face during the opening song. Still not sure what went on there, but he graciously laughed it off and they rocked out to a pretty full hall. I remember Donnie's quip about the great reaction the band had from the audience: "We must play Dudley More!" (A pun on the diminutive comedian and Hollywood comedy actor, of course.) 'It was a great show, with Alex Kane of AntiProduct joining Enuff Z'Nuff for the encore. It was also wonderful to witness the guys knocking out Beatles covers and some of their own ballads in the after-show acoustic set. I managed to catch Ricky and Johnny in the bar afterwards for a photo that reminds me of the show to this day. They've returned to the UK many times since with many different line-ups, but this was one of their best ever headlining shows. Thank you JB's!"

The 1998 gig list is, again, sporadic, but records show that Hugh Cornwell was invited back after his earlier debacle with The Stranglers. The Selecter, who seemed to be there every ten minutes, came in August, and The Quireboys, a hard-rock outfit that had been favourably compared to The Faces, arrived late September. November welcomed Jimmy Pursey with Sham 69. The band, formed back in 1976 in Hersham, has recorded 12 albums and 18 singles, including 'Hersham Boys', 'If the Kids are United', and 'Hurry up Harry'. Such was the draw of the West Midlands, Pursey even relocated from London to Stourbridge, probably so that he could get to JB's on the bus. Records for 1999, alas, are completely lost, but 2000 – the millennium year and also JB's 30th birthday – shows a very full itinerary, albeit dominated by the tribute acts. A band that stood out was Hogan's Heroes, with the guitar virtuoso Albert Lee. Lee, who moved to Los Angeles in 1974, has played with members of Deep Purple, Emmylou Harris, Eric Clapton, The Everly Brothers, and many more. He has also won many awards, including Guitar Player magazine's 'Best Country Guitarist'. Lee is highly rated by his peers and thought of as 'the guitarist's guitarist', though surprisingly, his career never reached the heights that some thought it might. Maybe this is because, as Clapton and Jimmy Page put it, the man has no ego whatsoever. Lee also appeared regularly with Bill Wyman's Rhythm Kings, alongside local hero, Mike Sanchez.

In April, Miles Hunt of The Wonder Stuff, played a solo gig, followed closely by Danny Vaughn, ex-member of Tyketto, the American hard-rockers. Blaze Bayley – ex-vocalist of heavy-rock outfits Wolfsbane and Iron Maiden – followed hot on his heels, which probably explained why most of the youth of Dudley were stone deaf following the summer of 2000.

In July, Sam decided to arrange a spectacular

Mick Taylor, who used to be lead guitarist with that little-known outfit, The Rolling Stones.

A nameless Castle Hill customer succumbs to the power of Newcastle Brown.

Keith 'Frogman' Curtis of the Soul Survivors.

THE SELECTER

A Selecter flyer. Pauline Black and the band were regular visitors, especially to Castle Hill.

10cc - albeit a few cubic centilitres short of their original load!

event to celebrate the club's birthday. He entered into talks with Peter Suddock, the chief executive of Dudley's Zoological Gardens, with a view to staging an outdoor concert in the castle grounds. Sam was convinced that the venue could be used regularly, and would help put Dudley, and of course JB's, on the map, musically speaking. An agreement was hammered out, which resulted in a great weekend of live music. The first of the two days would feature the Steve Gibbons Band, Curtis Little and the Receivers, The DTs (short for 'delirium tremens', the medical term for the effects of acute alcohol withdrawal. but known to their close friends as 'The Dog Turds'), and Dumpy's Rusty Nuts. The second-day headliners were Terrorvision, Miles Hunt, Ned's Atomic Dustbin, and Balaam and the Angel.

Terrorvision had also played at JB's just before the zoo and castle event, and they probably won't forget that particular evening in a hurry. Try to imagine, if you will, a heaving mass of pogoing punters enjoying themselves. Then, around halfway through the band's performance, imagine Johnny Bryant's beautifully renovated and oiled dance floor suddenly collapsing under the strain with an almighty, sickening crack, and dispatching around 30 audience members into the abyss. It was lucky that no one was killed or seriously injured, as the cavity between the floor and the ceiling below was around five feet deep. It would have been far better, from a comedian's perspective at least, if Terrorvision had disappeared instead, because then we could have used the classic line, 'It's just a stage they were going through!'

The following day, emergency repairs were carried out, as a touring band was due on stage that evening. Sam, meanwhile, was so embarrassed that he had let down 30 members of his audience in such a manner, he wanted the floor to open up beneath him.

The open-air concert was a huge success. The music was good, the weather behaved itself (as did the audience), and Dudley had found itself a top-class venue for future events. The only problem was, the chief executive wasn't the least bit interested in doing it again, a decision that saw Sam deeply frustrated. To this day, he cannot understand why the council and Mr Suddock were so unenthusiastic about holding more events there. Instead of welcoming a music club that now had a national reputation for bringing top-class

acts to Dudley, they seemed – to Sam's way of thinking at least – to be placing obstacles in his way rather than encouraging a potential new partnership, because they didn't really want him there. To add insult to injury, the zoo and castle venue had cost Sam around £5,000 to hire, which he'd agreed to in the belief that the event would hopefully be the first of many. In the zoo management's defence, they argued that the foot and mouth disease outbreak prevented them staging another event. Interestingly, they didn't ban everyday visitors to the castle, just rock bands, who some animal experts strongly believe are carriers of the disease.

It was mooted at around that time that the zoo and castle should join up with the Black Country Museum, to create one giant tourist attraction that stretched from Castle Hill to the museum site in Tipton Road. The plan was to have a central car park, with access to both attractions made possible with a single entrance fee. This meant that the properties situated between the two sites were, shall we say, inconvenient. The historic Hippodrome was one of them, and, of course, JB's was another. Certain factions were all for demolishing the Hippodrome, whilst others vehemently opposed it and demanded that it be renovated and reopened. The comparison to the fate of The Robin rock club on Pedmore Road, Quarry Bank, and its relationship with the Merry Hill developers suddenly became blindingly obvious. The council, for all we know, may well have finally come to realize that having a renowned music venue was good for the town, but the fact remained, it was inconveniently situated. It just seems a shame that no one bothered to tell Sam before he spent all of his hard-earned savings on it. Sam was also upset about the car-park deal that had been struck with the zoo. He had to rent space from them, which cost him a considerable amount of money, only to find that the zoo had installed pay-and-display meters. This meant that his customers were feeding the meters, the proceeds of which benefitted the zoo, when he had been led to believe that he was handing over money in order that they could park free of charge.

All this left a nasty taste, but the club soldiered on regardless. Again, the gig lists for 2001 and 2002 are missing, but the list for 2003 showed positive signs of improvement, in terms of the quality of acts. All of a sudden, the tributes had receded, and instead there was a healthy percentage of original bands on

Buddies Glenn Hughes and Tony Iommi take advantage of the 'Buy One Get One Free' sunglasses offer at Specsavers, Merry Hill.

Roy Williams makes a good point, for once.

Sam at Castle Hill. Worryingly, this wasn't a fancy dress night. He just liked to wear gorgeous glittery grass skirts (try saying that when you've had a few!).

Fan, Iain Black, schmoozes with his heroes, Illinois rockers Enuff Z'Enuff.

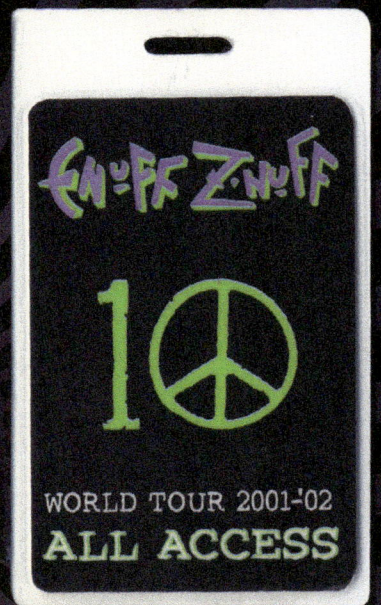

offer again, including Debbie Bonham, Pretty Boy Floyd, a glam-metal band (these music categories are getting dafter!), the Levellers, The Soul Survivors, Faster Pussycat (more glam metal – whatever that is when it's at home), Curtis Little, The Beat, Steve Gibbons, Laika Dog, Glenn Hughes (of Trapeze and Deep Purple), the Heavy Metal Kids (with Gary Holton, the young, cocky cockney one with blue streaks in his hair, from Auf Wiedersehen, Pet), the Mick Taylor Band (Taylor being an ex-member of The Rolling Stones, no less!), Shed Seven, and Blaze Bayley.

2004 continued in this promising vein with Curtis Little again, Bad Manners, LA Guns, The Hamsters, and the Michael Schenker Group (Schenker being the ex-lead guitarist of UFO and ex-member of the Scorpions). It seems, on the evidence of the gig lists, that tribute bands had taken a back seat and in their stead were the heavier rock bands, though Sam was still catering for other musical tastes too. The Levellers returned, followed by Glenn Hughes, so the new, larger venue seemed to be paying off in terms of the size of act it could now book. While all seemed well on the music front, there were still problems with the day-to-day running of the club. It still rankles with Sid that the police at that time seemed to adopt a policy of deliberate provocation and bloody-mindedness, and so did Dudley Council. For example, there was a raid on the club during the Glenn Hughes gig mentioned above. This resulted in total chaos, when the police insisted that the room was emptied, because, in their opinion, members of the door staff were not badged properly. Sam refused to act on this, and was duly charged, only for the judge to throw the case out of court, adding that the police should apologize and pay compensation. Sam is still waiting for that to happen.

On another occasion, a young lady, who was drunk (what, a drunken young lady in Dudley?), walked out of the club in an attempt to flag down a taxi, fell over in a heap and snapped the heel of her shoe. As a result, Sam was taken to court, with the council arguing that he should have spotted that she was non compos mentis and allowed her to use his phone to call a cab. Sam argued that if the shoe was on the other foot, so to speak, and he had been similarly tanked up at Dudley Leisure Centre and had demanded to use their private telephone, he'd probably have been told to go away and annoy someone else. Again, the case was laughed out of court. Sam may well have won the day

yet again, but none of this helped with his burgeoning persecution complex.

2004 continued strongly, with Girlschool, Bev Bevan (of The Move, ELO, and Black Sabbath), and – wait for it – 10cc, admittedly not featuring Lol Creme and Kevin Godley by that point, but undoubtedly a huge band in terms of its many hits, and quite a coup for Sam. The year also finished well with the return of Blaze Bayley, Budgie, EdGuy, and Tyketto.

2005 was another splendid year, band-wise at least, with Hughes returning yet again, Nazareth, Enuff Z'Nuff, Rage Against The Machine, UK Subs, and just when you think it couldn't get better, The Jam, Foo Fighters, Diamond Head, and Y&T. Castle Hill was getting pretty heavy and the lions and tigers were beginning to wear earplugs.

2006 was the year that the founder committee member, Sid (remember him?), retired from his job. After getting a few things out of his system – driving all the way from Chicago to LA on the classic Route 66 trip for starters (amusingly, he arrived at the end of his marathon journey, parked the car, and turned the radio on in time to hear JB's regular, Steve Winwood, sing 'So Glad We Made It', bang on cue!) – he decided to visit JB's once more. He and Sam had grown up on the same street, and been best mates since they were 11 years old, so it was nice to have the time on his hands once again to drop by and socialize occasionally. He was a little concerned that his old mate was not so much burning the candle at both ends as just throwing the thing into the fire. Sam had never been a good delegator. He was a workaholic and liked to be 'hands-on', and this meant being first there and last to leave. For the benefit of those who are not familiar with rock clubs, that can mean lunchtime till 4 or 5am. This was a workload that would kill a youngster, let alone a middle-aged man. A bigger club sounds great, but with that comes bigger bills, more staff, and a constant need to attract bigger audiences to fill the place. It was really a time to be slowing down, but that wasn't in Sam's nature.

The Wonder Stuff returned in 2006, and it is interesting to see how bands' fees had rocketed since those early days, when the club could secure the likes of the Average White Band for £75 plus VAT, a crate of Newcastle Brown, and fish and chips. Now, top-name acts like The Wonder Stuff had proper

American rocker, Jeff Scott Soto, formerly the vocalist with Talisman.

Gilby Clark, formerly the rhythm guitarist with Guns n' Roses, discovers the delights of Dudley.

JB's Castle Hill was used as a backdrop for the plush Laney Amplification catalogue.

DANIELZ
T·REXTASY

T-Rextasy, one of the many tribute bands to play at the Castle Hill venue.

management agencies, and their agency was asking for £5,000, which meant that Sam had to sell a hell of a lot of tickets to get his money back. Quite often, a band's fee could not be met by ticket sales alone. The bar takings obviously helped, but if they weren't sufficient, the club made a loss and hoped to redress the balance with other nights in the near future. Not the ideal way to run a business, but what could be done? Sam recalls the night that the American band Wheatus played at the Castle Hill site, with the horror of it all still etched on his face. The band had been very successful with their singles 'Teenage Dirtbag' and 'A Little Respect' (the old Erasure cover), reaching number 2 and 3 respectively in the UK charts. It had been a considerable coup to get them to Dudley, only for the band to be greeted by a club that was almost empty. Apparently, the club members had wrongly presumed they were a tribute band, and not the real thing, and had subsequently stayed at home to watch TV instead. This little misunderstanding might seem quite funny in hindsight, had it not cost Sam a cool £7,000.

The nature of booking bands was also changing. In the olden days, bands were very much in control of their own destinies. The Boomtown Rats, for example, were riding high with a number 1 single when they arrived at King Street. They could easily have reneged on their deal with Sam and backed out, choosing instead a far more prestige concert hall that was offering far more money. To their credit, they honoured their commitment, just as The Beatles did, when they played the Plaza Ballroom in Old Hill in the very early '60s. The Beatles went down well (there's a surprise) and were booked again for the following year, by which time, all hell broke loose and the lovable moptops were world superstars. No matter. They returned to the Plaza, because it was the right thing to do. (I still remember an entry in my little diary at that time – when I was ten years old – that read: The Beatles are playing just up the road from my house tonight, but mom and dad won't let me go because of the Teddy boys.)

In the Castle Hill era, however, bands were ruled by management agencies and more or less did what they were told. If another club was offering, say, £200 more than JB's was, the band went there instead. There was little loyalty shown, which was quite immoral in many ways, when one considers how Sam and Co. had nurtured generations of bands over the years that had

gone on to become millionaires. Thankfully, acts like The Wonder Stuff, The Neds, and other home-grown talent, remained faithful.

2007 was a strong year in terms of quality bands, such as LA Guns, Steve Winwood, Danny Vaughn, the Happy Mondays, and Big Country, but the highlight of the year was a special birthday party. We'll let Roy Williams take over the story.

Roy Williams reaches sixty. Who'd have thunk it?

An abiding memory for me was my 60th birthday party at the Castle Hill site, on the 14th February 2007. Around that time I was working as front-of-house sound engineer for Robert Plant. Robert had reformed The Honey Drippers for a local charity gig (the charity being The Proton Effect, which raises funds to help and support cancer sufferers and their friends and families) at Kidderminster Town Hall on December 2006. During a conversation Robert asked me what I had planned for my 60th. I told him that I'd probably go to JB's and get pissed with my mates, seeing as I'd spent half of my life at one JB's club or another. He suggested that he'd play at my party if possible, so I contacted Sam, and we sorted out a date. The deal was, all the bar takings went to JB's, and the door takings and ticket sales went to The Proton Effect charity. I talked the Big Town Playboys into reforming for the evening – largely because I'd left JB's to work on the road with them for ten years. A couple of days before the gig, I had a call from Ralph Baker, who managed Jeff Beck at the time. He said that Jeff would be coming along to the party, and had been rehearsing a few numbers with bassist Ian Jennings from the Playboys, as well as Jimmy Copley, who had previously played at JB's with Upp. Jeff had been known to change his mind, so I thought it best not to mention this to anyone. I told Ralph that Jeff was more than welcome to join in, and we'd play things by ear on the day. Jeff did turn up, deciding to play in-between the Playboys and The Honey Drippers. The place was sold out, and not many folks had known that Beck was going to be there. Ricky Cool, who was also acting as compère for the evening, announced that Jeff Beck and his band would be playing a few numbers for them. The audience stood there *in a state of shock, and it took them a song or two to fully realize what was happening. I loved that element of surprise; it was a wonderful birthday present! Incredibly, £15 tickets were changing hands for £100 on eBay, as word got round. An incredible £4,950 was raised that night. However, the evening was also tinged with sadness, as Richard Willis, a JB's sound engineer, had passed away only a few days before the gig.*

The following year welcomed Nazareth, The Wonder Stuff, Budgie, Bad Company (unfortunately minus frontman Paul Rodgers, which is a bit like ordering an omelette without the eggs), and The Damned, in a period that, again, saw a far better ratio of original acts versus tribute bands. Paul Gilbert, ex-member of Mr. Big and a superbly talented guitarist, arrived in November, followed by prog-rock favourites, Marillion. Spencer Davis made a welcome return to the club in November, accompanied by The Animals. Where else could you get both of them on the same night, we ask! EdGuy, a power-metal band from Germany (here we go with the silly music categories again), opened 2009, with Lordi from Finland, another heavy-rock outfit, hot on their tail. JB's was now extending its tentacles to all corners of the USA and Europe in search of bands, and boy, some of them were loud. The Dan Reed Network, a funk-rock band from Portland, Oregon, strutted its funky stuff on the 2nd of May, and Black Stone Cherry, another American hard-rock combo, shook the walls in June. Club favourites, The Wonder Stuff and The Damned, made their yearly commitment to the Dudley scene, and in August, Terry Reid, the man who gave away two of the choicest jobs in rock music to mates of his, played his inaugural gig at Castle Hill.

Before you knew it, it was JB's 40th anniversary party, featuring Seasick Steve. Roy Williams, who was working with Seasick Steve at the time, had told Steve about the club and its history, and asked him if he fancied the idea of playing at JB's for the anniversary. After talking it through with Sam, Roy also contacted the other artistes – Ian Parker, Scott Matthews, and Lisa Mills – to arrange putting a night together. Everyone played for expenses only, and the door profit once again went to The Proton Effect charity, with JB's keeping the bar takings. This time, £9,241 was raised on the night.

Most will be familiar with old Seasick, but maybe not the other three artistes mentioned. Scott is a guitarist, Ian, a folksy songwriter, and Lisa, a fairly gorgeous country-style singer-songwriter. As to Seasick himself, by all accounts he was – and still is – a lovely-natured, self-effacing chap. He left home at 16, having been on the wrong end of some nasty beatings by his stepfather. He then rode the trains across the USA, often sleeping rough at wherever he ended up. When he became famous, his life changed dramatically, as one would expect, but fundamentally, he hasn't changed at all. He told JB's staff that he was used to huge limousines picking him up from hotels and taking him to his shows, in halls so large he couldn't see the audience without binoculars. After a show, he was whisked straight back to his hotel, and he never got to see much of anything, or talk to many people. Playing at JB's was heaven for him, with its homespun attitude, the comparatively small room, and the fans he could spend time with at the bar afterwards. He explained to them that he had negotiated his latest record deal so that he didn't take as big a percentage as usual, but in return he wanted the record company to buy him a nice new John Deere tractor! When Sid mentioned that he and his wife had visited Memphis whilst on holiday, Seasick Steve asked if they'd treated themselves to staying at The Peabody hotel, which is apparently the nicest one in town. When Sid said they had, Steve informed them that he'd never stayed there himself, but in the olden days he'd slept in the doorway a few times!

Gotthard was an extremely good band (filling stadia elsewhere in Europe), who arrived by Swissair in November (are the Swiss allowed to have rock bands, incidentally?), and shortly afterwards came Y&T for a return visit. Sonata Artica, a Finnish power-metal band, was the next big name to turn up in the capital of the Black Country. Apparently, they had eager fans snaking right back up Castle Hill as they waited for tickets; all very exotic for Dudley! One of the highlights of 2010 was a visit by American guitarist Kip Winger, who was with Alice Cooper before branching out on his own as a guitarist and singer with Winger (if you will excuse the unintentional rhyme).

Then, just as it looked as if things were levelling out a little, fate crept up behind Sam and whacked him on the back of the head with a cosh.

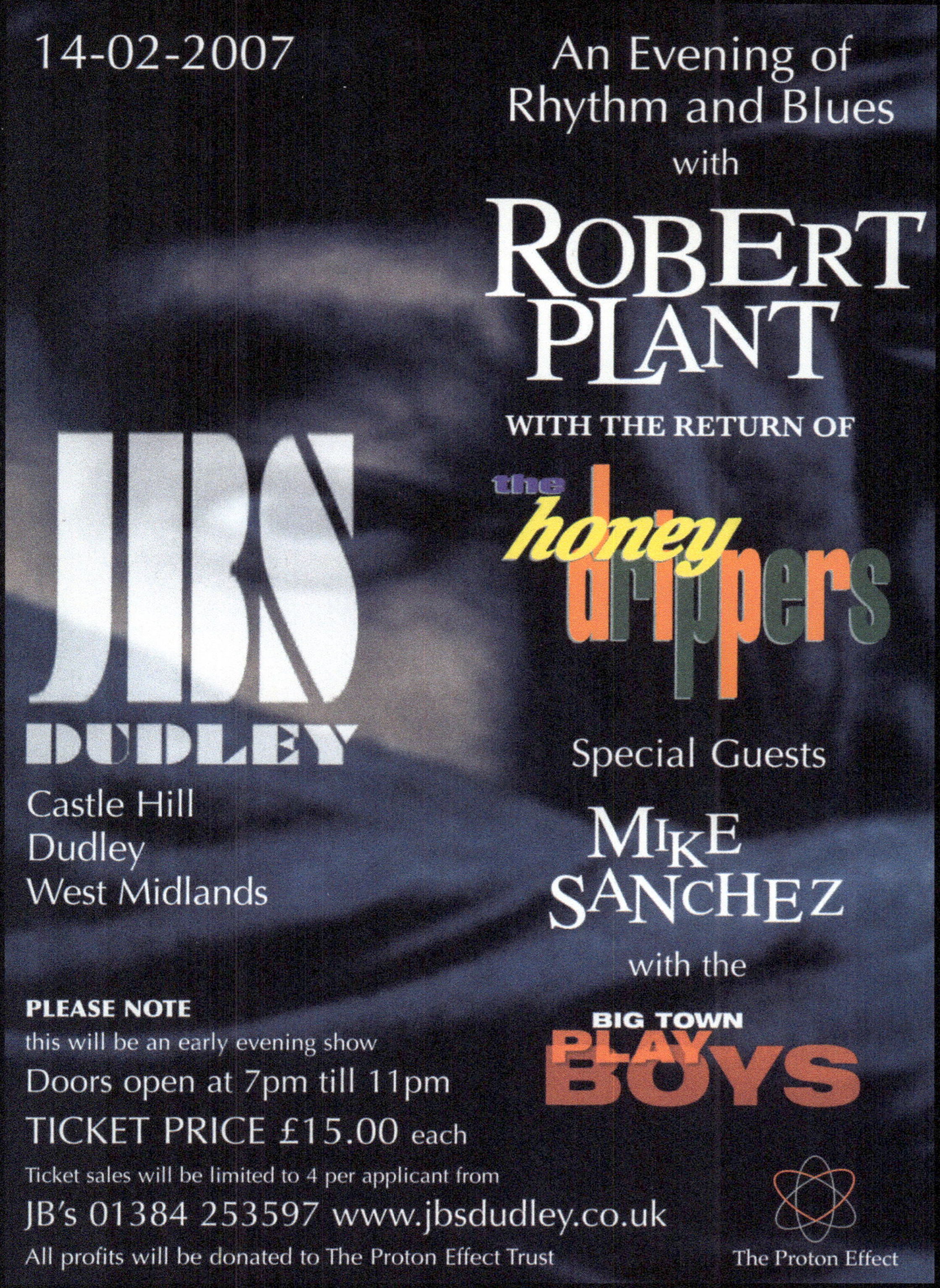

The poster for Roy Williams' 60th birthday bash.

14-02-2007

An Evening of
Rhythm and Blues
with

RoBErT PLANT

WITH THE RETURN OF

the
**honey
drippers**

JBS
DUDLEY

Castle Hill
Dudley
West Midlands

Special Guests

MiKE SANChEZ

with the

**BIG TOWN
PLAY
BOYS**

PLEASE NOTE
this will be an early evening show
Doors open at 7pm till 11pm
TICKET PRICE £15.00 each
Ticket sales will be limited to 4 per applicant from
JB's 01384 253597 www.jbsdudley.co.uk
All profits will be donated to The Proton Effect Trust

The Proton Effect

Colin 'Sam' Jukes

The 6th of January 2011

The day the Music died

"A long, long time ago
I can still remember
How that music used to make me smile
And I knew if I had my chance
That I could make those people dance
And maybe they'd be happy for a while...
But something touched me deep inside
The day the music died...
But I knew I was out of luck
The day the music died "

Don McLean

"Don't it always seem to go
But you don't know what you've got till it's gone
They paved paradise and put up a parking lot "

Joni Mitchell

Sadly, the records show that the 6th of January 2011 was the date of the JB's closing-down party, or maybe 'wake' is a better word. Forty-one years after Sam and Johnny Bryant had hatched their plans for world domination in a Tipton youth club, the music had finally died. There was no single catastrophic incident that caused the club to close. It was the steady build-up of a number of seemingly unrelated factors which combined to create the perfect storm. The first nail in the coffin was the smoking ban. Like it or loathe it, it contributed to the mass emptying of British pubs and clubs, from which many never recovered. Then the credit crunch arrived, chronically depleting people's disposable income. Cheap alcohol in supermarkets meant that folks were choosing to drink at home and not go out to pubs, restaurants and clubs, where a round of drinks cost far more. Instead of going out with friends to watch a live band, couples chose to drink and smoke in front of their nice, new 40-inch high-definition television sets, with takeaway Domino's margherita pizzas on their laps. Add to that the rising cost of hiring a good band, the ever-increasing cost of food, gas and electricity, council tax, etc., and things began to get tight. Then factor in the customers that were being allowed into the club without paying – friends of the door staff let in with a nod and a wink, probably because they were skint and couldn't afford to pay. All this was picking Sam's pocket far better than the Artful Dodger could ever do. The Performing Rights

Society added greatly to Sam's woes, by demanding 3% of his door takings, so in turn they could pay bands their dues. For those not familiar with this organization, it is their role in life to collect a fee from radio stations, discotheques, and businesses where music is played in any form – even a hairdressing shop's CD player or an old office wireless. A blanket percentage is charged to cover every time that a performer's song is played on the radio or TV, so that he or she or the band can receive a royalty, and this is fine in theory, but Sam argued that his club was a live-music venue, where mostly bands performed their own songs anyway. When a tribute band played there, they were, in effect, earning their living by stealing the material of the band they were imitating, so surely they, rather than Sam, should be made to cough up. All of this, however, went in one ear and out the other, and the PRS issued a solicitor's letter demanding an incredible £18,000. When this was not paid, they sent the bailiffs in. Clearly upset, Sam added that for 41 years he had supported live music, and 90% of the bands who played at the club were not even members of PRS (the society that, incidentally, once tried to demand money from me for having the radio on in my own house, where I paint my pictures and write my stories, because once in a blue moon a client might choose to visit me and accidentally hear a snippet of someone's tune while they were there).

With the bailiffs from PRS beating at the door, Sam and Sue Jukes reluctantly applied for administration. Those who possess an understanding or irony will appreciate the fact that PRS was doing its level best to close down a club that has arguably done more for music than virtually any other establishment or person has in this country over a period of 41 years. They should be proud!

The headlines in the Express and Star stated that JB's had £450,000 of creditors, but the truth was that the only creditors were Sam and Sue. They had drawn their pensions of £84,000 and £83,000 and put them into the club's bank account in an effort to keep the place running. They had a mortgage of £200,000 on the club building secured against their home. Not only had they dedicated their talents and working lives to the club, but they had given it every penny they had earned, and all of their future security. Sue's sister, Pat Marsh, came to the rescue with £9,000 of her own money to pay off the car-park debt, which

Peter Suddock was personally pursuing Sam for, in spite of Sam being seriously ill with stress. As if all this wasn't enough, during this fraught period, Sam's health took a drastic downward turn. Sue came home one day to find two ambulances outside her house, due to her husband having suffered a potentially life-threatening stroke. The stroke affected his speech and short-term memory, and though his speech is back to normal, his memory loss is still problematic. Another stroke followed, then sadly a third, and there have been several more hospital visits since. No matter how tragic all of this was, in true JB's tradition, comedy wasn't far away. Towards the end of the Castle Hill era, a theatrical rock band had used a coffin on stage, presumably so that the singer could rise from it at some point. This rather morbid prop was accidentally left at the club when the band was loading its equipment into the van, and it had remained at the club ever since. When Sam suffered his first stroke, an old friend, Cliff Whiteley (who Sam assures me was the first black chap to live in Tipton), was informed, quite erroneously, that Sam had died, by someone who'd been told the news second-hand by a neighbour's granny's window cleaner. The usual Chinese whispers routine, in other words. Distraught, Cliff dashed to the club, and bursting into the reception, he came across the coffin. Presuming that the staff had decided to let Sam lie in state for JB's members to pay their respects, he broke down and wept. Meanwhile, Sam was probably a few miles away at Russells Hall Hospital, sipping on a nice cup of tea and perusing his 'Get Well Soon' cards.

Sam had to sell the Castle Hill premises by auction, which was held at Aston Villa Football Club. It sold for £225,000, around the figure he'd paid for it, and was bought by a West Midlands business consortium headed by Raj Kumar, who spent a load of money on the place and turned it into an Indian and Caribbean wedding venue. It looks great inside, by all accounts. Raj also elected to keep the name JB's, for some obscure reason, in spite of the fact that the two businesses had little in common. Sam agrees that he made a lovely job of the renovations, but the new business was subsequently not granted any car parking by the zoo (even though they have acres of it). Nor was Raj given permission by the council for catering on site, even though without it a wedding venue is about as useful as a chocolate fireguard. Maybe this is cynical, but the expression 'history repeating itself' springs to mind. A newspaper article in the Express and Star, published around the same time that this chapter was written, tells of the troubled venue becoming a music club once more, presumably because they weren't allowed to function properly as a wedding venue. Sam and Sue wish the new owners good luck in whatever they do. They'll probably need it.

Having spotted an article in the same newspaper a few years back, about the Wolverhampton Civic Hall's wall of fame, Sid Weston decided to ring the venue with a view to including his old mate, Sam Jukes. Jonn Penney, the vocalist with Nec's Atomic Dustbin, now works for the Civic Hall as its media officer, and he agreed that Sam would fit the various criteria for such an honour, but would need someone to induct him. Up stepped Miles Hunt of The Wonder Stuff, and so Colin 'Sam' Jukes now sits alongside the likes of Lenny

Henry, Miles himself, of course, rock band Magnum, John Bonham, Noddy Holder, and Glenn Hughes, which rightly makes him very proud. It's nice to see the back-room boys honoured in this way, as well as the ones in the spotlight.

John Lennon once famously said that life is what happens to you while you're busy making other plans. In Sam's case, this was certainly true. All he ever wanted to be was a footballer, and then, when that went wrong, a speedway rider. Somehow, he accidentally became the owner of arguably one of the best-loved, most influential, career-changing, eccentric, and longest-running live-music venues in Great Britain. Thank you, Sam. Football's loss was our gain.

Miles Hunt, of the Wonder Stuff, with Sam Jukes at the Wolverhampton Wall of Fame event.

JB'S

A quick word from Robert Plant

Maybe it's the same twitch, rumble, and search for each generation; that special time – voices to be heard, opinions to be considered (tribal or individual). All of us down the years gravitate to our 'like-kind'. And totems... for many, music – the opiate, the pacifier, the 'freak flag', the lingua franca of generations, one from another – which represents so much.

JB's club was the Shining Light – the Big Black-Country Totem.

With graft, love, and energy, a small bunch of eager loons created a home for thousands of disaffected music lovers and subterranean socialites. Far from mainstream pop fodder, JB's club presented powerful new acts on their way to glory and mass audiences. All paraded before the crowd with 'no nonsense' rougher than rough charm. Society had a home, a place to be – with all its dramas played out before an amazing alternative soundtrack.

I enjoyed my connections with the club – mostly playing, in or out, fringe projects, or just sneaking past the disguised narcotic agents hiding in the parking lot to try to convince Jimmy the Con, ferocious doorman, that I was 'with the band'.

A truly valuable, much loved, and sorely missed beacon of Black Country life.

Robert Plant, New York, September 2014

Laura Tristram

The Editor

I was given the unenviable task of editing and proofreading my dad's 63,000 words – not out of nepotism, but because that happens to be what I do for a living. He is a very funny writer. I'll begrudgingly admit, and it was a joy to read, but, like most writers, he wouldn't know the difference between a hyphen, an N-dash, and an M-dash if one of them bit him. And don't get me started on possessive apostrophes or the Oxford comma. No, when I said unenviable, I was referring to having to check the spelling of every band name and artiste (and there are lots of them), the dates, song lyrics, grammar, punctuation, and the chronology, all on my meagre wage.

I have heard countless tales from my mom and dad of their time spent at JB's in their youth, but after reading everyone's memoirs, it really feels as if I knew the place, and I am disappointed that I was too young to witness the many great bands, as well as the bizarre, humorous and extraordinary events that occurred there.

The JB's book is a fantastic read, and was put together by some brilliant characters. I have tried my utmost to do the book justice and ensure there are no errors or factual discrepancies; however, putting a book together is, as you can imagine, a very complex process involving a good many people, so if there is the odd error here and there, I apologize (and will 'lump hommer me dad', as they'd say in the Black Country, for accidentally inserting said errors by accident after he'd received the corrected text from me; you just can't get the staff these days). Also, with some 10,000 or more band appearances over 41 years, it was impossible to name them all, much as we would have loved to. All we could do was provide you with a brief snapshot of what the place was like – an attempt to bring back to life this remarkable little club for all the people who spent countless, enjoyable, and crazy nights there, and at its associated gatherings. And a big thank you to all who contributed. I hope you all enjoy reading it as much as I enjoyed editing it.

Laura Tristram, BA History of Art; MA Publishing

Steve Jolliffe

The Graphic Designer/Photographer

Steve has been an artist and designer for 40 years, and in this time he has worked, either in-house or freelance, for hundreds of direct clients, design studios and advertising agencies all over the country. At the age of fifty, he belatedly fulfilled a life-long desire to play the drums. He bought himself a cheap kit and had a handful of initial lessons. In his typical doggedly determined way he watched and learned from other drummers, played at open-mic nights to get the necessary live music experience, before landing a job with his first band playing original music. Four years after buying his first set of drums, he played at JB's, Castle Hill, in 2010, just before it closed.

Check out Steve's website at www.stevejolliffe.co.uk

The somewhat foreboding front door of JB's King Street. Abandon all hope, ye who enter here!

The Committee

If I Could Turn Back The Hands of Time

" *How did I ever let you slip away?*
Never knowing I'd be singing this
song some day
And now I'm sinking, sinking to rise
no more
Ever since you closed the door "

R Kelly

I would like to thank the following people for their help and guidance with this book.

Sam and Sue Jukes, Sid Weston, John Weston, Roy Williams, Johnny Bryant, Colin Pugh and family, and Larry Oakley (who kindly asked me to write this book for them), Dermott Stephens, Les Bates, Roz Hardwick, Robin Wilson, Dr Howard Williamson, Chris Lea, Robert Plant, Steve Gibbons, Abacus Books, Macmillan Publishers (Picador imprint), David Newton, Shaun Payne, Jonn Penney, Glenis Smythe, Richard Rodgers, Steve Jolliffe, Laura Tristram (for continuing to edit this book whilst seriously ill in hospital), Tina Virr, John 'Vessel' Cartwright, members of the JB's Dudley – King Street back of the Pathfinder Facebook site, the photographers – both amateur and professional – who have kindly allowed us to use their images, the people – too numerous to mention – that have lent us their treasured memorabilia or supplied an anecdote, the Black Country Bugle, Stourbridge News, and Express and Star for allowing us to quote their articles, The Queen's Head, Wolverley (for loaning the committee their 'operations room' free of charge), Sylvia Hackett (for the rare photos from Down Under), Steven and David Webb, Larry and Anne Homer (for the photographs and stories), CPI Antony Rowe (for doing a lovely job of printing the book, we hope), and last but not least, all the people I have forgotten to mention but who helped nevertheless. Blame your glaring omission from this list on my incompetence, not malice. I'll remember you in time for the inevitable reprint!

GT

Sam Jukes

Sid Weston

Sue Jukes

John Weston

Roy Williams

Johnny Bryant

Colin Pugh

Dermott Stephens

Larry Oakley

John Weston's Visitors' Book
Revisited

Ask your favourite artistes to sign below, to increase the value of your book on eBay!

John Weston has been an avid autograph hunter since his youth. To his knowledge, he has given away at least eleven complete sets of Beatles autographs to friends, but still owns several sets. He probably has one of the best collections in the world, and all the signatures except one – Marlon Brando's (the only one he ever paid for) – were signed in his presence, so he knows they are genuine! His collection now numbers at least a thousand, and that doesn't include the JB's visitors' book autographs, some of which are reproduced within.

If you would like to see the 1969 to 2010 gig lists, visit our website **www.jbsbook.com**, where you can order copies of the book online. You can also order the book from any bookshop, simply by quoting the title, the author's name or, if you have it to hand, the ISBN number, which is 978-0-9926208-3-7.

The PRS (Profanities Revenue Service) has levied a percentage of the profits from this book for allowing us to use the 'F' word 19 times and the 'C' word twice. There is currently still no charge for domestic use, so feel free to eff and blind in the comfort of your own home to your heart's content. However, if you swear in the workplace you may be subject to a hefty fine. Be warned that this could easily be large enough to bankrupt your business, even after 41 years of successful trading.

Did you know?

The last band to play at JB's was...

Mantis Defeats Jaguar.

A serious word about copyright

This detailed and complex book has been physically created and assembled by just three hard-working people, namely, the writer, the designer and the editor. At Penguin, for example, it would have taken a huge task force comprising writers, designers, typesetters, artists, marketing and advertising executives, proofreaders, sub-editors, editors, secretaries and runners. The photographs within have been sent to us by multiple sources, so if we have unwittingly infringed copyright or misappropriated images, spelt a name incorrectly or whatever, please contact us and we will endeavour to put things right in the next reprint, and also on our **www.jbsbook.com** website. If that is not satisfactory, we will simply remove the photograph and replace it, but obviously, we'd rather not! We would ask you to please be sympathetic with regard to these issues and remember the spirit of altruism that helped create JB's club in the first place. Mistakes are inevitable, but our motives are pure. When all is said and done, we are advertising your talents, recording your work for posterity and trying to serve your interests, as well as telling the JB's story. If copyright has been accidentally breached, we simply cannot afford predatory reproduction fees, and any requests for such payments would jeopardize the existence of this very worthy and much awaited publication. Besides, we know you're better than that!

Finally, on a legal note, remember that there is a huge difference between someone printing something you don't care to read about yourself, and someone printing a lie. The former is uncomfortable, undoubtedly, but not illegal. The latter is libel, which you have to prove in a court of law at great expense!